W9-CLH-827

① 9/13
① 5/14

LEVITICUS AND NUMBERS

LEVITICUS AND NUMBERS

ATHALYA BRENNER AND ARCHIE CHI CHUNG LEE, EDITORS

Fortress Press

Minneapolis

LEVITICUS AND NUMBERS

Texts @ Contexts Series

Cover image: Christian Hugo Martin, *Forms*, Oil on canvas, 100×225 cm. 2009

Cover design: Laurie Ingram

Library of Congress Cataloging-in-Publication Data

978-0-8006-9936-9

CONTENTS

Other Books in the Series

Athalya Brenner and Nicole Wilkinson Duran
Series Editors
Editorial Committee
Hebrew Bible
Athalya Brenner, Cheryl Kirk-Duggan, Kari Latvus, Archie Chi-Chung
Lee, Gale A. Yee
New Testament
Nicole Wilkinson Duran, James P. Grimshaw, Yung Suk Kim, Teresa
Okure, Daniel Patte, Volumes
Hebrew Bible
Genesis
Exodus and Deuteronomy
Leviticus and Numbers
Joshua and Judges
New Testament
Matthew
Mark
John
First and Second Corinthians

SERIES PREFACE

THE EDITORS

TEXTS IN/AT LIFE CONTEXTS (UPDATED)

Myth cannot be defined but as an empty screen, a structure.
. . . A myth is but an empty screen for transference.[1]

שבעים פנים לתורה ("The Torah has seventy faces.")[2]

The discipline of biblical studies emerges from a particular cultural context; it is profoundly influenced by the assumptions and values of the Western European and North Atlantic, male-dominated, and largely Protestant environment in which it was born. Yet like the religions with which it is involved, the critical study of the Bible has traveled beyond its original context. Its presence in a diversity of academic settings around the globe has been experienced as both liberative and imperialist, sometimes simultaneously. Like many travelers, biblical scholars become aware of their own cultural rootedness only in contact with, and through the eyes of, people in other cultures.

The way any one of us closes a door seems in Philadelphia nothing at all remarkable, but in Chiang Mai, it seems overly loud and emphatic—so very typically American. In the same way, Western biblical interpretation did not seem tied to any specific context when only Westerners were reading and writing it. Since so much economic, military, and consequently cultural power has been vested in the West, the West has had the privilege of maintaining this cultural closure for two centuries. Those who engaged in biblical studies—even when they were women or men from Africa, Asia, and Latin

America—nevertheless had to take on the Western context along with the discipline.

But much of recent Bible scholarship has moved toward the recognition that considerations not only of the contexts of assumed, or implied, biblical authors but also the contexts of the interpreters are valid and legitimate in an inquiry into biblical literature. We use *contexts* here as an umbrella term covering a wide range of issues: on the one hand, social factors (such as location, economic situation, gender, age, class, ethnicity, color, and things pertaining to personal biography) and, on the other hand, ideological factors (such as faith, beliefs, practiced norms, and personal politics).

Contextual readings of the Bible are an attempt to redress the previous longstanding and grave imbalance that says that there is a kind of "plain," unaligned biblical criticism that is somehow "normative," and that there is another, distinct kind of biblical criticism aligned with some social location: the writing of Latina/o scholars advocating liberation, the writing of feminist scholars emphasizing gender as a cultural factor, the writings of African scholars pointing out the text's and the readers' imperialism, the writing of Jews and Muslims, and so on. The project of recognizing and emphasizing the role of context in reading freely admits that we all come from somewhere: no one is native to the biblical text; no one reads only in the interests of the text itself. North Atlantic and Western European scholarship has focused on the Bible's characters as individuals, has read past its miracles and stories of spiritual manifestations, or "translated" them into other categories. These results of Euro-American contextual reading would be no problem if they were seen as such; but they have become a chain to be broken when they have been held up as the one and only "objective," plain truth of the text itself.

The biblical text, as we have come to understand in the postmodern world and as pre-Enlightenment interpreters perhaps understood more clearly, does not speak in its own voice. It cannot read itself. *We* must read it, and in reading it, we must acknowledge that our own voice's particular pitch and timbre and inflection affect the meaning that emerges. Biblical scholars usually read the text in the voice of a Western Protestant male. When interpreters in the Southern Hemisphere and in Asia have assumed ownership of the Bible, it has meant a recognition that this Euro-American male voice is not the voice of the text itself; it is only one reader's voice, or rather, the voice of one context—however familiar and authoritative it may seem to all who have been affected by Western political and economic power. Needless to say, it is not a voice suited to bring out the best meaning for every reading community. Indeed, as biblical studies tended for so long to speak in this one particular voice, it may be the case that

that voice has outlived its meaning-producing usefulness: we may have heard all that this voice has to say, at least for now. Nevertheless, we have included that voice in this series, in part in an effort to hear it as emerging from its specific context, in order to put that previously authoritative voice quite literally in its place.

The trend of acknowledging readers' contexts as meaningful is already, inter alia, recognizable in the pioneering volumes of *Reading from This Place* (Segovia and Tolbert 1995; 2000; 2004), which indeed move from the center to the margins and back and from the United States to the rest of the world. More recent publications along this line also include *Her Master's Tools?* (Vander Stichele and Penner 2005), *From Every People and Nation: The Book of Revelation in Intercultural Perspective* (Rhoads 2005), *From Every People and Nation: A Biblical Theology of Race* (Hays and Carson 2003), and the *Global Bible Commentary* (*GBC*; Patte et al. 2004).

The editors of the *GBC* have gone a long way toward this shift by soliciting and admitting contributions from so-called third-, fourth-, and fifth-world scholars alongside first- and second-world scholars, thus attempting to usher the former and their perspectives into the *center* of biblical discussion. Contributors to the *GBC* were asked to begin by clearly stating their context before proceeding. The result was a collection of short introductions to the books of the Bible (Hebrew Bible/Old Testament and New Testament), each introduction from one specific context and, perforce, limited in scope. At the Society of Biblical Literature's (SBL) annual meeting in Philadelphia in 2005, during the two *GBC* sessions and especially in the session devoted to pedagogical implications, it became clear that this project should be continued, albeit articulated further and redirected.

On methodological grounds, the paradox of a deliberately inclusive policy that foregrounds differences in the interpretation of the Bible could not be addressed in a single- or double-volume format because in most instances those formats would allow for only one viewpoint for each biblical issue or passage (as in previous publications) or biblical book (as in the *GBC*) to be articulated. The acceptance of such a limit may indeed lead to a decentering of traditional scholarship, but it would definitely not usher in multivocality on any single topic. It is true that, for pedagogical reasons, a teacher might achieve multivocality of scholarship by using various specialized scholarship types together; for instance, the *GBC* has been used side-by-side in a course with historical introductions to the Bible and other focused introductions, such as the *Women's Bible Commentary* (Newsom and Ringe 1998). But research and classes focused on a single biblical book or biblical corpus need another kind of resource: volumes exemplifying a broad multivocality in themselves, varied enough in contexts from various shades of the confessional to various degrees of the secular, especially since in most previous publications, the contexts of communities of faith overrode all other contexts.

On the practical level, then, we found that we could address some of these methodological, pedagogical, and representational limitations evident in previous projects in contextual interpretation through a book series in which each volume introduces multiple contextual readings of the same biblical texts. This is what the SBL's Contextual Biblical Interpretation Consultation has already been promoting since 2005 during the American annual meeting; and since 2011 also at the annual international SBL conference. The consultation serves as a testing ground for a multiplicity of readings of the same biblical texts by scholars from different contexts.

These considerations led us to believe that a book series focusing specifically on contextual multiple readings for specific topics, of specific biblical books, would be timely. We decided to construct a series, including at least eight to ten volumes, divided between the Hebrew Bible (HB/OT) and the New Testament (NT). Each of the planned volumes would focus on one or two biblical books: Genesis, Exodus and Deuteronomy, Leviticus and Numbers, Joshua and Judges, and later books for the HB/OT; Mark, Luke-Acts, John, and Paul's letters for the NT.[3] The general HB/OT editor is Athalya Brenner, with Archie Lee and Gale Yee as associate editors. The general NT editor is Nicole Duran, with Daniel Patte and Teresa Okure as associate editors. Other colleagues have joined as editors for specific volumes.

Each volume focuses on clusters of contexts and of issues or themes, as determined by the editors in consultation with potential contributors. A combination of topics or themes, texts, and interpretive contexts seems better for our purpose than a text-only focus. In this way, more viewpoints on specific issues will be presented, with the hope of gaining a grid of interests and understanding. The interpreters' contexts will be allowed to play a central role in choosing a theme: we do not want to impose our choice of themes upon others, but as the contributions emerge, we will collect themes for each volume under several headings.

While we were soliciting articles for the first volumes (and continue to solicit contributions for future volumes), contributors were asked to foreground their own multiple "contexts" while presenting their interpretation of a given issue pertaining to the relevant biblical book(s). We asked that the interpretation be firmly grounded in those contexts and sharply focused on the specific theme, as well as in dialogue with "classical" informed biblical scholarship. Finally, we asked for a concluding assessment of the significance of this interpretation for the contributor's contexts (whether secular or in the framework of a faith community).

Our main interest in this series is to examine how formulating the content-specific, ideological, and thematic questions from life contexts will focus the reading of the biblical texts. The result is a two-way process of reading that (1) considers the contemporary life context from the perspective of the chosen themes in the given biblical book as corrective lenses, pointing out specific problems and issues in that context as highlighted by the themes in the biblical book; and (2) conversely, considers the given biblical book and the chosen theme from the perspective of the life context.

The word *contexts*, like *identity*, is a blanket term with many components. For some, their geographical context is uppermost; for others, the dominant factor may be gender, faith, membership in a certain community, class, and so forth. The balance is personal and not always conscious; it does, however, dictate choices of interpretation. One of our interests as editors is to present the personal beyond the autobiographical as pertinent to the wider scholarly endeavor, especially but not only when *grids of consent* emerge that supersede divergence. Consent is no guarantee of Truthspeak; neither does it necessarily point at a sure recognition of the biblical authors' elusive contexts and intentions. It does, however, have cultural and political implications.

Globalization promotes uniformity but also diversity, by shortening distances, enabling dissemination of information, and exchanging resources. This is an opportunity for modifying traditional power hierarchies and reallocating knowledge, for upsetting hegemonies, and for combining the old with the new, the familiar with the unknown—in short, for a fresh mutuality. This series, then, consciously promotes the revision of biblical myths into new reread and rewritten versions that hang on many threads of welcome transference. Our contributors were asked, decidedly, to be responsibly nonobjective and to represent only themselves on the biblical screen. Paradoxically, we hope, the readings here offered will form a new tapestry or, changing the metaphor, new metaphorical screens on which contemporary life contexts and the life of biblical texts in those contexts may be reflected and refracted.

Notes

1. Mieke Bal 1993: 347, 360.

2. This saying indicates, through its usage of the stereotypic number seventy, that the Torah—and, by extension, the whole Bible—intrinsically has many meanings. It is therefore often used to indicate the multivalence and variability of biblical interpretation, and does not appear in this formulation in traditional Jewish biblical interpretation before the Middle Ages. Its earliest appearances are in the medieval commentator Ibn Ezra's introduction to his commentary on the Torah, toward the introduction's end (as in printed versions), in Midrash *Numbers Rabbah* (13:15-16), and in later Jewish mystical literature.

3. At this time, no volume on Revelation is planned, since Rhoads's volume *From Every People and Nation: The Book of Revelation in Intercultural Perspective* (2005) is readily available, with a concept similar to ours.

Contributors

Amadi Ahiamadu is lecturer in the Department of Religious and Cultural Studies, University of Port Harcourt, Nigeria, and a research fellow of the Department of Old and New Testament, University of Stellenbosch, South Africa. He is also a member of the Nigerian Association of Biblical Studies. In partnership with Wycliffe Bible Translators he produced the Ogba New Testament translation. His areas of specialization and research interest include Old and New Testament studies, biblical and literary hermeneutics, ecotheology, and Hebrew and Old Testament translation.

Athalya Brenner is emerita professor of Hebrew Bible/Old Testament at the Universiteit van Amsterdam, currently teaching biblical studies at Tel Aviv University. She is the editor of *A Feminist Companion to the Hebrew Bible*, first and second series (nineteen volumes). Her research interests are biblical poetics and philology, feminist criticisms, and cultural studies as applied to biblical studies.

Kristel A. Clayville is a PhD candidate in Religious Ethics at the Divinity School, University of Chicago. She is currently writing her dissertation, titled "Responsible Hermeneutics: The Interpretation of Religious Texts in the Environmental Ethics of Hans Jonas and Holmes Rolston III." Her main research interests are in the areas of ethics of biblical interpretation, land ethics, and Bible and ethics, with ecological concerns anchoring these interests practically.

Yonina Dor was chair of the Bible Department at Oranim Educational College, Qiryat Tiv'on, Israel. Her PhD (Hebrew University, Jerusalem) is about the expulsion of foreign women in Ezra-Nehemiah. Her research interests are Ezra-Nehemiah, the marriage of Israelites with foreign wives, biblical ethics, and biblical myths. Another area of interest is the didactics of Bible teaching in contemporary Israeli state education and the teaching of the Bible within a humanistic framework.

Carole R. Fontaine is the Taylor Professor of Biblical Theology and History at Andover Newton Theological School. She studied at Yale Divinity School and Duke University, and is the author of *Smooth Words: Women, Proverbs and Performance in Biblical Wisdom*, and *With Eyes of Flesh: The Bible, Gender and Human Rights*. She is vice president of the International Federation of Women against Fundamentalism and Equality (WAFE), and has volunteered for the NGO Women's United Nations Report Network (WUNRN) for over a decade. A lifelong student of Judaism, she also hugs Muslims with backpacks on purpose.

Wil Gafney is associate professor of Hebrew and Old Testament at the Lutheran Theological Seminary at Philadelphia. She is an Episcopal priest at the historic African Episcopal Church of St. Thomas, founded by Absalom Jones in 1792. She is also a member of the Dorshei Derekh (Reconstructionist) Minyan of the Germantown Jewish Centre; both church and Minyan are in Philadelphia.

Helen R. Jacobus received her PhD from the University of Manchester (2011) for her thesis on Aramaic calendars in the Dead Sea Scrolls. She is an honorary research associate at University College London, Department of Hebrew and Jewish Studies. Her paper on the zodiac and its role in early Jewish calendars received the Sean W. Dever Memorial Prize, 2011.

Joseph Ryan Kelly is a PhD candidate at the Southern Baptist Theological Seminary, Louisville, Kentucky. He is interested in Hebrew Bible/Old Testament theology and ethics. His published work can be found in *Antiguo Oriente, Bulletin for Biblical Research, Journal of Hebrew Scriptures*, and *Exodus and Deuteronomy* in the Texts @ Contexts series. He blogs on the Hebrew Bible at kolhaadam.wordpress.com.

Archie C. C. Lee is professor in the Department of Cultural and Religious Studies, the Chinese University of Hong Kong. He has written books and articles in the areas of Old Testament studies, the Bible in China, cross-textual hermeneutics and Asian biblical interpretation. He is the president of the Society of Asian Biblical Studies and one of the editors (with Athalya Brenner and Gale Yee) of *Genesis: Texts @ Contexts* (Fortress, 2012).

Diana Lipton read English at Oxford University and earned her PhD in biblical studies at Cambridge University. Her publications include *Revisions of the Night: Politics and Promises in the Patriarchal Dreams of Genesis* (1999) and *Longing for Egypt and Other Unexpected Biblical Tales* (2008), along with several edited volumes. She was a Fellow of Newnham College, Cambridge, and a Reader in Hebrew Bible and Jewish Studies at King's College London. She is now a visiting lecturer at Tel Aviv University.

Anthony Rees is lecturer in Old Testament at Pacific Theological College, Fiji. He completed his doctoral work at Charles Sturt University in Sydney, Australia, before taking up his position in Fiji.

Yael Shemesh is senior lecturer in Hebrew Bible at Bar-Ilan University. Her main fields of interest are the poetics of biblical narrative, prophetic stories, measure for measure, feminist interpretation, animal ethics, and mourning in the Bible. Among her publications are "Rape Is Rape Is Rape: The Story of Dinah and Shechem (Genesis 34)," *ZAW* 119 (2007), and "Jephthah—Victimizer and Victim: A Comparison of Jephthah and Characters in Genesis," *JANES* 32 (2011). She recently completed a study on mourning in the Bible.

Nāsili Vaka'uta, born and raised in the Polynesian kingdom of Tonga, is Ranston Lecturer in Biblical Studies at Trinity Methodist Theological College (Auckland, New Zealand) and honorary teaching fellow at the School of Theology (University of Auckland). His publications include *Reading Ezra 9–10 Tu'a-wise: Rethinking Biblical Interpretation in Oceania* (SBL, 2011), and several other peer-reviewed articles and book chapters. His research interests are contextual biblical interpretation, indigenous methodologies, and Oceanic hermeneutics.

Sonia K. Wong is a doctoral student in Hebrew Bible at Vanderbilt University. Her research interests include postcolonial biblical criticism and feminist criticism.

Abbreviations

AB Anchor Bible

AbB *Altbabylonische Briefe in Umschrift und Übersetzung.* Edited by F. R. Kraus. Leiden, 1964–

ABD *Anchor Bible Dictionary.* Edited by D. N. Freedman. 6 vols. New York: Doubleday, 1992

AfOB Archiv für Orientforschung: Beiheft

AJSL *American Journal of Semitic Languages and Literatures*

ANET *Ancient Near Eastern Texts Relating to the Old Testament.* Ed. James B. Pritchard. 3rd ed. Princeton: Princeton University Press, 1969

AOTC Abingdon Old Testament Commentaries

ATD Das Alte Testament Deutsch

BA *Biblical Archaeologist*

BDB Brown, Driver, and Briggs. *A Hebrew and English Lexicon of the Old Testament*

BibInt *Biblical Interpretation*

BN *Biblische Notizen*

BT Babylonian Talmud

BT The Bible Translator

BZAW Beihefte zur Zeitschrift für die alttestamentliche Wissenschaft

CAT The Cuneiform Alphabetic Texts from Ugarit, Ras Ibn Hani and Other Places (KTU: second, enlarged edition), eds. Manfried Dietrich, Oswald Loretz and Joaquín 1995. Sanmartín, Münster: Ugarit-Verlag.

CBC Cambridge Bible Commentary

CBQ *Catholic Biblical Quarterly*

DSD *Dead Sea Discoveries*

DJD Discoveries in the Judaean Desert

EdF Erträge der Forschung

EI *Eretz-Israel: Archaeological, Historical and Geographical Studies.* Jerusalem: Israel Exploration Society. 1951–

FAT Forschungen zum Alten Testament

H Holiness Code

HBT   *Horizons of Biblical Theology*

HR   *History of Religions*

HSM   Harvard Semitic Monographs

HTR   *Harvard Theological Review*

IBC   Interpretation: A Bible Commentary for Teaching and Preaching

ICC   International Critical Comentary

Int   *Interpretation*

JANESCU   *Journal of the Ancient Near Eastern Society of Columbia University*

JBL   *Journal of Biblical Literature*

JCS   *Journal of Cuneiform Studies*

JHS   *Journal of Hebrew Scriptures*

JJS   *Journal of Jewish Studies*

JNES   *Journal of Near Eastern Studies*

JQR   *The Jewish Quarterly Review*

JSOT   *Journal for the Study of the Old Testament*

JSOTSup   Journal for the Study of the Old Testament: Supplement Series

JSSR   *Journal for the Scientific Study of Religion*

Jub.   *Jubilees*

LCL   Loeb Classical Library

LXX   Septuagint

MT   Masoretic Text

NCB   New Century Bible

NIB   New Interpreters Bible

NIBCOT   New International Biblical Commentary on the Old Testament

NICOT   New International Commentary on the Old Testament

NJPS   Jewish Publication Society Translation, 1985

NovTSup   Supplements to Novum Testamentum

OTL   Old Testament Library

OTS   *Oudtestamentische Studiën*

P   Priestly source

ScrHier   Scripta Hierosolymitana

SemeiaSt   Semeia Studies

TDOT   *Theological Dictionary of the New Testament*

TSAJ   Texte und Studien zum antiken Judentum

UF *Ugarit-Forschungen*

TWOT *Theological Wordbook of the Old Testament*

VT *Vetus Testamentum*

VTSup Supplements to Vetus Testamentum

WW *Word and World*

WBC Word Biblical Commentary

ZAW Zeitschrift für die alttestamentliche Wissenschaft

Introduction

Athalya Brenner

Both Leviticus and Numbers begin with the claim that what is set out in them was delivered by the Hebrew God to Moses at the Tent of Meeting, in the desert, on the way from Egypt to the promised land (Lev. 1:1; Num. 1:1). Numbers goes further, giving the date of delivery as well, as the second month in the second year of the exodus from Egypt (1:1). Leviticus ends on this note: "These are the commandments that the Lord gave Moses for the Israelite people on Mount Sinai" (Lev. 27:34).[1] Numbers ends with, "These are the commandments and regulations that the Lord enjoined upon the Israelites, through Moses, on the steppes of Moab, at the Jordan near Jericho" (Num. 36:13). Even assuming that the notations back and front are bookends added by editors, Leviticus is largely static topographically and chronologically, whereas Numbers is more dynamic in this respect and takes us almost to the point of entry into the land. In this respect it is much like the end of Deuteronomy, which goes one step further, including Moses' death and the transfer of his authority to Joshua, already mentioned in Numbers 27 and actualized in Deut. 34:9.

The frame, then, is similar if not identical, and materials parallel to and overlapping Exodus and Deuteronomy appear frequently, albeit with variations. Though Leviticus and Numbers in many ways differ in content and presentation, several distinct features unify the two books. Those are: insistence on a desert community that accepts Moses' leadership at times grudgingly and unwillingly; the centrality of the Tent of Meeting, already built and functioning; the centrality of Aaron and his priestly family for the community, in a cultic role but in other roles as well; the importance of properly conducted cult and worship, including minute instructions for priestly functioning and behavior; and the contention that social legislation and the hoped-for ethical performance it would safeguard, partly repetitive (see Leviticus 19, unanimously assigned to the H source [Holiness Code: Leviticus 17–26], and the Decalogue [Exodus 20 = Deuteronomy 5], falls within the sphere of religious regulation and religious ethical behavior. Since the latter feature is pronounced in both books, it is of little consequence for the end-product text (MT) whether the H source, to which part of Leviticus is assigned, predates most or part of other chapters in Leviticus and Numbers, most of which are assigned by scholars to various versions of the P (Priestly) source.

It is therefore no surprise that, out of the thirteen essays in this volume, five are focused on cultic, priestly, and theological matters (in order of appearance: Shemesh, Wong, Lipton, Lee, and Fontaine). It is also not surprising, given the interests of our contributors in general, that six essays deal with matters of social ethics, especially as they are applied to gender matters and community identity (Jacobus, Dor, Rees, Vaka'uta, Geffney, Ahiamadu), with Shemesh and Lipton's essays dealing with both clusters of topics. Two essays extend the ethics discussion into present-day ecology concerns (Clayville and Kelly). The remaining essays, once again, are about the ethics of religious behavior and human rights (Lee and Fontaine). In sum, then, our contributors are more interested in the ethical implications of the so-called Holiness Code and Priestly source than in their formal features of arranging the community as a cultic entity and of regulating the cult itself.

Four of the contributors are American (Clayville, Kelly, Gafney, Fontaine), one of whom is African American (Gafney). Two are British (Jacobus and Lipton, the latter a new immigrant to Israel). One contributor is from Australia (Rees), one from Oceania (Vaka'uta), one from Nigeria (Ahiamadu), two from Hong Kong (Wong and Lee), and four from Israel (Shemesh, Dor, Brenner, now also Lipton). Most of the contributors are Christian or post-Christian of various affiliations; the British/Israeli ones are Jewish of diverse faith convictions. Since several of the essays focus on the same text (notably in the case of Numbers 25) or issue, we leave it for our readers to ponder to what extent any particular authorly faith conviction, in addition to the obvious geographical and community factors, influences the readings here offered.

Part 1: Issues in Leviticus

Kristel Clayville and Joseph Kelly focus on environmental issues that can be linked to Leviticus. In so doing they center a topic that, for most readers, would be considered marginal within the frameworks of the P and H writings.

Clayville, in "Landed Interpretation: An Environmental Ethicist Reads Leviticus," is concerned about land agency from an ethical viewpoint. Having explained her own liminal position personally, religiously, and geographically, she claims that the whole of Leviticus can be read from an environmental ethics angle but limits herself to a discussion of the Holiness Code. She reads mainly from the perspective of Aldo Leopold's *Land Ethic*, and this enables her to distinguish two competing systems concerning the land and its ecology and human ecology in the Holiness Code, leading to conclusions about human liminality as exemplified by the sojourner, the *ger*: "The *ger*'s liminality situates him or her between nature and culture, pointing both backward and forward to Israel's past experiences and future life with the land." Clayville sees the tension between the two ethical systems concerning the land in Leviticus as an opening rather than a hindrance.

In "USDA or YHWH? Pursuing a Divinely Inspired Diet," Kelly's "interest in the text of Leviticus (and by extension Deuteronomy), specifically the legislation surrounding food, is shaped largely by current ethical issues surrounding industrialized agriculture and foodways in America." Concerns about hunger, food health, food, and democracy and capitalism in an age of technology and industrialization may contribute to understanding religious dietary laws, and vice versa. He analyzes the dietary laws of Leviticus 11 and Deuteronomy 14, as well as several New Testament sources, to see how those operate in his specific North American, Christian, democratic contexts. He concludes that, between biblical traditions and contemporaneous state regulations, an ethical moral ground concerning many aspects of food production and consumption is possible to achieve.

Yael Shemesh discusses another ethical matter in her essay, "'Do Not Bare Your Heads and Do Not Rend Your Clothes' (Leviticus 10:6): On Mourning and Refraining from Mourning in the Bible." Following the personal experience of her father's death and the mourning customs her family practiced, Shemesh discusses four cases in which biblical characters did *not* mourn for their dead: Aaron for his sons (Leviticus 10), David for his infant son (2 Sam. 12:15–25), the Shunammite for her son (2 Kgs 4:8–37), and Ezekiel for his wife (Ezek. 24:15–24). In two of these cases, the first and last, a divine command prohibits the mourning rites. Shemesh, an Israeli and a practicing Jew, considers the social and moral significance of mourning rites and of refraining from them, in addition to the role women must have played in such rituals and occasions.

In "Slave Wives and Transgressive Unions in Biblical and Ancient Near Eastern Laws and Literature," Helen Jacobus contends that much of the drama of marital relations in the Torah, in stories as well as in legal codes, is based on the original, implied audience's knowledge of the biblical as well as the Ancient Near East (ANE) law codes. She finds that the narratives on sexually transgressive behavior in Genesis and beyond are mirrored in a group of relevant ANE laws and corresponding biblical laws. Therefore, she writes, "Without modern interpreters aligning knowledge of ancient legal texts with the biblical narratives, the story lines lose their dramatic impact, significant layers of meaning, and possible legal and societal implications." Once again, this essay proves the value of demarginalization and recentering, in that it works from contemporary experience to a notion of recentering ancient sources.

"The Notion of כפר in the Book of Leviticus and Chinese Popular Religion," by Sonia Wong, is one of the two essays in this volume from the background of Chinese/Hong Kong culture. Wong begins by problematizing the term "Chinese popular religion," applying it to both indigenous and diasporic systems. Then, following Archie Lee's cross-cultural method, she reads the Levitical notion of כפר, *k-p-r* Piel, often rendered as "expiate, atone, purify," in dialogue with Chinese popular religious culture. She concludes that recognizing the mechanism of *k-p-r* is invalid for her culture, even reprehensible; according to her, "The [Levitical] cathartic power of purification and reparation offerings is absent in Chinese popular religion. The complex and elaborated rituals in Leviticus function as a kind of penance and passage to the reintegration of the guilty party into the community. In contrast, in Chinese popular religion, ritual offerings are not efficacious: they do not contribute to the absolution of sins and the resolution of guilt."

In the last essay of part 1, "Golden Do's and Don'ts: Leviticus 19:1-17 from a Human Rights-Based Approach (HRBA)," Carole Fontaine insists that in her capacity as both bible scholar and sociopolitical activist she feels that texts of the Holiness Code, and Leviticus is general, has much to offer to issues of human rights in our contemporary world, or in her language, HRBA issues. Her case study is Leviticus 19, which she analyzes in detail to show—whatever its provenance—that it can function as a blueprint for a just, contemporary society.

Part 2: Issues in Numbers

With Diana Lipton's essay, we move from Leviticus to Numbers, and to a cluster of articles that has gender and violence, especially violence against women, as its focus. Finally, the last two essays in this section branch out from gender rights to human rights.

In "'Bitter Waters' (Numbers 5), Flood Waters (Genesis 6–9), and Some Theologies of Exile and Land," Lipton writes: "In this essay, I offer an intertextual reading of the Sotah ritual of the bitter waters (Num. 5:1-31) and the flood narrative (Gen. 6:1—9:28). I argue that they function as structural, ritual, literary, and theological equivalents of, respectively, divorce as described in Deut. 24:1-4 and exile as interpreted in many prophetic texts, especially in Jeremiah (e.g., Jer. 29:1-14) and Ezekiel (e.g., Ezekiel 36), as a punishment and solution for wrongdoing." Her essay, which developed over time from an earlier version, exemplifies how conscious contextualization of one's unique journey can fruitfully work for understanding biblical passages and for creating links and productive associations beyond the personal and even the narrowly communal.

Numbers 25 is a difficult passage. Structurally, since it moves from an incident with "the daughters of Moab" at Baʿal Peʿor to one with a woman "Midianite" and back, raising the question, first, of how many incidents and, second, from what locations/periods and provenances this one story is amalgamated; ethically, since it involves killing in the name of Yhwh and a plague caused by Yhwh; gender-wise, since females are accused of "whoring" in the sense of pagan worship; othering, since the accusation is leveled at ethnically foreign women and the Israelite men they presumably "seduce"; and ethically again, since the revenge killing is carried out by the priests, headed by the priest Phinehas, overlooking the proscription of bloodshed and killing by priests. One chapter in a whole book. Perhaps not so very significant considering that the preceding stories of the spies (Numbers 13–14) and Balaam (chs. 22–24) are longer and perhaps more meaningful for the whole journey described. Nevertheless, and probably because of the problems underlying it—problems of violence, xenophobia, identity versus the other, gender stereotypes—this passage has received much attention in recent scholarship, which is reflected in this contextual collection. Four contributors chose to write about this passage, each from her or his own context. In "From the Well in Midian to the Baal of Peor: Different Attitudes to Marriage of Israelites to Midianite Women," Yonina Dor writes from an Israeli context. Anthony Rees, in "Numbers 25 and Beyond: Phinehas and Other Detestable Practice(r)s," writes from an Australian aboriginal context. In "Indicting YHWH: Interpreting Numbers 25 in Oceania," Nāsili Vakaʿuta writes from an Oceania (Tonga) context. Finally, Wil Gafney, in "A Queer Womanist Midrashic Reading of Numbers 25:1-18," writes from an African American context.

Still within gender relations but from another viewpoint, Amadi Ahiamadu considers female inheritance in "Assessing Female Inheritance of Land in Nigeria with the Daughters of Zelophehad Narrative (Numbers 27:1-11)." In his own words, "The choice of the narratives about Zelophehad's daughters is intended to highlight its relevance to understanding the inheritance rights of women in Nigeria. The side-by-side reading of the two disparate cultures, across time and place, helps us analyze a problem in the Niger Delta areas that demands an attitudinal change with respect to female inheritance of land. . . . It serves as a textual example from the Bible that can be used to assess the Nigerian understanding of the whole concept of inheritance."

Moving from gender to the more general human rights sphere, in "Reading Iconoclastic Stipulations in Numbers 33:50-56 from the Pluralistic Religious Context of China," Archie C. C. Lee describes his personal experience of evangelical Christian missionaries' forced iconoclasm and the cultural trauma, crisis, and loss that Christian converts of Chinese descent experienced as a result. He then contextualizes his family's experience against the background of the Chinese Taiping movement of the nineteenth century, then reads the iconoclastic passage of Num. 35:50-56 in the light of his own contextualization. Most of us are hardly aware, in our religious and/or cultural zeal for betterment, of the cultural price asked and paid in conversion. Lee's essay is a timely reminder about the price paid and the damage done in the wholesale annihilation of the old rather than its integration with the new, even when the recipients are willing.

With this essay we conclude. Fontaine (in chapter 6) is explicit about her wish to "defend" Leviticus as a worthy human rights document. This is far from older scholarly treatments of the P and H sources, which insisted on the formal, narrower, self-interested nature of these alleged Torah sources. Other contributors, as well, focused on issues that may seem less important to mainstream scholarship on these Torah books. In this volume we may have skipped a lengthy discussion of technical cultic minutiae or foregrounded events, but the contributors, and we the editors, have tried to demonstrate how such texts, perhaps despite themselves, can serve as positive or negative teachers in disparate contemporary communities.

Editorial Notes

The editors worked to make this volume accessible both to scholars and to interested readers who have no knowledge of Hebrew. Throughout the volume Hebrew words are presented either in transliteration or in Hebrew letters. In the latter case, a transliteration of the Hebrew words usually follows in italics, in popular rather than academic transliteration, for the sound of the original language. Translations of the Hebrew words are supplied, be they in Hebrew font or in transliteration. Authors in this volume, as in other volume, use various forms of the Hebrew God's names: YHWH, Yahweh, and Yhwh.

Notes

1. Biblical quotes in this introduction are from the JPS translation unless otherwise stated.

PART I

Issues in Leviticus

1

Landed Interpretation

An Environmental Ethicist Reads Leviticus

Kristel A. Clayville

LANDED CONTEXT

The title of this essay is a little misleading, suggesting that I write from a single location, when in fact my training in multiple disciplines gives me liminal academic status. I am not only an environmental ethicist; I am a former biblicist and archaeologist who has chosen ethics as her academic home because it is an ideal place for posing questions about ancient texts and modern life. I was raised in the Disciples of Christ, a low-church Protestant denomination that developed in rural Kentucky and whose sole article of faith is, "No creed but Christ, no book but the Bible."[1] I was always more comfortable with the second half of that statement of belief, and so I organized my studies around archaeological and textual studies of the Bible. Thus I am an environmental ethicist with training in critical methods of engagement with the Hebrew Bible, and one who has gotten her hands dirty at the archaeological sites of Castra, Ein Gedi, Sepphoris, and Kirbet Cana.

Not only do I have a liminal academic context, but I also have a liminal personal context. I spent my early years in Kentucky, where the Appalachian Mountains give us a different view of what is possible. There is quite a bit of both looking up and climbing up to be done, but there are also physical barriers to vision and long paths around mountains to be plotted. The mountains form a culture by isolation, but also by nourishment. And so I have a strong sense of the constructive force that place has in making people who they are, both socially and religiously. I come from the blending of two farming families, and I was always aware that my parents had chosen to leave the life of the land. My liminality comes from having one foot in the modern world, full of its technological advances, and one foot in an older, almost tribal culture that prioritizes kinship ties and insider status while shirking much of what the modern world has to offer. It is no small wonder that I, having been formed in this environment, gravitate toward environmental ethics. I was reared with a love of nature, skepticism toward modern inventions, and an emphasis on the Bible. Bringing all of these parts of myself together without demonizing any one of them has been part of my long academic journey.

In addition to living in this liminal space academically and personally, I also inhabit it legally. As a woman married to a woman, my travels from place to place result in legal confusion. Am I in a state that recognizes the legal standing of my relationship? Do the state laws or the city laws govern my relationship at this time? These questions and others plague my movements and push me to think critically about place and its relationship to law. I am often put in the position of asking the question, Where am I? as the necessary precursor to, Who am I?—at least in relation to the other people of the lands that I traverse. This liminal legal status allows me to think of myself analogically as a *ger* in the land of Israel, who in Lev. 19:33 is extended the courtesy of legal standing. Yet the explicit mention suggests that the people did not simply assume the legal standing of strangers.

Of course, my marriage is also a contentious subject religiously. My social location pushes back against that simple reading: "No book but the Bible," forcing an abundance of meaning for me or no meaning at all. I cannot read the statement as reductionistically limiting my own self-definition, but rather, I must engage the Bible as a polyphonous text, polyvalent and overflowing with meaning. In an effort to preserve meaning, I develop interpretations of the biblical text that honor my own investment in it but that don't result in self-immolation. To this end, I often rely on an intertwining of premodern interpretive principles with the historical-critical method. Or more to the point, I embrace the Documentary Hypothesis while also affirming the superabundance of meaning within the biblical text. In short, an interweaving of my personal and academic contexts shapes my relationship to the biblical text and influences my reading.

My own commitments to the biblical text do not allow me to ignore Leviticus, but in fact demand that I engage it to bring about meaning in a modern, liminal context. Scholars have recognized Leviticus as a treasure trove of information on ancient Israelite cultic practice, family organization, legal reasoning, and social ethics (for instance, Douglas 2002 [1966] and Milgrom 2004). Yet much of the significance of this text has been relegated to informing how we think about the past. In fact, the Revised Common Lectionary includes only selections from Leviticus 19, and in public debates one hears only citations of the antihomosexuality passages (Lev. 18:22; 20:13). In many ways, the content of Leviticus has determined not only our approaches to the text but also what we expect to be the fruitful significance of any of our readings of it. Yet when Leviticus is read from an environmental ethics perspective, it proves to be a valuable source for cultivating an ecological imagination, which gives a historically specific religious text a constructive voice in contemporary environmental ethics.

While the entire text of Leviticus can be read from an environmental ethics perspective, I will limit myself to the Holiness Code (chs. 17–27), due to the specific references to land and family in that section. As mentioned, previous studies of Leviticus have argued that the text doesn't have any contemporary relevance. We can only glean more information about the ancient cult, family structure, or legal reasoning, objects of study that are really only of academic interest. But within the Holiness Code, the content specifically about the land is a good starting place for interpreting the text to speak to a modern context. My approach locates the significance in our modern context rather than gleaning information about social history. Before narrowing this study to focus on the Holiness Code, however, I will go into more detail about what reading from an environmental ethics perspective means for my approach to the text.

LANDED READING

Environmental ethics is a broad field of study. It includes animal studies, sustainability studies, ecojustice, and ecotheology, just to name a few subfields. The overarching thematic unity of all these studies is that they investigate and make normative claims about the human relationship to nature. Within these studies, scholars must define *humans* and *nature*, as well as the unit of moral considerability for each. Does *human* mean "individuals," or does it refer to a group? Are animals individuals that need to be protected, or do their habitats simply need to be protected? Is nature composed of individuals or species? Will normative judgments be based on value theory, on the preservation of human freedom, on theological principles, on the premise of limiting the aggregate amount of suffering in the world? These are only a few of the various options available to environmental ethicists, who engage conceptually and practically with the relationships between living entities in the world. While environmental ethicists interpret the world using these questions and categories (among others), these questions and categories need not be relegated to this one academic sphere. We can borrow these questions and concepts to orient our reading of the Holiness Code.

Certain assumptions about the world are embedded in these questions and concepts; so we must ask, what does asking these questions and using these concepts imply about the biblical text? First, it implies that the text has an ethical outlook and is seeking to regulate behavior. Given that Leviticus is a legal text including apodictic and casuistic laws, considering it to have an ethical outlook does not seem like much of a stretch. The difficulty lies in seeing these apodictic and casuistic formulations as part of a larger ethical outlook that includes the deontological elements drawn from them, but that is not defined by them. This larger and encompassing ethical outlook leads to the second point; namely, the main topic of Leviticus is the human relationship to nature. Asserting such a claim means that the creation of holy space is a subcategory of this larger theme. Third, importing questions and concepts from environmental ethics in reading Leviticus suggests that the referents in the text have real-world analogues. Since the questions and concepts were formulated to navigate relationships between real-world entities, one may assume that using them would make a similar claim about the text of Leviticus—that, in fact, it makes claims about the world as it exists and ought to exist rather than about a merely textual world or the world described in the text, which is a world we do not physically inhabit. With Leviticus, this is not a pressing concern. The text contains mainly objects, animals, and categories of people that we would find in our everyday lives,[2] even in a modern context. The normative ethical warrant is presented as an imitative theological model,[3] which could confound the idea that objects in the text have real-world analogues. But my reading of the Holiness Code does not rely on that theological context for ethical grounding. Rather, I contend that this theological warrant frames the entire ethical outlook of the text, adding a layer of normativity instead of defining the contours of normativity. Within that theological framing, there is still the need to further investigate the kinds of relationships presented.

In short, reading from an environmental ethics perspective shifts the kinds of questions that we ask of the Holiness Code. Rather than asking questions driven by the historical particularity of the text, we can formulate questions about the relationships between human and nonhuman entities, values embedded in the text, and duties prescribed by the text. While I have outlined some of the broad questions and concepts that will orient reading the Holiness Code from an environmental ethics perspective, we can narrow into a particular environmental perspective that is consonant with the concerns and worldview of the Holiness Code, namely, the *Land Ethic*, an approach to thinking about nature that focuses on ecosystems as the locus of value rather than human interests or individual animals.

Aldo Leopold, the founder of the Land Ethic,[4] has been called a prophet by many later thinkers. J. Baird Callicott offers two reasons for this: "Leopold studied the Bible, not as an act of faith, but as a model of literary style. . . . And he thought far ahead of his time" (Callicott 1999: 7). The consonance of the worldviews of the Holiness Code and the Land Ethic could be attributed to Leopold's study of the Bible (1989)—after all, it is hard to ignore content even if one is reading only for literary style. If this is so, then contrary to Callicott's characterization of Leopold's prophetic abilities, it is not his forward thinking or prognostications about the future that make him a prophet, but rather his backward gaze to a past that articulated an ethical model with potential in a contemporary situation. Leopold as prophet reinvigorates an ethical worldview from the biblical text that has lost force in the modern world. Like the biblical prophets, he looks not simply to the future but also to the past for models of ethical action that can be given new life.[5]

Leopold articulated the Land Ethic based on his observations and interactions with the ecology around his farm in Wisconsin. These observations and interactions are organized by month, so the changing seasons and the cyclical nature of time are built into Leopold's experiences. Leopold's presentation of time in his writing is not unlike the Levitical model of cyclical time governed by ritual. Additionally, Leopold's Land Ethic espouses an ecological holism, meaning that the unit of moral considerability is the whole, not the part or the individual. Leviticus also concerns itself mainly with the whole—that is, the community of the Israelites—and the land itself. Again and again we see in the text that individuals who are considered טמא, tame' ("impure"), are segregated from the community until they can regain their טהור, ṭahor ("pure"), status. And if becoming ṭahor again is not possible, then the individuals are excommunicated for the sake of the holiness of the community. Temporality and community focus are not the only overlaps between the Levitical worldview and that of Leopold's Land Ethic. As we will see, the Holiness Code can be read as embodying the logic of ethical development and the warrant for extending the community that funds the Land Ethic, but further explication of the logical structure of the Land Ethic is needed before we proceed.

Leopold summarizes his *Land Ethic* with the moral maxim: "A thing is right when it tends to preserve the integrity, stability, and beauty of the biotic community. It is wrong when it tends otherwise" (Leopold 1989: 224–25). This summary comes after pages and pages detailing his interactions with the land

and his experiences with it over multiple seasons. Land is not the only subject of Leopold's ethics, but it is the largest part. One of the main questions that leads scholars to dismiss the Land Ethic is Leopold's lack of definition for the term "biotic community." Does it reference a whole (rather than an individual), and how would we value a system?

Callicott, one of the few academic proponents of the Land Ethic, attributes much of the dismissal to Leopold's concise writing style. Callicott offers an interpretation of the Land Ethic that fleshes it out with some of Leopold's other works, bringing two significant points about Leopold's terse style to the forefront while also unpacking the logical structure undergirding Leopold's thought.

First, Leopold begins his ethical section by referencing ancient Greek ethics, suggesting that land today is enslaved just as humans were in ancient Greece. As time has passed, society has decided to extend moral considerability to many different groups of humans who would have been excluded in the past. Here Callicott makes a cogent argument for the simple progressive view of the history of morality that Leopold implies. Leopold suggests, Callicott points out, that moral consciousness can make huge leaps even if moral practice doesn't follow on its heels. Humans can come to the conclusion that enslaving each other is immoral long before abandoning the practice.

Second, Callicott points out that Leopold pushes us to think about the history of ethics in biological as well as philosophical terms. He defines an ethic as "a limitation on freedom of action in the struggle for existence" (Leopold 1989: 238). There are clear echoes of Darwin here, which poses the question of how ethics originated and developed in complexity. Leopold embraces Darwinian morality, which is rooted in the sentiments. In contrast to the theological and rationalistic accounts of morality's origins, the theory of the sentiments more fully complements evolutionary theory. Briefly put, Darwin's account of morality begins with bonds of affection (sentiment) between parents and offspring, which are common to all animals. This very basic bond of affection and sympathy facilitates the creation of small, close-knit social groups—mainly kin groups. The family group enlarges by extending sympathies and affection to more distantly related individuals. As the family group grows, the social group grows and extends to even more individuals. In short, the parent-offspring bond becomes the fertile ground for thinking about others and considering them for inclusion in the community (Darwin 1874: 98–100). For Leopold, natural selection endowed humans with an affective moral response to perceived bonds of kinship, community membership, and identity. This affective response works against and augments our egoism. The common psychological narrative of the development of ethics is that one becomes aware of his or her own intrinsic value, then generalizes and analogizes from that awareness to include others. Thus a focus on the self is the beginning of ethical thinking, whereas in Leopold's Darwinian model of development, focus on relationships sparks ethical thinking. The fundament of Leopold's work is therefore the extension of familial kinship ethics to nonmembers, and even to nature. In fact, Callicott draws attention to the language of "evolutionary possibility" that Leopold uses to describe the extension of moral considerability to nature (Leopold 1989: 239). Though Leopold admits that the timeline may be long, the extension of human ethical categories to nature would mark the coevolution of human moral consciousness and action.

The cyclical temporality and ecological holism in the Land Ethic are consonant with Leviticus's approach to time and its community focus. In Leviticus, especially in the Holiness Code, the community eclipses the individual. In fact, reading Leviticus as a single narrative suggests an ever-narrowing concern from the beginning of the text to the end. The priests are holy and create a holy space for the community, which must prioritize self-preservation at the expense of individuals. And after Leviticus 19, the family becomes a metonymy for the community, so that the social existence of the Israelites relies on the holiness of the family. I want to suggest that the Holiness Code broadens in a way that we are often unaware of due to its emphasis on sexual deviations and its overt misogyny. In that broadening, talk of familial relationships extends the community to include the land itself. This extension of ethical concern becomes evident when we look at the passages where the land is personified and/or in parallel construction[6] with daughters.

LANDED AGENCY: THE LAND IN THE HOLINESS CODE AS SEMIAUTONOMOUS AGENT

While Leviticus has garnered academic attention, much of that attention has been paid to the strange rituals, cosmology, and dietary laws. Of note is Jacob Milgrom's three-volume Anchor Bible commentary on Leviticus (1991–2001), which is encyclopedic in scope, but emphasizes ritual. And anthropologist Mary Douglas has written influential books on the analogical structure of thinking in Leviticus both early and late in her career (2002 [1966], 1999). Land in the Bible has also been thoroughly studied: much of that work has been organized around the idea of land as a theological-political category or as the necessary territory for a polity created by God. Walter Brueggemann (2002) and Martin Buber (1997) have written on the land as a central category of thought in biblical religion, as did both Wellhausen (1885: 92–99) and von Rad (Rad 1962: 296–305) before them. In order to think about land more generally as an entity with agency, my reading in the Holiness Code focuses on the land's personification in the text.

I am not the first person to notice that the land is personified in the Holiness Code, nor am I the first person to suggest that the land as central to biblical faith can also be the starting point for constructive theological and ethical work. In his 1996 book, *People and Land in the Holiness Code: An Exegetical Study of the Ideational Framework of the Law in Leviticus 17–26*, Jan Joosten (1996) devotes a section to the personification of the land in his book, but due to the parameters of his project, he does not discuss the implications for other areas of study or contemporary ethical problems. I am also not the first person to suggest that the land in Leviticus is an agent. In her recent book *Scripture, Culture, and Agriculture*, Ellen Davis concludes her chapter on Leviticus by referring to the personified land as a "semi-autonomous moral agent" (Davis 2009: 100). As the subtitle of this section makes clear, I refer to the land as simply a semiautonomous agent because "moral" as a descriptor of the land itself implies that the land has consciousness, takes initiative in acting, and possibly that it reasons self-reflectively about its actions. In short, I don't think that "moral" can be applied to the land, even though I think the land has some agency in the text, since it participates in moral discourse and outlining the framework of a moral world that requires maintenance. But still, the question remains: What is the definition of agency that the personification of the land points to, and what are the implications of this recognition of the land as an agent for reading the Holiness Code through the lens of the Land Ethic? In demonstrating that the land in fact does have some agency in the Holiness Code, I will concentrate on a core set of verses that—taken as a group—show the land is independent from its inhabitants, comes under the same laws as humans, and has some similarity with humans in terms of needs and preferences.

Within the context of the sexual purity laws in Leviticus 18 and 20, we find two passages that suggest the land is an entity distinct from its inhabitants. Both of these passages are part of the summary sections in which YHWH warns Israel of the consequences of the listed sexual impurities and illicit relationships. In 20:22-24 YHWH says to Israel (NRSV),

> You shall keep all my statutes and all my ordinances, and observe them, so that the land to which I bring you to settle in may not vomit you out. You shall not follow the practices of the nation that I am driving out before you. Because they did all these things, I abhorred

them. But I have said to you, you shall inherit their land, and I will give it to you to possess, a land flowing with milk and honey; I am the Lord your God; I have separated you from the peoples.

The first verse in this passage is clear—the land vomits out inhabitants who don't keep YHWH's statutes and ordinances. In this first part of the passage, it is the land that responds to impurity by expelling the inhabitants who cause the impurities. There is also no conflation of the people and the land, or to put it another way, there is no identification of the people with the land. The land can belong to others, and in fact it has. In the second part of the passage, YHWH says that the people who lived in the land before the Israelites were driven out by YHWH's own agency. YHWH possesses the land and can give it to another people, but the land itself can also vomit them out for the impurities that accrue in it. The potential agency of the land is hinted at here but is also coupled with YHWH's agency. It is not clear whether inhabitants are expelled from the land due to YHWH's initiative or due to the land's response to them.

In Leviticus 18:24-28, we find a similar passage. YHWH instructs Moses to relate certain sexual laws to the people of Israel and then gives the warrant for these laws:

> Do not defile yourselves in any of these ways, for by all these practices the nations I am casting out before you have defiled themselves. Thus the land became defiled; and I punished it for its iniquity, and the land vomited out its inhabitants. But you shall keep my statutes and my ordinances and commit none of these abominations, either the citizen or the alien who resides among you (for the inhabitants of the land who were before you committed all of these abominations and the land became defiled); otherwise the land will vomit you out for defiling it, as it vomited out the nation that was before you.

In this passage, YHWH again casts out the inhabitants of the land and the land vomits them out due to the buildup of impurities. Possibly we should think of the exile of the nations from the land in terms of a two-stage process of eviction. The land becomes defiled and vomits them out, and YHWH observes this and takes initiative to act, finishing the eviction. This two-stage process sets up the land as an index of impurity, but also describes it as having an initial responsiveness to this impurity, which sparks action on the part of YHWH.

Another aspect of the personification of the land in this passage is that it is subject to the same kinds of punishment that humans are. The land becomes defiled by the actions of the humans living on it, but simply by being defiled it suffers the punishment of YHWH. What is the relationship between the land's being punished and the land's vomiting out its inhabitants? Is the expulsion of the inhabitants a reaction to both the human action and divine punishment? Does YHWH's taking action against the land in any way set up the response of the land to its inhabitants? What is at stake in this question is the characterization of YHWH's relationship to nature within the Holiness Code. The Song of the Sea in Exodus 15 provides an interesting point of comparison, though I am sure that there are many other good comparisons in other theophanic texts. Exod. 15:8 describes the parting of the Sea of Reeds as follows:

> At the blast of your nostrils [YHWH's nostrils] the waters piled up,
> the floods stood up in a heap,
> the deeps congealed in the heart of the sea.

Here, the waters respond to YHWH's actions, but it is clear that the initiative comes from YHWH. In the Holiness Code, it is unclear whether the land responds to human action, divine action, or both. But the text is clear on this point: the suffering of the land is a human problem, not a natural problem. Humans are the initial cause of the suffering, while the category of natural evil is foreign to the text's worldview.

Complicating the idea of the land as an agent is its appearance in parallel constructions with human agents. In Lev. 19:29, the land is described as coming under the same kinds of purity regulations as daughters. The verse instructs fathers on the treatment of their daughters. It reads, "Do not profane your daughter by making her a prostitute, that the land not become prostituted and full of depravity." Both the land and women are described as reacting to the same kind of mistreatment. They are each subordinates in the relationship, daughters to fathers and the land to humans, and they each respond to this mistreatment by changing states—the daughter to a defiled state and the land to a state of depravity. I do not wish to discuss the long history of interpretation regarding the possibility of cult prostitution in Israel. I am focusing on the relationship between the entities mentioned in the verse, and to that end, the main difficulty lies in determining what kind of action by an agent causes what kind of response. Does the father's action simultaneously cause the defilement of the daughter and the land, such that the daughter and the land are represented as similar objects for certain actions? Or is it a more explicitly causal relationship, with the father's action defiling the daughter and the daughter's actions afflicting the land? In each of the questions above, the inclusion of the land as part of the family relationship is assumed and, consequently, an ethical extension to the land of moral concern based on kinship ties. So it is not simply that the father-daughter relationship has consequences for the land, but rather, the land in the Holiness Code is considered the backdrop and regulating ideal for family relationships.

The land is also parallel to people in two passages in Leviticus 26. This chapter is characterized by blessings, curses, and the necessity of exile and repentance for the renewal of the covenant. The first passage is 26:34-35. It reads:

> Then [after you have been exiled] the land shall enjoy its Sabbath years as long as it lies desolate, while you are in the land of your enemies; then the land shall rest, and enjoy its Sabbath years. As long as it lies desolate it shall have the rest it did not have on your Sabbaths when you were living on it.

The land is described as requiring Sabbaths, which are instituted as the final act of creation in the first creation account in Genesis (2:1-4a). YHWH rests after creation and institutes it for humans. Here in Leviticus we see the land needing a Sabbath from agricultural practices. And while it is a stretch, it could be said that, like humans, the land is participating in the Sabbath, and consequently in being holy, since holiness and purity are the ways that Leviticus describes being like YHWH. Sure, giving the land a Sabbath is part of the law for humans, but the land is personified to the point that it is said to enjoy its Sabbath; thus rest for the land is not simply part of the laws governing human relationships with nature. As a divine institution, the Sabbath applies to the land too.

Finally, in Lev. 26:42, the land is remembered as part of the covenant. YHWH says, "Then will I remember my covenant with Jacob, I will remember my covenant with Isaac, and also my covenant with Abraham, and I will remember the land." The covenants with Jacob, Isaac, and Abraham are named individually, and then YHWH mentions that YHWH will remember the land. The mention of the land along with these three people implies the land as part of the content of the covenant; thus the mention of the land is a bit superfluous. But taken with the other passages that more explicitly personify the land, it is possible that this passage also does so, and that the land is viewed as a separate entity: not merely as the content of the covenant but also as a member of it.

The contours of the land's agency in the Holiness Code are somewhat nebulous. The kind of agency that the personification of the land points to is defined mainly by responsive activity. The land responds both to human action and to divine action. Through its responsiveness, the land shows preferences for certain kinds of actions. While the land doesn't have a mental or emotional life, it is a separate entity that sometimes shares in having equal consideration with humans under the sexual purity laws and the Sabbath requirements.

I contend that the readings above are funded by thinking about the text of the Holiness Code through the Land Ethic. When we think from a Land Ethic perspective, our imaginations make connections at the *peshat* ("simple") or surface-level meaning of the text. For the most part, the interpretations above rely on grammatical relationships between words and the concretization of metaphorical language used to describe the land. While imagination is always part of the interpretive process, it often exerts its influence at the *derash* ("theological/exegetical") level of interpretation, where part of the task is to go beyond the text itself to reestablish its significance in the world.

CONCLUSION

By reading the Holiness Code through the lens of the Land Ethic, we uncover two models of ethical thinking about land that are in tension in the text. First, the land is an ecosystem that imposes its needs on the people who inhabit it. Through its responsive agency, the land can expel those who disregard its needs, and sometimes YHWH is part of this process of expulsion. Furthermore, the land is a preexistent ecosystem with regulations and needs that predate the current inhabitants (Israelites). In this model, the inhabitants are akin to an invasive species that must be controlled. The text offers a theo-legal method of control, suggesting that one function of the laws in Leviticus is to inculcate and habituate the Israelites with behaviors and attitudes that will help them live with the land. Second, we have another ethical model in which the land is subordinate to humans, and the familial language in the Holiness Code is suggestive of extending human ethics to the land. In this model, humans have priority and use their relationships with one another to think analogically about their relationships with nature. Ultimately, individuals transfer the value of their interhuman relationships to their dealings with nature. In this perspective, the ritual and legal structure of Leviticus as a whole has a pedagogical function. The analogical thinking that presents the legal form of cultic life in the early chapters of Leviticus begins the process of extending ethics to the land in the Holiness Code, where we see the human-land relationship described in familial language. In short, for this ethical model, Leviticus both forms people who can think analogically and provides theological and ethical warrants for this kind of thinking.

At the hinge of these two ethical models—ecosystemism and extensionism—stands the גר, *ger* ("foreigner, sojourner"). While Lev. 19:33 is firmly in the Holiness Code, the entirety of chapter 19 bridges the cultic ritual with the outside world. The early chapters of Leviticus show natural objects being brought into holy spaces, while chapter 19 marks the move to bringing holiness into natural spaces. At this juncture, the *ger* not only reminds the Israelites of their past foreign status, becoming the warrant for the extension of ethics, but also points forward to the Israelites' foreign status with respect to the land. Thus the Israelites are called to remember their own foreignness not simply to prod them to include the *ger* but also to suggest that their thinking about the relationship between human action and nature will rely on their memories of being strangers themselves, and these memories will enable them to act in conformity with the land's needs. The *ger*, though silent in the text, speaks critically and constructively to the Israelites and the reader about the relationship between culture (cult, ritual, law, memory) and nature. The *ger*'s liminality situates him or her between nature and culture, pointing both backward and forward to Israel's past experiences and future life with the land. This liminality with regard to conceptual categories and the law opens up a space of possibility for the *ger* to bridge the two dominant patterns of ethical thinking about the land in Leviticus.

Notes

1. It was brought to my attention in writing this piece that this is only half of the citation. The full statement reads, "No creed but Christ, no book but the Bible, no law but love, no name but the divine." My own church only mentioned the half of the statement that I have cited. For more information, see Foster and Dunnavant 2004: 188.

2. Except maybe the sorcerers mentioned in Leviticus 19.

3. "Be holy because I, the Lord your God, am holy."

4. Aldo Leopold articulated the Land Ethic in 1949 in *A Sand County Almanac*. The 1989 edition in the bibliography is a reprint of the original.

5. I realize that with this statement I am entering a long-standing debate about the historical development and significance of the cult and the biblical prophets' relationship to both cult and law. On my reading of the book of Amos, 2:4-16 and 5:7-15 outline the social and ethical problems that have caused exile, and 5:21-27 criticizes ritual that is devoid of the accompanying ethical worldview. This makes my position sympathetic to Yehezkel Kaufmann's in *The Religion of Israel* rather than Julius Wellhausen's in *Prolegomena to the History of Israel*.

6. I do not mean the technical term that is used to describe Hebrew poetics.

2

USDA or YHWH?

Pursuing a Divinely Inspired Diet

Joseph Ryan Kelly

Old Testament Theology and the Interpreter's Context

Recent work in Old Testament theology has focused attention on the context of the interpreters and the role this plays in orienting and shaping their studies. In a chapter titled "What is a 'Theology of Genesis'?" in his *Theology of the Book of Genesis*, Walter Moberly writes, "There is something intrinsically contextual and provisional about theological use of the biblical text. Theology is not a once-for-all exercise in finding right words and/or deeds, but rather a continuing and ever-repeated attempt to articulate what a faithful understanding and use of the biblical text might look like in the changing circumstances of life" (Moberly 2009: 19).[1] According to Moberly, the context of the communities of faith in which theology is done is a part of what shapes the kind of work that falls under the rubric of Old Testament theology: "The context of the interpreter becomes significant in a variety of possible ways. The entrance point into working theologically with Genesis need not arise from systematic reading of the biblical text itself, but rather from some issue or challenge within continuing Christian life" (p. 17). John Rogerson concurs: "However hard scholars may strive for objectivity, however hard they may try not to read their own interests and assumptions into the way they organize their work, they will not be able to avoid the fact that they are situated in times and circumstances that inescapably affect and shape what they do" (Rogerson 2010: 10). Rogerson is not greatly concerned about the question of how to organize a theology of the Old Testament—the well-known debate between Walther Eichrodt and Gerhard von Rad notwithstanding—because he understands the interpreter to contextualize the activity.[2] He describes his own

Theology of the Old Testament as "a scholarly exercise, with Old Testament texts being interrogated and expounded with the help of critical scholarship, but in accordance with an agenda set by one person's [Rogerson's] perception of the human condition in today's world(s)" (p. 11). As a self-described humanist and socialist, Rogerson frequently interacts with like-minded writers to develop his own theological reflection. For Moberly, the contemporary creationism-evolution and science-religion debates; the (ab)use of natural resources in a warming world; interfaith dialogue among Jews, Christians, and Muslims; and new-atheist critiques of religious faith—specifically of the God of the Old Testament—are some of the contextual issues and challenges that shape his book's theological agenda.

These two interpreters exemplify one way in which one might approach the task of Old Testament theology, whether of a particular book or of the larger canon.[3] In what follows, I intend to adopt a similar posture.

INTEREST IN BIBLICAL FOOD LEGISLATION IN LIGHT OF CURRENT ETHICAL CONCERNS

My own interest in the text of Leviticus (and by extension Deuteronomy), specifically the legislation surrounding food, is shaped largely by current ethical issues surrounding industrialized agriculture and foodways in America. I am sympathetic to the notion that food systems provide a center, moral or otherwise, that helps shape the physical and spiritual health of a society (Davis 2009). We live in an age of impressive technological innovation. Industrialized agricultural methods of food production produce an unprecedented volume of food, so much so that "enough food is grown worldwide to provide 4.3 pounds of food per person per day, which would include two and a half pounds of grain, beans, and nuts, a pound of fruits and vegetables, and nearly another pound of meat, milk, and eggs" (Kimbrell 2002: 7). Unfortunately, this does not mean that industrialized agriculture has brought an end to world hunger. As I write this essay, East Africa is experiencing a drought-induced famine that threatens the well being of over 13 million people. Industrialization may produce enough food to feed the global population, but it does not guarantee equitable distribution. The humanitarian aid response thus far has been insufficient, and insurgency continues to exacerbate the crisis in East Africa. According to Kimbrell, the very idea that a surplus of food produced by industrialized agriculture will end world hunger is a misguided notion: "World hunger is not created by lack of food but by poverty and landlessness, which deny people access to food. Industrialized agriculture actually increases hunger by raising the cost of farming, by forcing tens of millions of farmers off the land, and by growing primarily high-profit export and luxury crops" (6). Indeed, the World Bank's Poverty Reduction and Equity Group identifies the high fluctuation of domestic food prices in the area of East Africa as a contributing factor to this famine (World Bank Poverty Reduction and Equity Group 2011). While shortfalls in yields can and do contribute to these unstable food prices, the report lists other, nonagricultural factors such as global stocks and, in the case of maize, increased demand for the production of biofuels (2). It is disquieting news that some people in East Africa may starve to death so that other countries can satisfy their energy appetite.

Hunger is not, however, the only enemy we face in an industrialized age. Industrialization has introduced new moral dilemmas about the health of our food, from what we grow and raise, how we grow and raise it, through processing, packaging and distribution, marketing, and finally to consumption. Should we eat meat (Foer 2009), and if so, how much (Pollan 2008)? How important is growing and raising organic foodstuffs (Rodale 2010)? What constitutes something grown or raised organically (Pollan 2006)? Are genetically modified organisms (GMOs) safe to produce and consume (Smith 2003)? Might they be necessary in a warming world (Lappé 2010)? Should consumers be concerned about concentrated animal feeding operations (CAFOs) or the methods of production used in slaughterhouses (Imhoff 2010)? Clearly, we are faced with numerous ethical dilemmas as both consumers and citizens. As consumers in a capitalist society, the food items we purchase—and avoid—influences the future trajectories of agribusiness. As citizens in a democracy, our voices influence politicians and legislators who establish the standards that govern agribusiness.

While these two aspects of our society, capitalism and democracy, play a profound role in shaping and developing industrialization and agribusiness, a third aspect has in times past also proven immensely influential—religion. For example, Protestant Christian denominations and parachurch organizations like the Women's Christian Temperance Union played a considerable role in promoting the cause of alcohol prohibition in America, enacted in the Eighteenth Amendment to the Constitution, which governed the manufacture, sale, transportation, and consumption of alcohol.[4] Even today, religious dietary traditions create a demand for kosher and halal food products, increasingly commonplace in grocery chains across America. That having been said, the concerns raised by industrialization do not necessarily fall within the immediate purview of religious dietary traditions. From a historical perspective, this is natural. But the ability of these traditions to address emerging concerns raised by industrialization will prove significant in determining their role, and that of religion more generally, in shaping the moral sensibilities of an industrialized (or postindustrialized?) society.

DIETARY TRADITIONS IN THE CHRISTIAN-AMERICAN CONTEXTS

No dominant dietary traditions shape the larger food culture today within my own particular context, American Christianity. This should be attributed, at least in part, to the instructions stemming from the New Testament that suggest dietary traditions are not central to the Christian gospel (Rom. 14:17; Col. 2:16). There are some Christians, however, who suppose that the Bible may yet have something to contribute to the discussion of diet. In the final chapter of his book *What Did the Ancient Israelites Eat?* Nathan MacDonald addresses the phenomenon of so-called biblical diets—programs promoted by individuals who identify within the pages of the Bible a divinely inspired diet. They tend to romanticize the dietary lifestyle of ancient Israelites and/or early Christians (especially Jesus), promising exceptional physical and sometimes even spiritual health benefits. A common denominator among these diets is the relevance of Israel's dietary legislation in Leviticus 11 and Deuteronomy 14 for modern-day Christians. "Although this is a departure from traditional Christian thought and some New Testament texts, the dietary laws are important to the authors of 'biblical diets' because they appear to justify the view of the Bible as a nutritional handbook. . . . Through an American Protestant lens, however, these cannot be laws that have to be obeyed, merely the Creator's advice that we would do well to heed" (MacDonald 2008b: 96–97). As MacDonald recognizes, "biblical diets" are most likely to attract adherents from American evangelicalism, particularly those who subscribe to the "theory about and style of using the Bible" described by Christian Smith as *biblicism*. Its assumptions and beliefs culminate in the following outlook: "The Bible teaches doctrine and morals with every affirmation that it makes, so that together those affirmations comprise something like a handbook or textbook for Christian belief and living, a compendium of divine and therefore inerrant teachings on a full array of subjects—including science, economics, health, politics, and romance" (Smith 2011: 5).[5]

Biblicists advocating biblical diets express the Christian conviction that Scripture is divine spiration (θεόπνευστος) and relevant to the Christian life (2 Tim. 3:16-17). The question of the relevance of texts like Leviticus 11 and Deuteronomy 14 is not a matter of *if* but of *how* MacDonald's critique of the biblical diets posture is sensitive to this conviction. He distinguishes between "Biblical Food" and the "Bible on Food," arguing that "the Bible does not purport to offer dietary advice, but it does frequently touch upon food and human responses to it. . . . The Old Testament presses for food to be grown responsibly, received with thankfulness and rejoicing, given generously to others, and enjoyed in moderation" (MacDonald 2008b: 98–101).

MacDonald's four observations are cogent and relevant, though one might struggle from these to see the influence of texts like Leviticus 11 and Deuteronomy 14, the texts most influential to American evangelicals or biblicists adopting a "biblical diet." While we should recognize that these texts are not, strictly speaking, "dietary advice" to modern-day communities of faith, they do belong to Scripture and should contribute to our theological understanding of their respective contexts. In this respect, questions of their presence and function within Scripture are appropriate.

Leviticus 11 and Deuteronomy 14: Diet in Theological Perspective

In considering the theological significance of Leviticus 11 and Deuteronomy 14, it is advantageous to first highlight their distinctiveness. While biblicists, generally speaking, prefer that related passages like these cohere "like puzzle pieces into single, unified, internally consistent bodies of instruction" (Smith 2011: 5), Leviticus 11 and Deuteronomy 14 challenge this assumption. Christophe Nihan painstakingly lays out the issues involved and convincingly demonstrates that, rather than construe one text as having derived from the other, each stems from a common source (Nihan 2007: 283–99). This analysis is built largely on the observation that each text contains unique features not found in the other, and that neither trajectory can account for both the expansion and the omission of material: "Attempts to derive Deut 14 from Lev 11 or Lev 11 from Deut 14 are too simple to be regarded as satisfactory, and the parallels between the two texts are best explained by the assumption of a common source" (Nihan 2007: 288). We need not concern ourselves too much with this hypothetical *Vorlage* beyond the fact that, inasmuch as this is true of Leviticus 11 and Deuteronomy 14, it provides a window, however partial, into the diet of ancient Israel (MacDonald 2008a: 60–65; 2008b: 33, 91–93). Neither of the two biblical texts is the origin of Israel's dietary tradition, as though the distinction between clean and unclean animals is something that YHWH establishes ex nihilo on Mount Sinai (Houston 2003: 159; Gen. 7:2-3, 8-9; 8:20). Rather, each text assumes an established Israelite dietary tradition with its attendant concerns, and each invests this tradition with its own language and theology (Nihan 2007: 288).

From this, we can draw two important theological conclusions about the role of Leviticus 11 and Deuteronomy 14 in contributing to a theological perspective on food. First, the abiding value of these texts for subsequent communities of faith is in the theological worldview(s) with which they invest ancient Israel's dietary tradition. The prohibited and permitted meat belongs to the culturally situated and temporally restricted context of ancient Israel. Christianity has largely adopted this opinion, though often for theological motivations arising from the New Testament, not from a close reading of the texts in the Hebrew Bible. But even when one restricts oneself to the Hebrew Bible, one must come to grips with the limited (in scope) and irreconcilable advice of Leviticus 11 and Deuteronomy 14. The legislation does not anticipate the dietary concerns or opportunities of people living beyond Iron Age agriculture, nor are many of the dietary dilemmas facing ancient Israelites addressed by this legislation.[6] This dietary advice is not comprehensive in scope, not even for ancient Israelites. Moreover, the legislation in each text cannot be entirely reconciled together. This is most obvious and problematic with respect to the legislation concerning insects—Leviticus allows for the consumption of certain clean insects where Deuteronomy prohibits all insect consumption (Lev. 11:20-23 and Deut. 14:19). For the interpreter involved in Old Testament theology, attention is misplaced if it is focused on the dietary advice divorced from the unique language and theology of each text. If we want to learn from these texts, we must focus our attention on the significance of the theology, not become preoccupied with the language.

Second, we must recognize legal development as a canonical reality and follow the implications for what this implies of divine law as conceived in the Hebrew Bible (Fretheim 2005: 152–56). The fact that Leviticus 11 and Deuteronomy 14 are ultimately irreconcilable must reflect something of their different circumstances. According to the biblical narrative, a forty-year interval separates them. We might say with Terence Fretheim that "God moves with this people on their life's journey, and God's will for them changes because they are changing" (2005: 153). Even if the circumstances at the beginning and end of this forty-year interval do not provide the historical circumstances that occasioned the differences between them, the development of law within the Pentateuch is a significant reality for those who see themselves as spiritual heirs of these laws. If law can develop within the canon of Scripture as it charts the development of Israel, why should this not continue as the spiritual heirs of these texts continue to develop as well?

The postbiblical formulation of new laws by human beings should be seen as being in tune with the divine intention regarding creational life and well-being evident in biblical law. Because these ever-emerging laws, however, are usually associated with legislatures, courts, and church assemblies and developed by human beings, we tend not to think of them as God's laws: but of course, they are. It may well be that some of these newer laws will stand over against their biblical predecessors, but this would be not unlike their biblical predecessors in, say, Deuteronomy. (Fretheim 2005: 155)

This provides a way forward for taking seriously the theological witness of Leviticus 11 and Deuteronomy 14 while at the same time addressing concerns that require new insights and the integration of new laws into the life of faith.

LEVITICUS 14 AND ITS PRIESTLY CONTEXT

How, then, might Leviticus 11 speak to the particular questions raised earlier in this essay? In his essay "Towards an Integrated Reading of the Dietary Laws of Leviticus," Walter Houston moves this kind of discussion forward by evaluating how three interpreters—Philo, Jacob Milgrom, and Mary Douglas—each "view the ritual and morality of Leviticus as parts of a unified whole," and then he shares his own reflections on the matter (Houston 2003: 143). For Houston in particular, it is not necessary to find a single principle or ethical system that explains every minutia of these laws; rather, "the dietary laws are part of a much broader structure of moral and cosmological thinking, and serve to maintain not only the specific holiness of Israel in relation to YHWH, but cosmic righteousness or right order in general" (Houston 2003: 160; cf. 1993: 253–58). The role of the larger narrative story line of the Pentateuch is important to this argument, specifically the literature recognized by scholars as belonging to the Priestly strata of the Pentateuch. To begin with this involves Gen. 1:26-30, where the primeval situation envisioned is one in which all humanity participates in a vegetarian diet. This text is not, strictly speaking, promoting vegetarianism, something towards which the Hebrew Bible has a generally negative posture (MacDonald 2008b: 25–26; Prov. 15:17). Rather, "vegetarianism is a way of describing a world at peace with itself" (Rogerson 2010: 44). As Rogerson capably demonstrates, Genesis 1 stands over against the world that humanity creates at the conclusion of the flood narrative (another Priestly text):

> This [Genesis 9:1-3] is no longer a vegetarian world at peace with itself. It is a world in which the human race may kill and eat animals provided that they avoid eating their blood (Genesis 9:4). . . . If Genesis 1 and Genesis 6–9 are compared, it will be seen that Genesis 1 is a critique of the world described in 6–9. The former world results from the creative word of God. The world of our experience is a compromise world, born of human wickedness and necessarily adapted to the destructive creature that humanity is, or has become. (Rogerson 2010: 48)

For Rogerson, the story of the Old Testament can be read as a divine project in which humanity is (re)created to live in the kind of world envisioned in Genesis 1 (Rogerson 2010: 48, 171–95). Eschatological texts like Isa. 11:6-9 and 65:17-25 also contribute to this narrative arc. As Houston observes, Leviticus 11 functions as one step in this direction:[7] "It is only when each creature observes its place in the cosmic order, and humanity, in dominion over them all, preserves the place of each, that justice and harmony can be maintained in the world." Recognizing that this falls short of the primeval or eschatological ideal, he concedes that "it is an acceptable substitute" (Houston 2003: 160). The challenge of Leviticus 11 for contemporary people of faith is to invest their own cultural dietary values and traditions with such an orientation.

BACK TO THE PRESENT: APPLICATION TO THE AMERICAN CONTEXT?

In my own American context, there is currently great concern for the health and well being of both consumers and for what is raised for consumption. Americans are increasingly overweight and unhealthy, and the way in which we raise our food, both animal and vegetable, gives us cause to question the wholesomeness of our material culture (Davis 2009: "A Wholesome Materiality: Reading Leviticus," 80–100). With these concerns in mind, it is difficult to see how an American culture could benefit from adopting a biblical diet, so-called. Leviticus does not address healthy meat-consumption practices and does not encourage a diet that includes mostly vegetables. There is no concern in the text about how to raise "permitted" animals, whether for human health or for animal welfare. But even still, communities of faith that abandon the biblical distinctions between clean and unclean animals have not abandoned the God who declares all creation to be good. Rather, they continue the pursuit for justice and wholeness within God's good creation.

The pursuit of a divinely inspired diet follows the path of law as it develops over time, and invests the laws of one's culture with the values and ideals that transcend that which is culturally relative in the Hebrew Bible (Houston 2003: 161; cf. 2008). It is not a question of either/or—of USDA or YHWH—but rather both/and. The laws of legislatures, courts, and church assemblies are not absolute (just as the laws in ancient Israel were not!), but when they are understood, critiqued, and invested with a theological vision like that to which Leviticus 11 belongs, they are no less divinely inspired.

Notes

1. Moberly's vision strikes me as congruent in significant ways to concerns raised by James Barr in his analysis of the discipline of Biblical/Old Testament theology (Barr 1999: 53-84, esp. 60-61, 74-75, 79-80, 83-84).

2. Rogerson argues concerning the work of von Rad that it "was fundamentally shaped by the dominating concerns of German protestant Old Testament scholarship of the 1930s and 1940s." He also wonders "whether von Rad's stress on Israel's confession of its faith was in any way influenced by his opposition to National Socialism and his involvement with the Confessing Church" (2010: 11).

3. For an outline of a Jewish approach to biblical theology with similar interpretive concerns, see the proposals by Benjamin Sommer (2009) and Marvin Sweeney (2011: 3–41).

4. This is documented in the first episode of Ken Burns's PBS documentary *Prohibition* (Burns and Novick 2011: episode 1, "A Nation of Drunkards" [originally aired October 2, 2011]). Prohibition in America was subsequently repealed by the Twenty-First Amendment.

5. Smith's own thesis is that biblicism is impossible, undermined by pervasive interpretive pluralism (chs. 1 and 2). As an alternative, he suggests that (Christian evangelical) communities of faith adopt a Christocentric hermeneutical key (ch. 5) to help them navigate the complexity and ambiguity of Scripture (ch. 6). In the final analysis, I am unsure how Smith's proposal sufficiently distinguishes itself from certain aspects of the biblicism that he finds untenable (Smith 2011: 134–39, esp. 136).

6. According to MacDonald, the evidence suggests the existence of nutritional deficiencies in the diet of ancient Israelites (MacDonald 2008a: 65–68; 2008b: 80–87). These deficiencies do not arise from Israelites' failing to adhere to the dietary constraints of Leviticus 11 or Deuteronomy 14.

7. Deuteronomy 14 has an altogether different orientation; exploring the unique language and theology of this text is outside the scope of this essay. In the secondary literature, the place to begin is Mayes 1994.

3

"Do Not Bare Your Heads and Do Not Rend Your Clothes" (Leviticus 10:6)

On Mourning and Refraining from Mourning in the Bible

Yael Shemesh

Many agree nowadays that objective research devoid of a personal dimension is a chimera. As noted by Fewell (1987: 77), the very choice of a research topic is influenced by subjective factors. Until October 2008, mourning in the Bible and the ways in which people deal with bereavement had never been one of my particular fields of interest, and my various plans for scholarly research did not include that topic. Then, on October 4, 2008, the Sabbath of Penitence (the Sabbath before the Day of Atonement), my beloved father succumbed to cancer. When we returned home after the funeral, close family friends brought us the first meal that we mourners ate in our new status, in accordance with Jewish custom, as my mother, my three brothers, my father's sisters, and I began "sitting *shiv'ah*" ("seven" [days])—observing the week of mourning and receiving the comforters who visited my parents' house.

The *shiv'ah* for my father's death was abbreviated to only three full days, rather than the customary week, also in keeping with custom, because Yom Kippur, which fell only four days after my father's death, truncated the initial period of mourning. Before my bereavement, I had always imagined that sitting *shiv'ah* and conversing with those who came to console me, when I was so deep in my grief, would be more than I could bear emotionally, and I thought that I would prefer for people to leave me alone with my pain. But as an Orthodox woman and lecturer in Bible at Bar-Ilan University (the only religious university in Israel), I knew that I could not avoid observing the prescribed rites of mourning. To my astonishment, I discovered the therapeutic and consoling side of the *shiv'ah*, the mourner's gratitude for the expressions of social support, and the relief of talking with people, especially when the focus is on the deceased.

I was always strongly attached to my father and had helped care for him during his last illness. After his death, I felt a strong need to consult psychological literature on mourning, where I learned that my experience was normal (yes, it turns out that heartache, in the most literal sense, is a well-known symptom of bereavement) and gained an idea of what I could expect throughout the rest of the long journey of mourning. Thirteen days after my father's death, while planning a bicycle tour with my husband in the hope that the physical activity would soothe my turbulent feelings, I decided, on the spur of the moment, to suspend my other academic projects and begin studying mourning in the Bible, because that was what I needed then, as therapy, and that I would dedicate the fruits of my research to my father's memory. During the cycling tour, I worked on a mental sketch of the introduction to that book. Thus my father's death spawned my current interest in mourning in the Bible and limited it to the specific category of mourning for the dead rather than other sorts of mourning, such as national mourning or petitionary mourning.

In the wake of my own experience with mourning customs, and starting from the story of Aaron and his sons, who were not permitted to indulge in the normal rites of mourning (Leviticus 10), the present article analyzes four cases in which biblical characters did not mourn and considers the main differences among them. Three of them involve the death of children (Aaron for his sons [Leviticus 10], David for his infant son [2 Sam. 12:15-25], and the Shunammite matron for her son [2 Kgs. 4:8-37]), and one involves the death of a spouse (Ezekiel for his wife [Ezek. 24:15-24]). In two cases, mourning is suppressed in compliance with the injunction of God or his prophet (Aaron and his sons as instructed by Moses, who interprets God's will; and Ezekiel directly at God's behest); in the other two cases it is the decision of the bereaved parent (David and the Shunammite matron). I will wind up with a consideration of the link between mourning and gender and point out the importance of women in mourning rituals.

I dedicate this essay to the memory of my beloved father, Robert Shemesh, who raised me with such great love.

"Do Not Bare Your Heads and Do Not Rend Your Clothes": Aaron and His Sons Are Forbidden to Mourn for Nadab and Abihu (Leviticus 10)

A terrible tragedy has struck the family of the newly installed high priest Aaron at an unexpected moment. Leviticus 8 and 9 recounts the ceremony in which Aaron and his sons were anointed with the consecrated oil and entered into their new function, after precise and meticulous preparations. Chapter 9 concludes on a particularly celebratory note:

> Aaron lifted his hands toward the people and blessed them; and he stepped down after offering the sin offering, the burnt offering, and the peace offerings. Moses and Aaron then went inside the Tent of Meeting. When they came out, they blessed the people; and the Presence of the Lord appeared to all the people. Fire came forth from before the Lord and consumed the burnt offering and the fat parts on the altar. And all the people saw, and shouted, and fell on their faces. (Lev. 9:22-24)[1]

But this pinnacle of spiritual exaltation is cut off tragically: the Lord's manifestation in the fire that blazes forth and consumes the sacrifice (9:24) evidently propels Aaron's two older sons, Nadab and Abihu, into a religious ecstasy in which they bring "strange fire before the Lord"—probably a flame not kindled from the perpetual fire on the sacrificial altar.[2] Their punishment is immediate and measure for measure, exacted by the very instrument of their transgression: "And fire came forth from the Lord and consumed them, and they died before the Lord" (Lev. 10:2).[3] Thus, in an instant, the collective elation gives way to desolation. Fire, so recently the symbol of the bond between the people and their God (9:24), has now become a means of punishment: the people's shouts of joy are replaced (we may conjecture) by screams of horror and a sense of shock.

The first reaction we hear of is Moses', who, seeking to attach meaning to his nephews' horrible deaths, tells Aaron: "This is what the Lord meant when He said: 'Through those near to Me I show Myself holy, and gain glory before all the people'" (10:3). This may mean that God is more punctilious with those who are closest to him.[4] It is true that Nadab and Abihu were punished, but in their death they sanctified the divine name. Did this idea provide some consolation to the bereaved father? According to the text, *vayiddom 'aharon* (v. 3)—which is generally rendered as "and Aaron was silent." But the verb used and thus his reaction are subject to various and even contradictory interpretations.

The normal understanding, as noted, is that the root *d-m-m* connotes silence. But this, too, can be understood in two totally different ways. The dominant interpretation in Jewish tradition is that Aaron held his peace and did not mourn, because he accepted the divine judgment and found consolation in what Moses had said (for instance, *Avot de-rabbi Nathan* A, 14 [Kister-Schechter edition, 30; *BT Zevahim* 115b). That is, the sense of *d-m-m* here is like that in Jer. 47:6, "rest and be still [*domi*]!"[5] Some, however, hold that Aaron was rendered mute by shock, accompanied by a deep depression. This reading is supported by Exod. 15:16: "Terror and dread descend upon them; through the might of Your arm they are still as stone [*yiddemu ka'aven*]." A mute reaction to bereavement is well known in the anthropological literature.[6] Some even believe that silence was a widespread mourning custom in biblical times, citing Job's friends, who sat silently with him for an entire week, contemplating his tragedy.[7] It seems more plausible, however, that silence was not a mourning custom of biblical Israel, and that when bereavement reduced mourners to silence it was a natural reaction to the shock rather than adherence to custom.[8]

Unlike the dominant reading that Aaron was mute (whether in acceptance of the divine judgment or because of his trauma), Levine (1993b) proposes understanding the verb *d-m-m* here in the sense of *d-m-m* II (BDB), "to mourn, moan."[9] He cites the similar Akkadian root *damāmu*, which has this meaning. He also proposes that we understand the Ugaritic *d-m-m* as cognate with the Akkadian *damāmu* and as parallel to the Ugaritc root *b-k-y*, "cry,"[10] and he cites texts from Ebla that also support a connection between the root *d-m-m* and mourning. Thus Levine (1993b: 89) proposes that "Aaron reacted in the customary manner; he moaned or wailed and was about to initiate formal mourning and lamentation for his two lost sons." But his plan is interrupted when Moses summons their cousins to bury the dead (v. 4) and explicitly forbids Aaron and his sons to mourn, so as to not to profane the sacred precincts: "And Moses said to Aaron and to his sons Eleazar and Ithamar, 'Do not bare your heads and do not rend your clothes'" (Lev. 10:6).

Although Moses mentions only two customs of mourning here, he certainly intends them to stand for the full gamut of associated practices, all of which are forbidden to Aaron and his sons. There is no single locus in the Bible that collects all of the various mourning customs, so we must assemble them from various passages. It is possible, too, that not all of them were followed in all periods or by all strata of biblical societies.[11] The rending of garments as a sign of mourning, forbidden to Aaron and his sons, is mentioned frequently.[12] The second practice forbidden them, loosing the hair or uncovering the head, is mentioned much less often.[13]

Other mourning practices mentioned in the Bible include weeping,[14] lamentation,[15] keening,[16] wearing sackcloth,[17] removing the shoes[18] and sometimes fasting,[19] refraining from bathing[20] or anointing the body with oil,[21] sitting or lying on the ground[22] or in ashes,[23] sometimes rolling in dirt or ashes,[24] strewing dirt or ashes on the head,[25] covering the lower part of the face (hiding the mustache),[26] and beating the breast[27] or thigh.[28] Although there is no explicit mention of abstaining from sexual relations, we may conjecture that it too was a mourning practice.[29] Bereaved wives marked themselves off from their surroundings by means of clearly recognizable "widow's weeds."[30] During the mourning period, relatives and friends visited the mourners to console them,[31] and took on several mourning practices themselves as a way to express their participation in the mourners' pain, nodding their head (or perhaps the whole body);[32] evidently they also provided the mourners with their first meal on the first day of mourning.[33]

In addition to these legitimate mourning rites, a number of customs are denounced as illegitimate by Leviticus and Deuteronomy and thus, it stands to reason, were widespread: self-mutilation[34] and shaving or plucking out the hair and beard.[35]

These and other mourning rites, across cultures, time, and place, play a major psychological function: they help mourners retain some degree of stability and structure in their lives at a time when their familiar world seems to have collapsed around them and the ground is disappearing from under their feet. Such practices help them internalize and adjust to their new status as orphans, widows or widowers, bereaved parents, and so on, and redefine their relations with the deceased and with those around them. In addition, of course, such practices make it possible for mourners to express their grief and unburden themselves of some of their pain.

Beyond all of these psychological benefits, however, the Bible takes it as axiomatic that the living have certain obligations toward the dead. (This seems to be almost universal in human societies throughout history.) Some of the survivors' duties to the dead, as found in the Bible, are fixed and apply to every death, such as burying the deceased[36] and mourning; other obligations obtain only in certain cases, such as blood redemption after a murder (Num. 35:19) and levirate marriage for the widow of a man who dies without offspring (Deut. 25:5–6). Thus Aaron and his sons are barred from fulfilling their duty toward their sons/brothers and from giving vent to their emotions in a way that might allow them to ease their pain.

Of all bereavements, the loss of children is the worst.[37] In patriarchal societies like that of the Bible, which attach major importance to sons, who continue the family name, we might go further and say that the most unbearable loss is that of sons. Sons are an extension of their father. This is why the wish expressed by David's courtiers as he lay on his deathbed—"May God make the renown of Solomon even greater than yours, and may He exalt his throne even higher than yours!" (1 Kgs. 1:47)—is no insult but in fact a blessing, which David accepts gladly. What is more, in the biblical era, male offspring served a practical function: they reinforced the power of the family and could support their parents in old age.[38]

Nadab and Abihu were Aaron's two oldest sons (Exod. 6:23). Only they had accompanied Moses and Aaron when they ascended Mount Sinai (Exod. 24:1). Aaron naturally would have seen them as his heirs, and his firstborn, Nadab, as his successor in the high priesthood. He was traumatized by their sudden death, but forbidden (along with his surviving sons, Ithamar and Eleazar) to mourn them, or even to accompany the dead to the grave. Moses summons Aaron's cousins, Mishael and Elzaphan, to do this instead.

But even though Aaron and his sons are instructed to stifle their mourning and to continue the ritual in the sanctuary—business as usual, as it were—they nevertheless find a way to express their grief by abstaining from the ritual consumption of the gift offering. Aaron allows it to burn to ashes, thereby turning it into a burnt offering. When Moses scolds him for this, Aaron associates his action with the calamity that has befallen him, without naming it explicitly: "Such things have befallen me!" (Lev. 10:19). This expresses his intense pain (Sharon 1999: 138).[39] Diane Sharon calls attention to the fact that this is a ritual meal; consequently, "In rejecting this meal, Aaron is also refusing to share a meal with the God whose fire has consumed his sons" (1999: 138).[40] According to her, a sin offering as described in Leviticus 10, part of which is eaten by the priests and part of which is reserved for the deity, can be viewed, in a certain sense, as a meal shared by the priests and the deity. By refusing to take part in this feast, Aaron is expressing, in the only way left to him, his grief and rage over what has just happened (Sharon 1999: 139). But such a personal expression of grief is not found in the case of a later priest, Ezekiel, when God forbids him to mourn for his dead wife.

"You Shall Not Lament or Weep or Let Your Tears Flow": Ezekiel Is Forbidden to Mourn for His Wife (Ezek. 24:15–24)

The Lord tells Ezekiel that a person who is very dear to him, "the delight of your eyes"[41] (Ezek. 24:16), is about to die. It is not obvious from this that the Lord is referring to his wife, whose existence the reader learns of for the first time only in this pericope, which relates her death. The phrase could equally refer to his children, if he had any. In any case, the Lord instructs Ezekiel to stifle his grief: "Son of man, I am about to take away the delight of your eyes from you through pestilence; but you shall not lament or weep or let your tears flow. Moan softly; observe no mourning for the dead: Put on your turban and put your sandals on your feet; do not cover over your upper lip, and do not eat the bread of men" (vv. 16-17).[42]

This pericope raises grave problems, both linguistic and thematic, that I cannot address here.[43] I will mention only that the Lord's injunction to Ezekiel at its beginning, rendered by the NJPS as "moan softly; observe no mourning for the dead," and by the RSV as "sigh, but not aloud," can be understood in several ways.[44] The most common interpretation derives the word *dom* from the root *d-m-m*, "be silent," and takes it as modifying *he'aneq*, "moan, sigh": thus "moan quietly." David Kimhi considers it to be an imperative and understands an implicit privative *me-* before *he'aneq*: "[*me-*]*he'aneq dom!* 'be silent [and refrain] from sighing,' that is, from crying out as other mourners do; but you be silent and do not cry out" (in Cohen 2000: 166). Abravanel's gloss is similar (1979: 537). More plausible, however, is the common view that the Lord is not forbidding him to moan (see v. 23, where groaning or moaning [*unehamtem*] is permitted to the people) and that the phrase indicates permission for the prophet to moan his loss quietly. Thus the meaning is something like "groan silently/moan silently [but] observe no mourning for the dead." By contrast, Levine (1993b: 99–100) and Greenberg (1997: 508–9) associate *dom* with *d-m-m* II, "to moan." Although they differ in the details,[45] they agree that Ezekiel is permitted to moan and sigh over his bereavement—but no more than that.

Whether we understand the passage as Kimhi and Abravanel do—namely, that Ezekiel was forbidden any manifestation, even private, of his sorrow—or that he was permitted to grieve quietly, he was clearly not allowed to engage in the standard mourning rites: lamenting or crying, baring his head and removing his shoes, covering his lip and eating the funeral meal. In contrast to Abraham, who in Gen. 23:2 mourns and weeps for Sarah (Gen. 23:2), Ezekiel, like Aaron and his sons, is told not to mourn his wife in the normal manner.[46]

But there is a major difference between the restrictions enjoined for Aaron and his sons and those laid on Ezekiel. In the former case, the purpose is to preserve the social order: as priests who have just been consecrated, Aaron and his sons must suppress their private grief in order to avoid profaning the sacred and in order to maintain the unity of the congregation for which they are responsible (Lev. 10:6-7). In Ezekiel's case, by contrast, the prophet's private life is cast as an emblem of the destiny of his people, as in the cases of Isaiah (Isa. 8:1-4, 18), Jeremiah (Jer. 16:1-9), and Hosea (Hos. 1:2-9; 3:1-3). Not only does Ezekiel's bottling up of his grief make no contribution to the social order; it actually expresses its fragility: just as Ezekiel does not mourn his wife, neither will the people mourn the awful tragedy that is about to overtake them—the destruction of Jerusalem, the razing of the temple, and the violent deaths of their sons and daughters (24:21). As the prophet puts it:[47] "You shall do as I have done: you shall not cover over your upper lips or eat the bread of comforters; and your turbans shall remain on your heads, and your sandals upon your feet. You shall not lament or weep, but you shall be heartsick because of your iniquities and shall moan to one another" (vv. 22-23).

Ezekiel's prophecy does not explain why the people will not follow mourning customs.[48] Some hold that there will be no mourning because the people have been commanded by the Lord to take their example from Ezekiel: not mourning for the sinful city of Jerusalem will show that they accept the justice of the divine decree and serve as a sign of their emotional detachment from Jerusalem and the temple.[49] It seems more likely, however, that we should understand the divine injunction here in light of Ezekiel's many other symbolic actions throughout the book and see his statement to the people as a prophecy rather than a command.[50] Just as the other examples of his unusual conduct are meant as omens of the people's destiny, not as divine injunctions to the people, so too here. When Ezekiel's prophecy is fulfilled and the exiles do not mourn the national disaster and the many dead, it will serve them as a portent (v. 24), that is, as evidence of the truth of Ezekiel's prophecy[51] and consequently of the existence of the Lord and his might, as the Lord tells the people through Ezekiel: "When this happens, then you will know that I am the Lord God." But if it is not a divine injunction to the people not to mourn, what will prevent them from observing the normal rites? The answer, I believe, is that the unprecedented scale of the catastrophe will bring the social order, including its mourning customs, crashing down, and leave the people paralyzed in their grief, too disheartened and depressed to even practice such rituals.[52] Moreover, when tragedy befalls an entire community, there is little point to institutionalized mourning, since there is no one to offer consolation.[53] The magnitude of the impending national calamity is such that the exiles will be able only to moan to each other, thereby expressing their collective grief for the destruction of Jerusalem and the temple and lamenting their private tragedy, the deaths of their sons and daughters, in a manner that is quite uncivilized, indeed animal-like.[54] This idea, that it is the intensity of the disaster that will deter the people from mourning, is confirmed by the parallel text in Jeremiah 16. Jeremiah is commanded not to marry and not to have children (16:2), and never to console mourners (vv. 5, 8[?]), so that his personal life will express the truncated future of the people in Judah, both parents and children, whose destruction has been decreed (vv. 5-7, 9). What is most important for us is that Jeremiah, too, describes the absence of mourning customs in the wake of mass death: "They shall not be buried; men shall not lament them, nor gash and tonsure themselves for them. They shall not break bread for a mourner to comfort him for a bereavement, nor offer one a cup of consolation for the loss of his father or mother" (vv. 6–7). I maintain that just as the people's failure to follow mourning customs in Jeremiah 16 is an effect of the scale of the disaster, so too in Ezek. 24:22-23.

In addition to the exiles in Babylon, we encounter parents who do not mourn the death of a child in David's reaction to the death of the boy born of his adulterous relationship with Bathsheba, although he had followed mourning customs while the infant was fighting for its life (2 Sam. 12:19-25), and again in the case of the Shunammite matron (2 Kgs. 4:18-37). In both of these, however, the parent is not commanded to stifle grief but elects to do so of his or her own accord. We now turn to an analysis of David's anticipatory mourning before the infant's death and to David's and the Shunammite's eschewing of mourning practices after the death of their sons.

"But Now That He Is Dead, Why Should I Fast?": David's Reaction to the Death of his Infant Son (2 Sam. 12:19–25)

The death of David's newborn son by Bathsheba, conceived in sin, is the first death in his immediate family known to us. It is also the only death in his family that is not sudden, but foreknown, given that Nathan prophesies the child's death in verse 14 and that the child lingers for seven days. This difference between the death of the newborn and other deaths in David's family sheds some light on why David reverses the normal procedure—mourning while the child yet lives, and stopping the moment he learns of the infant's death. The mourning customs observed by David during his son's illness, stated explicitly by the text, are fasting and lying on the ground: "David fasted, and he went in and spent the night lying [*veshakabh*] on the ground" (2 Sam. 12:16). The outcome of David's sin with Bathsheba—"he lay [*vayishkabh*] with her" (11:4)—is that he lies on the ground, in a vain attempt to atone for his sin and to annul the fatal decree passed against the son born of that sin. At the end of the story, the same words that designated the sin describe David's attempt to comfort Bathsheba: "He lay with her" (12:24).

David observes other mourning customs as well, although they are not mentioned in so many words. This may be inferred from the fact that, after the child's death, "he bathed and anointed himself, and he changed his clothes. He went into the House of the Lord[55] and prostrated himself" (v. 20).

The "elders of his house"—his counselors or ministers (see Gen. 24:2)—urge David to suspend his mourning—to rise from the ground and eat—certainly out of concern for his health, but in vain (2 Sam. 12:17). David pays no heed to their entreaties, even though they are among his closest confidants. The use here of the root *b-r-'/b-r-h*, which refers to the first meal after a mourning fast (2 Sam. 3:35) or illness (2 Sam. 13:5, 6, 7, 10), indicates that David was growing weaker before their eyes as a result of his intense mourning, which included fasting. We are not told at what stage of the child's illness David began observing mourning customs, but the statement that "on the seventh day the child died" (2 Sam. 12:18) evidently indicates that David's reaction to the child's illness began as soon as it became apparent. If so, we are talking of a weeklong fast, like that of the townsfolk of Jabesh Gilead after they bury Saul and his sons (1 Sam. 31:13). In addition to fasting and lying on the ground, David prays to the Lord.

David must have felt that he was to blame for the condition of the innocent child, who would soon die on account of his father's transgression, as the prophet Nathan had informed him even before the child was born (12:13-14). The link between forgiveness of David's sin and the child's death is clear. David regains his own life but must bury his infant son.

David's observance of mourning customs during his son's grave illness is not mourning for the dead but petitionary mourning, which is also an expression of penitence.[56] Such rites are appropriate as long as the petition is pending. As soon as David knows that the child is dead and that his entreaties are in vain, he terminates them. The narrator describes this in a series of short clauses that express vigorous activity and a return to life: "Thereupon David rose from the ground; he bathed and anointed himself, and he changed his clothes. He went into the House of the Lord and prostrated himself. Then he went home and asked for food, which they set before him, and he ate" (v. 20). David's conduct after the infant dies is the antithesis of his behavior while the child was sick (rising from the ground rather than lying on it, eating rather than fasting, and so on). The narrator expresses this by the divergent use of the roots *b-w-'* and *sh-k-b*: instead of "he went in [*uba'*] and spent the night lying [*veshakhabh*] on the ground" (v. 16), as part of his mourning, after the child's death the root *b-w-'* denotes resumption of his routine: "He went into [*vayabo'*] the House of the Lord. . . . Then he went [*vayabo'*] home" (v. 20). Shortly thereafter, the roots *b-w-'* and *sh-k-b* designate the renewal of sexual relations between David and Bathsheba: "he went in [*vayabo'*] to her and lay [*vayishkabh*] with her" (v. 24). David understands that Nathan's prophecy has been realized and that all his attempts to avert the evil decree were in vain. His behavior after he learns of the child's death is acceptance of the divine verdict.[57] What is more, as shown by Anderson (1991: 49, 82-84), not only do David's actions contrary to mourning rites express a return to normal life; but all of them are in fact associated with biblical expressions of joy. His conduct after the infant's death astonishes his courtiers, who misunderstand his mourning practices while the child was alive as evidence of a strong emotional bond with the child and an expression of his devastation over its impending death. So when the child dies, they are afraid to give David the bad news, lest he "do something terrible" to himself (v. 18). But their anxious whispering arouses his suspicion. "Is the child dead?" he demands. We can well imagine their trepidation as they replied with the single Hebrew word "[he is] dead" (v. 19), and their tense focus on his reaction. But seeing David's vigorous activity to end his mourning, contrary to what they have feared in light of his behavior thus far, they are bold enough to express their astonishment at this strange behavior, which does not correspond with what is expected of a bereaved father: "Why have you acted in this manner? While the child was alive, you fasted and wept; but now that the child is dead, you rise and take food!" (v. 21). Their puzzlement allows David to explain himself: "While the child was still alive, I fasted and wept because I thought: 'Who knows? The Lord may have pity on me, and the child may live.' But now that he is dead, why should I fast? Can I bring him back again? I shall go to him, but he will never come back to me" (vv. 22-23).

David's stoic response to the child's death does not resemble his reaction in other cases of bereavement. From the public and ceremonial perspective, his desire to eat after learning of the child's death stands in stark contrast to his refusal to do so after the death of Abner (2 Sam. 3:35). From the personal and emotional perspective, his pragmatic and rational response to the infant's death is not repeated following the slaying of Amnon (13:31, 36-37) and especially not after the death of Absalom (19:1-5). Fokkelman (1981: 90) conjectures that David's anticipatory mourning for his son, an entire week before the infant died, facilitated the resumption of his routine after the child's death. Although it is true that anticipatory mourning for a gravely ill person may reduce the intensity of the grief after the person breathes his or her last, it cannot explain David's sharp transition from intense mourning to perfectly normal behavior. As I read it, David's calm reaction is possible only because of his emotional distance from the dead child, with whom he never had a chance to bond. It corresponds to what we know from psychology and anthropology about parents' reactions to the death of infants, as opposed to the loss of grown children, especially in societies where infant mortality is high (Blauner 1966: 318 and n. 13 [bibliographical references]).[58] This is what David Kimhi writes about verses 22-23: "Nor is it worth weeping over the child after its death, as one weeps for the dead, because he was an infant and not a rational being for whose loss a man should weep. Yet David did cry for Amnon and Absalom, although it was not in his power to bring them back, as an expression of his pain and mourning" (Cohen 1993: 203).[59]

Perhaps, though, we can offer another explanation for David's indifference about the infant. Bathsheba's son is the fruit of their adultery, the result of an unplanned and distinctly unwanted pregnancy. His conception led David to murder Uriah, after he had failed in his valiant efforts to get Uriah to spend the night at home and sleep with his wife, so that he could plausibly be accounted the father of the child. Thus the innocent newborn is a reminder of David's terrible transgression, for which Nathan has already censured him: "Why have you despised the word of the Lord, to do what is evil in his sight? You have put Uriah the Hittite to the sword; you took his wife and made her your wife and had him killed by the sword of the Ammonites" (12:9). So we may conjecture that the infant's death bears with it a species of spiritual relief for the sinner; the reminder of the sin is buried, removed from sight and mind, and David can delude himself that by this loss he has paid for his sin and rehabilitated his relationship with God. The child dies instead of David, who accepts the verdict, unlike his howls of grief after the death of Absalom: "If only I had died instead of you!" (19:1 [18:33]).[60]

The sequence of actions by which David marks the end of his mourning—"He *went* into the House of the Lord. . . . Then he *went* home" (12:20)—is followed shortly by "he *went* in to her [Bathsheba]" (v. 24): a resumption of sexual relations and thus of normal life.[61] But here this has a special meaning—an attempt to console Bathsheba for the death of her infant: "David consoled his wife Bathsheba; he went in to her and lay with her." The language here is very close to that of their first and forbidden tryst: "She went to him and he lay with her" (11:4), but with such a great difference—then she was compelled to go and please him; now he goes to console her.[62] We can say that the child's illness and death opened David's heart to awareness of the misery of another person: first the child itself, as long as it was struggling for life, and then its mother, Bathsheba, after the death of her infant.

The events in chapters 11 and 12 have a chiastic structure:

Chapter 11	Chapter 12
Pregnancy	Death of the infant
Death of Uriah	Pregnancy

In chapter 11, Bathsheba's unwanted pregnancy leads to the murder of Uriah. In chapter 12, the death of Bathsheba's son leads David to console her, and she again conceives, but willingly this time. The conclusion of the story is a rectification of the sin and its punishment. In contrast to Nathan's earlier mission bearing a stern rebuke—"And the Lord sent Nathan to David" (12:1), the end of the story—"He sent a message through the prophet Nathan" (v. 25)—heralds hope and peace. In contrast to the death of the infant as a consequence of David's sin with "Uriah's wife" (v. 15), now we have the birth of the son who will continue his dynasty, a consequence of David's desire to console "his wife Bathsheba" (v. 24).[63] In contrast to the concluding sentence of the account of the sin—"But the Lord was displeased with what David had done" (11:27)—the second infant is the object of God's love (2 Sam. 12:24), which is reconfirmed by the name Nathan gives him at God's behest: "He sent a message through the prophet Nathan; and he was named Jedidiah [i.e., beloved of the Lord] at the instance of the Lord" (v. 25).

The name given him by his parents, too (by his father, according to the *kethib*; by his mother, according to the *qere*)—Solomon, which expresses wholeness and peace (v. 24)[64]—articulates their hope for a new beginning after the calamity they have endured. As Abravanel notes it in his commentary on verse 24: "He named him Solomon, to indicate that David and his father in heaven made peace through him" (1955: 349).

"ALL IS WELL": THE SHUNAMMITE MATRON'S RESTRAINED REACTION TO HER SON'S DEATH (2 KINGS 4:18–37)

Unlike David, who expresses no grief after the death of his infant son because he has accepted the heavenly verdict, the Shunammite matron suppresses all manifestations of mourning precisely because she has not accepted the death and is resolved to fight for her son's life. This requires that she conceal the fact of his death, for reasons I will explain below. First, however, let us consider the background of the story. In 2 Kgs. 4:8-17, we read that Elisha seeks to reward the Shunammite matron for her liberality in hosting him whenever he visits Shunem and for adding an upper chamber to her house for him to stay in. First he proposes to exercise his connections in high places on her behalf; but the matron rejects this offer and makes it clear that she is content with what she has. Elisha is not satisfied and still wants to reward her for her generosity. Here his serving-man Gehazi enters the picture, reminding his master that the woman has no son and that her husband is elderly. Gehazi is hinting that Elisha should exploit not his earthly but his heavenly entrée and work a miracle for the woman. Elisha accepts the advice and informs the Shunammite matron that within a year she will be embracing a son. The woman's anxious reaction—"Please, my lord, man of God, do not delude your maidservant" (v. 16)—does not indicate that she does not want a child but rather that, wanting one very much indeed, she is afraid of disappointment.[65] On the surface, however, her fears are pointless, and the prophet's promise is realized in full (v. 17). If the story ended here, we could read it as a freestanding account of a miraculous birth effected by Elisha. But the story has a second part in which the young boy, who has gone out to the fields to watch his father and the harvesters at work, succumbs to heatstroke or sunstroke. When the child cries out in pain, "My head, my head!" (v. 19), his father sends him back home to his mother. We read the heartrending details of how the mother cuddles him on her lap, powerless to help him, until he dies (v. 20). But the moment the child stops breathing, the Shunammite matron turns into a tigress fighting for the life of her son.

Instead of weeping inconsolably and starting to mourn, she lays the body on the bed in the room of Elisha, the "holy man of God" (as she refers to him in v. 9), shuts the door, and makes preparations for the long journey to Elisha on Carmel, where she will beg him to restore her son.

There seem to be three reasons for carrying the child's lifeless body to the man of God's room and bed. First, on the symbolic level, the man of God, who was responsible for the child's birth, is deemed by the Shunammite to be equally responsible for his "rebirth," and his bed symbolizes this responsibility. Second, on the magical level, her action expresses the common belief that the appurtenances of saints absorb some of their owner's holiness and thus have the power to effect miracles on their own (see Ganuz 1989). The Shunammite, who recognizes Elisha's holiness, identifies Elisha's bed as a protected space in which the process of death will be suspended until the man of God arrives and can restore the boy to life. Third, on the practical level, the Shunammite must conceal the child's death from everyone, and Elisha's shuttered chamber is the ideal hiding place. Her need to hide the death seems to combine practical consideration with mystical attitude. As a practical matter, had the child's corpse been left in a public space, the relatives might have buried him, putting an end to the Shunammite's hopes of regaining her son. On the mystical level, there is the idea that recognizing and accepting death gives it power and standing as an established fact. Note that she never utters the word "dead" in connection with the boy, not even to Elisha.

Before she reaches the prophet, though, she must overcome the obstacle of his servant Gehazi, whom Elisha, spying her in the distance and concerned by her unannounced arrival, sends out to make sure that she, her husband, and her son are well. The Shunammite dismisses Gehazi with the same answer she gave her husband, "All is well" (v. 26), because she understands that the situation is so serious that only direct intervention by the man of God will avail. (The accuracy of her perception is seen later, when Gehazi's mission with Elisha's staff fails, but the prophet is able to revive the child: vv. 29-37.) In contrast to her calm response to Gehazi, the Shunammite when she reaches Elisha is reduced to an act of desperation, which breaches the bounds of propriety, and seizes hold of the prophet's feet (v. 27). This utterly violates the distance that has always marked her behavior toward him, as manifested in the construction of his own room (v. 10) and in her standing in the doorway, rather than entering, when he summons her (v. 15). Falling on Elisha's feet is the woman's first expression of her anguish. Gehazi, shocked by her inappropriate behavior, tries to pull her away, but Elisha has understood that her shocking action stems from a shocking situation—"She is in bitter distress" (v. 27)—and instructs Gehazi to leave her alone. Only now does the Shunammite tell Elisha that her distress involves her son, when she complains to him: "Did I ask my lord for a son? Didn't I say: 'Don't mislead me'?" (v. 28). But she is still careful not to say that the child is dead. Elisha may believe, then, that the child is critically ill or unconscious, so that it would suffice to send his staff with Gehazi to rectify matters; the miracle of healing has little in common with the miracle of resurrection. Ultimately Elisha gives in to the Shunammite's insistence that he act directly to restore the child; at the end of the story, the Shunammite does again embrace a living son.

But in order to succeed in her mission, she has had to suppress her grief at her son's death and stifle every expression of mourning, to the point of falsely reassuring both her husband and Gehazi that "all is well." She avoids any manifestations of grief until the moment she grabs Elisha's feet in supplication. In this case, the strategy of not mourning is intended to bring the boy back to life.

"Summon the Dirge-Singers, Let Them Come":
Mourning and Gender (Jer. 9:16[17])

In Leviticus 10:6, Aaron and his two surviving sons are forbidden to mourn for Nadab and Abihu (see above). However, Moses tells Aaron that the entire nation will mourn the dead, a detail that may have offered some small consolation to the father and brothers, who could not mourn themselves. Although the text does not say so explicitly, there seem to have been other first-degree relatives who did mourn for Nadab and Abihu: their mother Elisheva (Exod. 6:23) and their sisters (Lev. 10:14).[66] It is true that there is no textual evidence of this mourning, but there is no reason why women who had not been anointed with the sacred oil should not express their grief. As such, their situation was better than that of the men in the family, who had to smother their pain and seclude themselves in the sacred precinct.

Anthropological research points to the important function of women in mourning rites.[67] Ethnomusicologists note that the singing of dirges, especially at funerals, is classically a female role.[68] In Sumerian literature, this is reflected by the dirges sung by Dumuzi's mother, sister, and wife after he dies and is transported to the underworld,[69] as well as by the "weeping goddess" who bewails the destruction of her city and sanctuary and the bitter fate of its citizens. The most impressive of these city dirges is that by the goddess Ningal for Ur.[70] There seems to be a parallel between the goddess who weeps for the destruction of her city and the personification of Zion in the book of Lamentations as a widow (Lam. 1:1), and as a mother traumatized by the suffering of her dying sons (2:19) and by the sight of their corpses (2:20). The motif of the weeping goddess is also evident in Jeremiah's image of the matriarch Rachel as the mother of the entire nation, weeping for her children and refusing to be comforted (Jer. 31:15).[71]

Although there is scant evidence in the Bible of mourning by specific women,[72] dirge-singing is represented as a women's profession. The role of the keeners is to arouse the mourners and comforters to tears, as we learn from Jeremiah: "Thus said the Lord of Hosts: 'Listen! Summon the dirge-singers, let them come; send for the skilled women,[73] let them come. Let them quickly start a wailing for us, that our eyes may run with tears, our pupils flow with water'" (Jer. 9:16-17 [17-18]). In the mishnaic era, too, this was a women's profession, as indicated by Rabbi Judah's dictum: "Even the poorest in Israel should not hire less than two flutes and one wailing woman" (m. Ketubot 4:4 [trans. Danby]. The Ugaritic myth tells of the women (referred to as weepers, mourners, and breakers of their skin) who lament Aqhat in the home of his father Danel for seven years before Danel expels them from his house (CAT 1.19 IV 9–22).[74]

It would seem, however, that aside from the professional keeners, for whom it was a livelihood, all women were expected to lament the dead or the catastrophe at times of private or collective mourning. "Daughters of Israel, weep over Saul," enjoins David (2 Sam. 1:24). Ezekiel instructs the daughters of the nations to sing a dirge for Egypt (Ezek. 32:16). Jeremiah calls on the Ammonite women, the "daughters of Rabbah," to cry out and observe mourning customs for the national calamity that will strike their country (Jer. 49:3). The daughters of Israel lament Jephthah's daughter four days every year (Judg. 11:40). The singing of dirges by women is one of the forbidden practices of idolatry, as indicated by Ezekiel's vision of the women sitting at the gate of the temple and weeping for the dead Tammuz (Ezek. 8:14), a ritual linked to the Sumerian myth of the death of Dumuzi, which spread throughout the Fertile Crescent and as far as Greece.

Isaiah has a vision of women who are "beat[ing themselves] on the breasts for the pleasant fields, for the fruitful vine" (Isa. 32:12). Here there is a play on words—*shadayim*, "breasts," and *sede hemed*, "pleasant fields"—plus the obvious allusion to women in "pleasant fields" and "fruitful vine."[75] On the explicit level, the women are to mourn for the fields and vines that no longer provide grain and wine; implicit, however, is that they are to mourn for themselves, for their sorry state in which they can no longer be seen as fruitful fields and prolific vines. As I understand it, the interplay of levels in Isaiah here provides an explanation of women's central role in mourning rites, as exemplified by the Sumerian weeping goddess/mother and by the matriarch Rachel weeping for her sons: women, who produce life from their bodies, like a field, and who nourish their infants with their own milk, are the first to mourn when the life that they brought into the world and lovingly nurtured suddenly withers and dies.

CONCLUSION

I have examined four biblical stories of mourners who do not observe mourning customs for dead relatives: Aaron and his sons are forbidden to mourn for their sons/brothers, Nadab and Abihu (Leviticus 10); Ezekiel is forbidden to mourn for his wife (Ezek. 24:15-24); David astonishes his courtiers by abruptly terminating his mourning when his infant son dies (2 Sam. 12:19-25); and the Shunammite matron does not display any grief for her dead son (2 Kings 4:8-37). In three of these cases the nonmourner is a parent (Aaron,[76] David, and the Shunammite matron); in the fourth, a husband (Ezekiel) who does not mourn his wife. In two of them, it is the Lord's prophet (Moses) or the Lord himself who prohibits the observance of mourning, but there is a significant difference between the situations: Aaron and his sons must eschew mourning in order to maintain the social order, whereas Ezekiel must suppress his grief for his wife as a sign of the collapse of the social order, soon to be manifested by the people's avoidance of mourning for the destruction of the temple and their loved ones. In the other two cases, it is the bereaved parent who decides not to mourn: David, by returning to his normal routine after the infant's death, expresses his acceptance of the divine judgment; whereas the Shunammite matron does not mourn precisely because she does not accept the verdict and is determined to do whatever she can to restore her son to life. In view of the immense psychological importance of mourning customs, we readily comprehend how difficult it must have been for Aaron and his sons, Ezekiel, and the Shunammite to stifle their anguish and behave as if nothing were wrong: Aaron and his sons did so in response to Moses' injunction; Ezekiel, in compliance with an explicit divine command; and the Shunammite, following her own intuition, which told her what would be the most effective manner to rectify the situation.

As I have argued here, it seems likely that Nadab and Abihu's mother and sisters were permitted to mourn for them, since they had not been anointed with the sacred oil and did not perform priestly functions. We know that women played a major role in mourning rites in the ancient world. I believe the key to their centrality in this domain is the notion that women, as the generators of life, are the most appropriate persons to lead the mourning for its loss.

Notes

1. Unless otherwise noted, the translations of biblical passages are from the NJPS.

2. See, e.g., Milgrom 1991: 598, 631; Hartley 1992: 131–32. For a summary of the rabbinic opinions about Nadab and Abihu's transgression, see Shinan 1978–79 and Kirschner 1983; for Philo's interpretation, see Kirschner 1983.

3. On the motif of fire as a means of expressing the principle of "measure for measure" in the Bible, see Shemesh 1999: 275.

4. Thus Abraham Ibn Ezra on Lev. 10:3 and, at greater length, on Amos 3:2; so too David Kimhi on Amos 3:2 and Abravanel on Lev. 10:1 (1964: 2:58–59). See also Noth 1977: 85; Milgrom 1991: 601–3; Hartley 1992: 134.

5. So too Odell 2000: 201.

6. The French sociologist Émile Durkheim (1965 [1915]: 437), who studied mourning customs among the Australian aborigines, reported that bereaved women were required to maintain strict silence for a period that might last as long as two years. According to him, it was not uncommon for this ban to reduce all the women in the camp to total silence. Even after the mourning period was over, the women would sometimes do without speech and continue to employ only sign language, in which they had become quite adept. On women's silence during mourning in Australia, see also Bendann (1930: 125, 138, 190–91, 229–30, 269); and the many examples offered by Gaster (1969: 819–25) of various primitive cultures in which widows (and

sometimes widowers) are required to remain silent (or speak only in a whisper) for a certain period of time. The anthropologists Huntington and Metcalf (1979: 49) say that both loud noise and extreme silence are familiar reactions to mourning. See there (103–17, 118) about the various times during mourning rituals when absolute silence is required among the Bara of Madagascar.

7. Feldman 1977: 97–99; Pham 1999: 29–31.

8. Ward 1972: 17–20; Levine 1993b: 95–96.

9. For a survey of literature on the root *d-m-m* in the sense of mourning, see Levine 1993b: 90, esp. n. 2 there.

10. See, e.g., Dahood (1960: 400), who cites a text from the Keret saga: *bn al tbkn al tdm ly* ("My son, do not weep for me, do not mourn for me" [CAT 1.16 I 25–26])

11. On mourning customs in biblical times, see, e.g., de Vaux 1961: 59–61; Ward 1972; Alster 1983; Pham 1999: 24–32; Olyan 2004: 31–34; Kruger 2005. For an analysis of several mourning gestures and postures, see Gruber 1980: 2:401–79.

12. On the rending of garments by mourners see, e.g., Gen. 37:34; 2 Sam. 1:2, 11; 3:31; 13:31; 2 Kgs. 2:12; Job 1:20. The rending of garments in the context of petitionary mourning is found, inter alia, in 1 Kgs. 21:27 and Esth. 4:1. For the rending of garments in the wake of some calamity and as a way of expressing distress, see Gen. 44:13 and 2 Sam. 13:19.

13. For uncovering the head as a sign of mourning, see Lev. 21:10; Ezek. 24:17, 23. See also Lev. 13:45 (the customs to be followed by a leper) and Num. 5:18 (the ritual of the *soṭah*).

14. E.g., Gen. 23:2; 50:3; Num. 20:29; Deut. 34:8; 2 Sam. 1:12; 3:32, 34. Anthropologists note that weeping is an almost universal reaction to death. See Rosenblatt, Walsh, and Jackson 1976: 15.

15. "Lamentation" *(hesped)* evidently refers to short cries of grief, as in "Alas, my brother!" (1 Kgs. 13:30; Jer. 22:18); "Ah, brother!" Ah, sister!" "Ah, lord!" or "Ah, his majesty!" (Jer. 22:18), or "Alas! alas!" (Amos 5:16). It is frequently associated with weeping: see Gen. 23:2; 2 Sam. 1:12; Ezek. 24:16, 23; 27:31; Esth. 4:3. Sometimes it is mentioned without weeping, as in Israel's mourning for Samuel (1 Sam. 25:1; 28:3) and Bathsheba's for Uriah (2 Sam. 11:26).

16. E.g., 2 Sam. 1:17; 3:33; 2 Chron. 35:25; Jer. 9:20; Ezek. 32:2.

17. On the wearing of sackcloth by mourners, see, e.g., Gen. 37:34; 2 Sam. 3:31; Isa. 22:12; Jer. 6:26, 48:37; Ezek. 7:18, 27:31. On sackcloth in the context of petitionary mourning see, e.g., 1 Kgs. 21:27; Esth. 4:1; Jon. 3:6, 8; Esth. 4:1.

18. Ezek. 24:17, 23; Mic. 1:8. For the removal of the shoes to express grief and distress, evidently as an expression of petitionary mourning, see 2 Sam. 15:30.

19. Fasting to express grief for the loss of a dear one is mentioned in 1 Sam. 31:13; 2 Sam. 1:12, 3:35. For fasting as part of petitionary mourning, see, e.g., Judg. 20:26; 2 Sam. 12:16; 1 Kgs. 21:27; Jon. 3:7; Esth. 4:16.

20. 2 Sam. 12:20.

21. 2 Sam. 12:20; 14:2; Isa. 61:3.

22. 2 Sam. 12:16; 13:31; Isa. 47:1.

23. Job 2:8; Isa. 47:1; Jon. 3:6. It is true that the mourners in these three passages are gentiles, but it is plausible that the mourning customs ascribed to them reflect those practiced in ancient Israel.

24. Job 16:15; Jer. 6:26; Ezek. 27:30.

25. See, e.g., 1 Sam. 4:12; Job 2:12. For sprinkling ashes on the head in petitionary mourning, see, e.g., Josh. 7:6.

26. Ezek. 24:17, 22. Covering the mustache is also one of the signs of mourning prescribed for the leper (Lev. 13:45); it is mentioned, too, as part of the garb of the disgraced seers and magicians who have received no answer (Mic. 3:7).

27. Isa. 32:12; Nah. 2:8.

28. Jer. 31:19; Ezek. 21:17.

29. This seems to be behind the story of Judah and Tamar in Genesis 38. Tamar, knowing that Judah has completed his period of mourning for his wife (v. 12), conjectures that he is in a state of sexual starvation. So she disguises herself as a prostitute and induces him to have sex with

her. On sexual relations as a sign of the conclusion of mourning see 2 Sam. 12:24. See also Anderson 1991: 27–37, 49, 72, 75–76, 80, 84, 86. According to *TB Ta'anit* 30a, mourners are not allowed to eat, drink, anoint the body, wear shoes, or have sexual relations.

30. Gen. 38:14, 19; 2 Sam. 14:2.

31. E.g., 2 Sam. 10:2; Job 2:11. Pham (1999) focuses on the role of the comforters.

32. E.g., Job 2:11; Jer. 15:5, 16:5; 22:10.

33. Jer. 16:7; Ezek. 24:17, 22.

34. For the ban on this custom, see Lev. 19:28, 21:5; Deut. 14:1. Evidence that it was practiced can be found, e.g., in Jer. 16:6; 41:5; 47:5; 48:37.

35. This custom, too, is forbidden by Lev. 21:5 and Deut. 14:1. There are many examples of its being followed: e.g., Job 1:20; Isa. 15:2; Jer. 7:29; 16:6; 41:5; 47:5; 48:37.

36. One who wishes to show further respect for the dead can erect a tombstone, as Jacob did for his beloved wife Rachel (Gen. 35:20).

37. The author of 4 Maccabees, astonished by the capacity of the mother of the seven sons to bear the loss of her children, makes clear the extent to which such behavior is unnatural, inasmuch as parents' love for their children is immense and the need to protect their children is natural. See also the examples he cites from the animal world—the birds and bees: 4 Macc. 14:11–20 [Charles 1913: 2:680]).

38. Ruth 4:14–15; Isa. 51:18. See also, in Ugaritic literature, the son's obligations to his father as detailed in the *Aqht* saga (CAT 1.17 I 23–33).

39. She cites examples, from ancient Near Eastern literature in general and from the Bible in particular, that a refusal to eat is a sign of a troubled spirit, whereas eating is an expression of tranquility.

40. Sharon 1999: 138. See also n5 there, about the notion that the sacrifice is a meal served to the divinity.

41. That is, someone whom your eyes desire, whom you love to look at (cf. Isa. 53:2). The expression may refer to objects or to people (1 Kgs. 20:6, and cf. vv. 3 and 5). In Lam. 2:4 it seems to mean "beloved children" (and cf. Hos. 9:16).

42. Translators and exegetes over the centuries have differed as to whether "men" here refers to "mourners" or "comforters." I tend to the second sense, along with Cooke 1936: 271; Greenberg 1997: 509; Friebel 1999: 331; Kasher 2004: 1:484; and Lapsley 2007: 97. See also Jer. 16:7. According to the Talmud (*TB Mo'ed katan* 24b), mourners may not eat of their own food on the first day of mourning. The custom that friends or relatives prepare the first meal after the funeral persists among Jews today.

43. For a discussion see, e.g., Stroete 1977.

44. For a survey of the various interpretations, see Zimmerli 1979: 502; Friebel 1999: 330–36.

45. Levine (1993b: 100) offers two different readings. The first understands *dom* as a noun and links it to the next word, *metim* ("dead"), in the sense of a moan or lament for the dead, and takes the noun phrase as the object of the following verb, *ta'aseh*: "Groan! But the lament over the dead [and] mourning do not perform." His second reading takes *dom* as a freestanding imperative: "Moan!" thus: "Groan! Moan! But do not perform mourning over the dead." Greenberg (1997: 508) connects *dom* (again as a noun) with the following *metim*, as in Levine's first construal, but takes the noun phrase as the object of the preceding verb, *he'aneq*: "Groan a moaning for the dead."

46. On the other hand, Lipton (2006) suggests that Ezekiel 24 deals not with mourning for the dead but with petitionary mourning: Ezekiel is forbidden to adopt the customs of mourning for his sick wife, in an attempt to persuade God to heal her, just as the exiles are forbidden to adopt mourning customs because of the temple and their relatives left behind in Zion, in an attempt to influence the Lord to show them mercy. But her reading does not persuade me. As I understand it, we should explain the ban on mourning by Ezekiel as similar to that on Aaron and his sons' mourning for Nadab and Abihu, who died an unnatural death (Lev. 10:6), discussed above, and the command to Jeremiah that he not mourn the dead (Jer. 16:1–9), addressed below.

47. Greenberg (1997: 515) finds an interesting parallel between the collapse of the social order in Ezekiel 24, in the wake of the great calamity, and an ancient Egyptian text, the "Prophecy of Neferti," which describes the collapse of the social order at the end of the Old Kingdom (see *ANET* 445b). In the latter, however, the failure to lament is a result of the lack of social solidarity (the text goes on to proclaim that the son will slay his father and brothers will turn foes), which, I maintain, is not the case in Ezekiel 24. See further below.

48. See the survey of various opinions in Stroete 1977: 164–66; Lapsley 2007: 95.

49. E.g., Odell 2000, especially 201–2 and, with some variants, Friebel (1999: 342–44), who argues that when the catastrophe actually strikes there is no longer any reason for mourning customs. He compares this to David's reaction to the death of his newborn son (2 Sam. 12:20) (342–43), to which we will return.

50. For symbolic actions related to prophecies of disaster, see Ezek. 4:1–17; 12:1–16, 17–20; 21:23-32 [18–27], and, with regard to prophecies of deliverance, 37:15-28.

51. Compare the role of the portent in Exod. 7:9; Deut. 13:2; 1 Kgs. 13:3; Ezek. 12:6. The last example is especially important for us, because it is another action by Ezekiel that serves as a prophetic symbol of the dismal destiny facing the people exiled from their land.

52. E.g., Cooke 1936: 269–70, 272; Allen 1990: 60–61; Greenberg 1997: 515.

53. This is Rashi's first explanation (Cohen 2000: 166).

54. The more usual sense of the root נחם, *n-ch-m* Qal, "groan, moan," used in v. 23, is to roar or bellow like an animal. For other uses related to human grief, see Ps. 38:9; Prov. 5:11. The optimistic reading that the exiles will not mourn because they will recognize that the destruction of Jerusalem and the temple heralds the dawn of a new age (e.g., Stroete 1977: 174; Block 1997: 794, 796; Friebel 1999: 348; Odell 2000) ignores the shocking description of the exiles as bellowing like animals.

55. The reference is evidently to the sanctuary that housed the ark of the covenant. See Avioz 2008.

56. See Judg. 20:26; 1 Sam. 7:6; 1 Kgs. 21:27; Jer. 36:9; Jon. 3:5-9; Esth. 4:1-4, 15-17. On petitionary mourning, see Olyan 2004: 62–96.

57. See Abravanel 1955: 349; Anderson 1991: 83; Sharon 1999: 41.

58. According to Blauner, primitive societies do not identify infants and children as "people."

59. So too Abravanel on 2 Sam. 13:37 (1955: 354).

60. This was noted by Sharon 1999: 145–46.

61. According to David Kimhi on 2 Sam. 12:20, David slept with Bathsheba on the very day that the infant died (Cohen 1993: 203).

62. Bar-Efrat 2009: 121.

63. On the different epithets attached to Bathsheba, see in Bar-Efrat there.

64. For the derivation of Solomon from "peace," see 1 Chron. 22:9: "Solomon [*shelomoh*] will be his name and I shall confer peace [*shalom*] and quiet on Israel in his time." For the paronomasia of the name Solomon and the various occurrences of the word *shalom* with reference to him, see, e.g., Garsiel 1991: 191–92, 204–5; Frisch 1999: 93–95. For the play between Solomon and *shelemut*, "wholeness, perfection," see Garsiel 1991: 206; Frisch 1988: 90–91.

65. *Pace* Shields 1993: 62–63, 67; Dijk-Hemmes 1994: 225, 228; and Amit 2003: 287–88. For a review of the argument that the matron actually does not want a son, see Shemesh 2008:15; for the refutation of that idea, see pp. 19–20 thereof.

66. Ugaritic literature offers several instances of mourning by sisters: the goddess Anat mourns for her brother Baal (CAT 1.6 I 1–29); Paghit mourns for her murdered brother Aqhat (CAT 1.19 I 34–37). Both of them take vengeance against the murderer (Anat's vengeance, CAT 1.6 II 4–37; Paghit's, CAT 1.19 IV 23–61). In the short Sumerian "Dream of Dumuzi," Dumuzi has a vision of his mother and sister mourning for him (Wolkstein and Kraemer 1983: 74). The sister, Geshtinanna, did not reveal Dumuzi's hiding place to the *galla*, even though they tortured her, unlike his friend, who revealed his secret for money (79–81). After Dumuzi's death, his wife

Inanna, mother Sirtur, and sister Geshtinanna sang a dirge for him (85–88). But it was Geshtinanna who sacrificed herself for him and shared his fate by agreeing to replace him in the underworld for six months out of every year (88–89).

67. E.g., Rosenblatt, Walsh, and Jackson 1976: 21–28, 145; Huntington and Metcalf 1979: 30, 36, 65, 77, 83, 102, 115–16. Durkheim (1965 [1915]: 436–41) notes that Australian aboriginal women are required to engage in especially cruel mourning rites (self-mutilation, cautery of their breasts and abdomen), which he ascribes to their inferior social status.

68. Feld and Fox (1994: 39), followed by Cooper in his article on Sumerian dirges (2006: 43–44), note that the importance of women as keeners may explain why the dirges are written in the Emesal dialect, conventionally viewed as a female dialect.

69. On the weeping-goddess motif, see Kramer 1982, 1983. On the dirges sung for Dumuzi by the three female deities (his mother, wife, and sister), see above, n. 66.

70. *ANET* 455–63.

71. Kramer (1982: 141*) proposes that the Sumerian text BM 98396, which describes the mourning by Ninhursag (also called Ningal) for the destruction of Ur, be taken as the prototype for Rachel's weeping for her children, "who are gone" (Jer. 31:15).

72. We read that Bathsheba mourned for her husband Uriah (2 Sam. 11:26) and that the wise woman of Tekoa disguised herself as a woman in mourning for her son (2 Sam. 14:2). We do read about the extraordinary attention paid by Rizpah daughter of Aiah to her dead sons (2 Sam. 21:10), but not that she actually mourned them.

73. "Skilled women" (*hakhamot*) means professional keeners. See, e.g., David Kimhi for the verse; Thompson 1980: 315 n. 2; Carroll 1986: 245.

74. In Israel today, at funerals of members of the Yemenite community, there are women who specialize in keening and singing dirges.

75. The metaphor of woman as a field is very common in Israelite culture and in both the ancient and modern world. See Shemesh 2011: 35–36. Woman as a fruitful vine can be found in Ezek. 19:10 and Ps. 128:3.

76. In this case, the surviving male siblings were included in the ban, but the narrative focuses on the reaction of the father.

4

Slave Wives and Transgressive Unions in Biblical and Ancient Near Eastern Laws and Literature

Helen R. Jacobus

Prologue

Several years ago, I attended a talk within the Orthodox Jewish community in London on monogamy among the patriarchs. As it sounded intriguing, given the polygamous situation in Jacob's household, I was curious to hear what this well-known rabbi had to say on the matter. The focus of the lecture was Isaac and Rebecca, who were indeed monogamous. The issue of polygamy among the patriarchs was never mentioned.

After the presentation, the rabbi asked the audience if there were any questions. As something was clearly missing from this talk, there was a pause, or perhaps the fall of silence may have been due to the awe the audience felt toward the speaker. Following what seemed like a very long time, a young man asked for the rabbi's opinion on Abraham's marriage. (No one, it seemed, dare ask about his view on Jacob.)

The rabbi replied that of course Abraham's marriage to Sarah was monogamous, and then, as an aside, he added, jokingly, "apart from the handmaiden." There was some laughter, possibly out of politeness for the revered man's joke, or embarrassment, or, who knows? But not everyone laughed. I was sitting near a young black woman, who had told me earlier that she was converting to Judaism. She and I exchanged glances, both of us feeling shocked.

I have no idea why I have always been interested in Hagar and Bilhah, and the issue of oppression. But my idea now, as a writer reading the biblical text, is that the composers and redactors of these richly layered, complex stories knew what they were doing. Those biblical characters were never meant to be understood in the way that this Orthodox rabbi does: inconvenient characters to be avoided, not to be looked at in the eye, mentally cast into the wilderness. I now see his attitude as a problem arises when institutionalized theology meets biblical literature: the two cannot interact openly and honestly without an enormous amount of difficulty.

Sometime later, I came across the ancient Near Eastern (ANE) law code, the Law of Hammurabi[1] 146, which I will look at later in this essay. In my view, the law seems to be dramatized in the text of Gen. 16:3-7. I put a bookmark on the page, and mentally filed away this information as an idea to research for an article one day. The call for papers for the Contextual Interpretation of the Bible was the starting pistol, an opportunity for me to bring together and explore all these disparate threads: the "joke" about "the handmaiden"; the dramatic characterization and writing in the biblical text, which is a never-ending journey; an endless fascination with the marginal women in the Bible, such as Hagar, Bilhah, and Tamar; and my surprise at the possible role that ANE laws may have played in biblical literary constructions.

INTRODUCTION

This essay contends that biblical narratives were composed in the knowledge that audiences were familiar with different ANE legal codes in cuneiform, as well as Hebrew biblical laws on conjugal relations and inheritance laws involving slave wives. I suggest that much of the drama in the Bible is created by main characters contravening written biblical and ANE laws, and that audiences would be aware that such frissons were being referenced. Furthermore, those breaches of legal codes form the subtext of the story lines; indeed, the characters' contraventions add so much depth and dramatic irony to the narratives that it is unlikely they have not been created or harmonized in this reverse way.

The narrative structures selected below work with proscriptive ANE laws on conjugal relationships with female slaves and free women in particular. Surprisingly, in the case of Hittite Laws,[2] there is a correspondence with the relevant group of laws on permitted sexual partnering and revisionist versions of this legislation in Leviticus 18.[3] On a similar note, David Wright, in his detailed study of the Covenant Code (CC) (Exod. 20:23—23:19) and the Laws Hammurabi (LH) noticed that the CC followed the LH in sequence (Wright 2009: vii). He concluded that "the role of the CC from beginning to end reflects a calculated use of LH" (Wright 2009: 344). His arguments, first put forward in 2003, have been critically accepted with reservations by Bruce Wells, who argues that Wright has probably overstated the case for an actual direct linear dependence of the CC on the LH (Wells 2006: 118). By contrast, Calum Carmichael relates biblical laws to biblical narratives, but his exegesis has not found wide scholarly acceptance (see, for example, Carmichael 2010; Fischer 2012). My postulations cover much the same ground as Carmichael, but my interpretations are completely different from his, and I bring ANE laws into the equation more frequently.

I put forward the proposal that the behavior of many main characters contravenes ANE family laws, some of which are neither replicated nor echoed in the Bible, but ancient audiences must have known of such codes because the references are so clearly marked in the stories. Furthermore, some of the laws in the biblical code were specifically invented to heighten the narrative. These did not emanate from ANE antecedents and had no other purpose other than as theatrical props in the story line. Other biblical laws are clearly signposted in the drama and have ANE precedents but have been specifically tailored from cuneiform legal codes to intersect with the stories. The narratives that they underline may have even been inspired by the earlier Mesopotamian material.

I argue that audiences would have understood the ironic literary conceit implying that biblical laws on transgressive unions postdate the characters' actions and choices; hence, the characters cannot be fully culpable of their offenses because those laws did not yet exist. Noticeably, however, they then become aware and consciously do not repeat the offense after the fact (for example, Gen 38:26d). The central story analyzed in this essay pertains to the Jacob cycle, with particular reference to Reuben and Bilhah (Gen. 35:22). The narratives of Judah and Tamar (Gen. 38), and Hagar and Ishmael (Gen. 16:1—18:5; 21:1-21; 22:2, 6-7, 10, 16) are discussed using the same paradigm.

The biblical dramas discussed here are created by deliberate, highly intricate paradoxes, lacunae in the biblical laws that bridge one statute to another, and by the ambiguity about which laws, precisely, are being referenced and crisscrossed in the text. Often, several laws are involved. The laws are characters; that is, virtual dramatis personae: they have a presence in the scenes selected and referenced in this study, and they interact with the wider narrative. My specific interest concerns the challenging nature of some of these stories that—as I argue—illuminate moral and legal codes. In the cases of Hagar, Zilpah, and Bilhah, the narratives sympathetically highlight the dearth of biblical laws concerning slave wives of the master. This is in clear contrast to the slave women's roles as second (and third and fourth) wives and surrogates in the biblical stories, and the plethora of legislation concerning them and their children in ANE laws. An "audience-aware, legal-literary framework" can be used to analyze difficult layers of text in the Bible, offering an integrated, holistic perspective, as opposed to taking a separate legal approach (such as Carmichael 1985, Levinson 1997, or Jackson 2007), or a literary critical analysis (such as Alter 1981) as single areas of study.

TRANSGRESSIVE RELATIONS IN DRAMA AND ANE LAW CODES: A COMPARATIVE CONTEXT

Human psychology and feelings seem to play less of a role as sources of motivation for actions and character development in the biblical stories, compared with Greek mythology and drama. One of the differences between the use of transgressed family laws and taboos in classical myths and plays is that classical dramatists may have been more interested in incest taboos as powerful thematic infrastructures in order to uncover the psychology of mythological dramatis personae such as Oedipus, Electra, and Phaedra. The characters' emotions propel them on journeys of personal inner change in order to effect inevitable tragedy. Hence, it may be suggested that ANE law codes in antiquity, particularly those on sexual and behavioral transgressions within the family group, may have inspired some of the most famous classical dramas, although in classical Greece the prohibition against incest was an "unwritten law."[4] There is no reason, though, why audiences would not have been aware of other written law codes and legal literature in the region.

Given that this idea is speculative, one may suggest that Sophocles's *Oedipus the King* (Storr 1932) could have been directly influenced by the law that a man should not have intercourse with his mother after his father's death (LH 157: Roth 1997: 111) or simply not have sexual relations with his mother (HL 189: Roth 1997: 236; Lev. 18:6-7a).

Euripides's (Kovacs 1998) and Sophocles's (Storr 1967) *Electra* may be not about suppressed desire for the father (a popular interpretation we owe to Jung [1912: 69]) forbidding father-daughter sexual relations (LH 154: Roth 1997: 110; no biblical prohibition), but about the implementation of the punishment for a wife who has her husband killed so as to marry another man. Legally approved retribution is explicitly stated in the final scenes of both versions of the plays. Given that the laws in the tragedies are not necessarily identical to the unwritten legal codes, some poetic license must be understood. The punishment in ANE law for the instigating, adulterous wife is impalement (LH 153: Roth 1997:110; no corresponding offense in the Bible). In Euripides's version of *Electra*, Orestes, Electra's brother, kills their mother, Clytemnestra, by driving a sword down her throat and murdering her husband.[5] Under Greek

Draconian law, the price would certainly be death; in later law, the penalty of death or exile would be decided by the family of the victim. Euripides, however, does not seem to approve of "blood for blood" in *Orestes* (Allen 2005: 508).

Forbidden relations between in-laws are reflected in Euripides's drama *Hippolytus*, where Phaedra is afflicted by an unrequited longing for her eponymous stepson (Kovacs 1995). The inspiration for a story line of emotional incest may have been inspired by the prohibition on such a union in ANE and Hebrew laws (LH 190: Roth 1997: 236; Lev. 20:11; Deut. 23:1; Deut. 27:20), creating a greater dramatic twist than a tale of unrequited love between nonrelatives. The familial relationship between Bilhah and Reuben, stepson and stepmother, is the same, but the story is different and the relationship rules much more complicated and unclear, as will be discussed below.

In the Bible, some threads of authorial interest in the literary reenactment of law codes revolve around the consequences of these broken taboos on inheritance, future generations, and the status of being an ancestor in the sacred genealogy of David. The purpose of the biblical legal-literary dramas may be to set boundaries and fixed social positions for the descendants to come.

Narrative-Dependent Laws

An example of a biblical law probably borne by the needs of the narrative is Deut. 21:15-17:

> If a man has two wives, one loved and one hated and both the loved and the hated have borne him sons, but the first born is the son of the hated one, on the day he bequeaths his estate to his sons, he may not treat the first-born son of the loved one in preference to the son of the hated one, who is the first-born. Instead, he must accept the first-born, the son of the hated one, and allot to him a double portion of all he possesses; since he is the first fruit of his vigor, ראשית אנו, the right of the firstborn is his.[6]

This is a key law in the story of the loss of Reuben's birthright, his punishment from Jacob for sleeping with Bilhah. A major theme in Genesis is the usurping by the younger brother of the elder, the overturning of primogeniture. The law alludes to Jacob's two elder sons by different wives. This rule appears to specifically refer to the inheritance rights of Reuben, a law tailored to give a double portion to the firstborn son of the hated wife. In particular, Deut. 21:17 seems to assume that the firstborn son of the hated wife is the father's "first fruit of his strength," ראשית אנו, *reshit 'ono*), hence a reference to Reuben. This is a wordplay on *Reuben* (רְאוּבֵן) and correlative with Jacob's direct oral reference to him when he revokes these rights to Reuben, "first fruit of my strength" (רֵאשִׁית אוֹנִי), on his deathbed in Gen. 49:3, since Reuben "went up to his father's bed" (Gen. 49:4). The Chronicler explains that this was a punishment for his incestuous liaison with Bilhah (1 Chron. 5:1) in Gen. 35:22, and that the birthright consequently went to Joseph (1 Chron. 5:2), the firstborn son of the loved wife, in contravention of Deut. 21:15-17.

Ancient Near Eastern laws protected a son from being totally disinherited unduly: he must commit a serious offense, not once but twice, to be so treated (LH 168–69: Roth 1997: 113). Biblical law says nothing about offenses that would be punishable by disinheritance, or of the loss of the right of the preferred heir, or under what circumstances the double portion would be removed. The amalgamation of biblical laws and situations, balancing and relating them to analogous ANE laws and biblical narratives, is, of course, prevalent throughout the Bible (see, for example, Brenner 1996: 129–31).

Using the legal-literary paradigm, I shall argue that Deut. 21:15-17 was created by the authors of the Bible solely for the purpose of the complex narratives behind Gen. 35:22. Here, there are two firstborns, and Reuben's story, so much briefer than Joseph's, may be in many ways far more complex psychologically, even if it is not the literary tour de force of the Joseph cycle. Westbrook states that Joseph's double portion was transferred to Ephraim and Manasseh when the tribes of Israel divided up the land of Canaan (Josh. 14:4, 17). Moreover, that the allotment of the double portion to Joseph was "legitimate" and did not contravene Deut. 21:15-17, due to "the sin of his first-born son against him [Jacob]" (Westbrook 1991: 136 and n2).

This biblical law works so well with the story that, I suggest, it is probably unlikely to have been composed before Gen. 29:1–30:24 and Gen. 35:22ab were authored. It could have been created at the same time, or afterward, but on balance I would suggest that Deut. 21:15-17 was part of the narrative, a kind of cross-reference. Joseph, as the firstborn son of the loved wife Rachel, receives Reuben's inheritance, as 1 Chron. 5:1–2 explains; and Judah, the fourth son of the primary (albeit hated) wife Lea, becomes through a process of elimination the blood-inheritor, the ancestor of kings (Gen. 49:10). This is curious because it is Judah's idea to sell Joseph (Gen. 37:26-27), and that is a capital offense in Deut. 24:7: "If a man is found to have stolen a soul from his brothers from the sons of Israel, enslaving him or selling him, that thief shall die." Reuben, however, is the hero who saves Joseph's life, wishes to rescue him, and mourns when he is sold (Gen. 37:21-22, 29). This behavior does not soften Jacob's attitude toward Reuben or absolve him of sleeping with Bilhah. The close narratological relationship between Deut. 24:7 and the selling of Joseph by all the brothers except Reuben, led by Judah, for twenty pieces of silver to the Midianites/Ishmaelites (evidence of redaction) in Gen. 37:28 would suggest that this law, too, is also probably part of the story. Were the law to be implemented, possibly all the brothers except Reuben and Joseph, the two firstborns signified in Deut. 21:15-17, would have to be punished by death. Joseph, however, excuses them all (Gen. 45:4-5; it is uncertain whether he actually forgives them).

Deuteronomy 24:7 is problematic as a general law code since the wording, if taken literally, really does refer to Joseph (taking Israel to mean Jacob); or, if the phrase "a soul from his brothers from the sons of Israel" is taken in the wider sense, the prohibition does not apply to Israelites who steal non-Israelites and sell them into slavery. Thus Israelites may kidnap gentiles with impunity. This rather perverse interpretation may be replaced by a more rational exegesis if one considers that Deut. 24:7 is intended to be part of the dramatic scenery to Genesis 37, and is not a real law at all.

REVISED LITERARY LAWS

The parallel biblical law that is integrated with Deut. 21:15-17, and is an interesting revision of an ANE law, is the prohibition on marrying two sisters in their lifetime, Lev. in 18:18: "Do not take a woman as a rival [לצרר] to her sister and reveal her nakedness in the other's lifetime.

According to Tosato, the law has been interpreted in the Damascus Document (CD A 4:19–21 and the Dead Sea Scrolls equivalent, 6Q 15 1 1-3. García Martínez and Tigchelaar 1997–1998: 556–57; 1152–1155) to mean a ban on polygamy, thereby taking "sisters" to mean "women" rather than biological relatives (Tosato 1984: 206–7). This may be the case in the Dead Sea Scrolls, but Schenker argues, alternatively, that "nowhere in the Old Testament is such a meaning for 'sister' attested" (Schenker 2003 [2011]:166, n. 9). Leviticus 18:18 would thus appear to be a succinct and interestingly worded prohibition on literally marrying the biological sister of one's wife, thereby creating a "rival wife" (from the root צרר Qal; BDB, 865) to the first wife during her lifetime.

This law seems to be a reference to the palpable unhappiness of Leah while her sister was the favorite wife (Gen. 29:30ab, 31-33; 30:15). It may be a derivation from the extant Hittite prohibition on marrying two sisters where both live in the same place (HL 191b: Roth 1997: 236). In HL 191 (Roth 1997: 236), (a) a free man may sleep with two free sisters and (b) with their mother (c) if they are in different countries, but not in the same geographical location, presumably because the potential for jealousy is lessened if they resided in different places. However, if a wife dies, a man is permitted to marry her sister

(HL 192: Roth 1997: 236; this is also the case according to the wording of Lev. 18:18). In Hittite laws, there are detailed codes distinguishing between sexual relationships that a free man is allowed to have with women who are related to each other if they are free, and if they are slaves (not in biblical law).

In the Bible, two adjacent edicts separate and revise the incestuous character of HL 191 by distinguishing between (d) a man sleeping with related women from three different generations and marrying the granddaughter (Lev. 18:17) and (e) having conjugal relations with two sisters (Lev. 18:18): "Do not uncover the nakedness of a woman and her daughter, nor marry her granddaughter and uncover her nakedness . . . it is depravity (Lev. 18:17). Lev. 18:17 partly repudiates HL 191 and extends the biblical version of the prohibition to marrying the granddaughter of the third generation of women (mother-daughter-granddaughter) with whom the man has had sex. This is a different incestuous pattern from that of HL 191 (the mother and her two daughters), which is not brought into the Hittite law at all. The scenario is extremely odd and has no connection with any biblical narratives.

The wording of Lev. 18:18 carefully absolves the husband from (e) practicing depravity by sleeping with two biological sisters, but rather focuses on producing unhealthy competition and unhappiness if the marriage to the two sisters takes place while they are both alive. It is possible that the audience was aware that Jacob was committing an offense in both HL 191 (a)(c) (sex with two biological sisters in the same location), and the Levitical Holiness Code (e) (marrying two sisters within their lifetimes, one as a rival wife). The unhappy story thus justifies the biblical law.

There were, however, extenuating circumstances for Jacob's marrying Rachel a week after his marriage to Leah (Gen. 29:23-28) that would be taken into consideration, so as not to condemn Jacob. The fact that Lev. 18:17 and 18:18 reflects all the prohibitions of HL 191 would suggest that the author of Lev. 18:18 and Gen. 29:1—30:24 may have been inspired by HL 191 (a) as the infrastructure for the narrative, and that these regional laws were well known.

In HL 194a, a man can have incestuous unions with slave sisters and their mother, in the same location, unlike with free women (HL 194a: Roth 1997: 236). Hittite Law 194b permits a father and son to have sex with the same prostitute. The reverse-gender incest case studies, a slave woman having sexual relations with a father and son in different locations (Gen. 35:21-22, Bilhah and Reuben and Jacob), or a free woman pretending to be a prostitute having sex with a father and his sons who are brothers who are her former husbands, each in their own lifetimes consecutively (Genesis 38, Tamar and Judah, Er and

Onan) could well constitute biblical case law while echoing a gender reversal of HL 191 and 194, and Lev 18:18.

While Jacob may have had a reason for marrying both Leah and Rachel, there were no extenuating circumstances for taking their servants Zilpah and Bilhah to bear more children for him as third and fourth wives. This situation occurred directly as result of the sister-wife rivalry (Gen. 30:4–13). According to *4QTestament of Naphtali* in the Dead Sea Scrolls (4Q215 fr. 1–3, Stone 1996) and the Book of Jubilees (*Jub.* 28:9), Zilpah and Bilhah were also sisters (Halpern-Amaru 1999). Their father, אחיות (*'Ahiyot*, meaning "sisters"), a member of Laban's household, was redeemed by Laban when he went into captivity. Their mother, Hanna (חנה), was a maidservant of Laban, whom Laban gave to Ahiyot. The Qumran text creates symmetry in Jacob's household: the familial relationship between Jacob and Zilpah and Bilhah, two biological sisters, mirrors his relationship with sisters Leah and Rachel. The emotional hierarchy of the relationships is also replicated.

A Closer Look at Genesis 35:22

In Gen. 35:22, Bilhah is referred to as a *pilegesh*, a free woman concubine of Jacob; that is, she is no longer a slave surrogate womb for Rachel. According to Bernard Jackson, the ownership of the woman slave who is given to the master to bear children for her mistress remains with the wife (Jackson 2007: 47). So upon her mistress Rachel's death (Gen. 35:18-19), Bilhah should be free. Or is she? For Ze'ev Falk, citing as an example the unfortunate "concubine" of Judges 19 (Falk 1964: 127), a *pilegsh* is free to leave. Confusingly, Bilhah is described as an אמה (*'amah*), which Jackson notes means a slave in perpetuity, and a שפחה (*shiphah*), a freeborn maid (Jackson 2007: 46–48). However, Edward Bridge argues that the meanings of the two terms are not dissimilar and that they both designate slave women (Bridge 2012).

One reading of Gen. 35:22, then, is that Bilhah, now a *pilegesh*, has, of her own free will, taken the place of Rachel sexually after Rachel's death. This, I suggest, needs an explanation. Having been made to be a surrogate for Rachel, why would she choose to become Jacob's concubine and not take her freedom? If there were an oral tradition, as reflected in Second Temple literature, that Zilpah and Bilhah were sisters whose parents were part of Laban's household, she may have chosen not to leave. Furthermore, if she left the clan, she would be leaving her two biological children, Dan and Naphtali, as well as Rachel's natural offspring, Joseph and Benjamin. Since the incident of Gen. 35:22 almost immediately follows the death of Rachel in the text (Gen. 35:16-20), the two notices are most probably linked.

The law of Lev. 19:20 appears to permit a slave woman who has not yet been freed and has been acquired by a man as his concubine (the Hebrew term is שִׁפְחָה נֶחֱרֶפֶת לְאִישׁ; see BDB, 358) to be able to be impregnated by another man before she is manumitted, both of them with impunity. What it actually states is that a man can impregnate a slave woman who has not yet been freed and has been acquired as a concubine by another man, but the second man must bring an indemnity. This law, written from the male point of view, is so specific and relevant to the discussion on Gen. 35:22 that it may be another theater-piece law. Given the incestuous nature of the relationships, concerning a father and son, the situation is more complicated. The wording of this law does not imply that force of any kind from the second man is permitted. (Incidentally, Leviticus 21–22 describes the second man's guilt offering as a ram with which his sin would be forgiven by a priest. If the law was invented for Reuben's liaison with Bilhah, as suggested here, could Reuben's indemnity be echoed with irony in Gen 37:31, where all the brothers, seemingly including Reuben, slaughter a ram and dip Joseph's garment into its blood?)

Hittite law codes allow a father and son to have intercourse with the same slave woman, or prostitute (HL 194: Roth 1997: 236), but a son is not allowed to sleep with his stepmother while the father is alive (HL 190: Roth 1997: 236). So, was Bilhah a stepmother (Lev. 18:8; Deut. 22:30; 23:1; 27:20), or a slave wife (Lev. 19:20; 25:44), or, as the mother of four of Reuben's half brothers, a maternal aunt (no biblical prohibition)? Did Reuben think that Rachel's death changed Bilhah's status so that she was due to be freed (Lev. 19:20), or so that she was already free? Is it a surprise to the audience that Bilhah is now described as Jacob's concubine? Which laws on sexual partners did Reuben transgress, exactly?

If Bilhah's status was that of a slave in perpetuity, she could be passed from father to son as a piece of property to be inherited (Lev. 25:44-46), a situation compatible with HL 194. However, since Rachel was dead, Bilhah may no longer have needed to provide her mistress's husband with wifely services. Of note is the information that Israel (Jacob) was in another location (Gen. 35:21-22a); thus the situation under Hittite legislation would have been permissible if Bilhah were a freeman and Jacob and Reuben were free females (HL 191).

Andrea Seri's important study on women domestic slaves in the Old Babylonian period (1894–1595 BCE), based on actual contracts, letters, and documents rather than on official law codes (Seri 2011), reveals that female slaves could be purchased as domestic servants for the mistress and as second wife for her husband where the wife was childless or had a disease (Seri 2011: 51–53, 56; Westbrook 1988: 107–9). In such cases, the slave's parents would receive the full betrothal price for their daughter (Seri 2011: 51–52). This does not seem to be the contract with which Bilhah was given to Rachel (Gen. 29:29; 30:3–8). Although Jacob worked for wages to pay for Rachel, Leah, and the flocks (Gen. 29–30:18), there is no mention of his paying the betrothal price for the intimate services of their slaves. In different contracts, upon a mistress's death, her slaves and her children could be set free (Seri 2011: 57, 59, 61), although here Dan, Naphtali, Gad, and Asher did not belong to Bilhah and Zilpah and were clearly adopted by Rachel, Leah, and Jacob (Gen. 30: 3–13); therefore, they were not slaves. Domestic slaves could also be passed to the mistress's descendants as inheritance as part of her estate, as they were considered property, along with crockery and furniture (Seri 2011: 54). They could also remain in the family if the slave were adopted by or married to a relative, such as a brother or son (Seri 2011: 59).

If we look at Gen. 35:22 in its legalistic context only, without any narratological information, the text may be raising several legal issues with regard to the status of Bilhah as Jacob's concubine after Rachel's death. As the contract with Rachel was no longer in place, if Bilhah was not to be inherited among the family in perpetuity as a piece of property like a pot or a chair (though this may have been the case according to Lev. 25: 44-46), was she obliged, or did she wish to continue providing, free martial duties for Jacob (as a favored sexual partner, like Rachel)? If Reuben thought that she had slave status, could he have been making a bid to marry her? Or, if Bilhah were part of Jacob's estate, inherited from Rachel, Reuben, if greedy, might try to claim her in lieu of his expected inheritance from Jacob. For an answer, we would need to take into account the literary characterization.

Suzanne Scholz argues, on the basis of the vocabulary used, that Reuben raped Bilhah (Scholz 2004). However, her textual argument is not watertight. The text states that Reuben "went" (וילך, vayyelekh) and "lay" (וישכב, vayyish-kabh) with Bilhah (Gen. 35:22b). There are no verbs connoting that Bilhah was forced or subdued in Gen. 35:22. In contrast, the language of Shechem and Dinah uses "he humbled" (ויענה, vaye'anneha) in addition to "he lay" (וישכב, vayyishkabh) and he "he took" (ויקח, vayiqqach; Gen. 34:2). The vocabulary of physical force is certainly used unequivocally in reference to Amnon's rape of Tamar (2 Sam. 13:14). Brenner argues that Reuben was trying to usurp his father's position as the head of the clan before Jacob's death (Brenner 1997: 106). According to Carmichael, Reuben was transgressing a prohibition on sleeping with his father's concubines while his father was still alive, and it was understood that a son would inherit his father's wives after his death (Carmichael 1985: 221–23). For Anthony Phillips, Deut. 23:1 was a response to the events of Gen. 35:22 (Phillips 2002: 247).

In biblical law, as Carmichael and Phillips argue, "Uncovering the father's skirt" by sleeping with his wife means that the son committed incest with the father. The three biblical laws forbidding sex with the father's wife all relate the crime to father-son incest. They are as follows:

- Lev. 20:11: "If a man lies with his father's wife, it is the nakedness of his father that he has uncovered: the two shall be put to death; their bloodguilt is upon them."
- Deut. 23:1: "No man shall take his father's wife nor uncover his father's garment."
- Deut. 27:20: "Cursed is he who lies with his father's wife, for he has uncovered his father's garment."

And in HL 190 we read: "If a man has sexual relations with his stepmother, it is not an offense. But if his father is still living, it is unpermitted sexual pairing" (Roth 1997: 236). Taking into account the Chronicler's explanation, it would appear that Reuben was being punished for a sexual offense against his father, albeit according to an anachronistic law from the future, rather than being disinherited for making a power bid, as reflected in the story of Absalom, who raped David's concubines (2 Sam. 16:22), and Adonijah, who asked for Abishag (1 Kgs. 2:13-25).

The same conclusion appears in Second Temple literature where the sexual intrusion itself is highlighted, such as *4QCommentary on Genesis* A (4Q252) 4:3–7; *Testament of Reuben* 1:37–41; and *Jub.* 33:6–9. In the *Testament of Reuben*, it is stated that Jacob did not touch Bilhah again; and in *Jubilees* it is also specified that Jacob did not touch her again because Reuben had uncovered his father's skirt, attesting to anachronistic legal knowledge. However, *Jub.* 33:15–17 adds that Reuben's crime was to sleep with Bilhah while Jacob was still alive, but that the law had not yet been revealed. This is interesting because not only does *Jubilees* accept that Reuben's lack of knowledge about Mosaic laws to come constitute mitigating circumstances (and is inconsistent with Jacob's final response), but also the legal reference to the prohibition on having relations with the stepmother while the father is alive is specified in ANE law only, not in the biblical codes.

The Mosaic laws against apparent incest by proxy ("uncovering the father's skirt" by sleeping with the stepmother) seems to extend to a prohibition on homosexuality by proxy, as reflected in Deut. 24:1-4. This law suggests that a former husband may be polluted by his ex-wife's second husband, if he remarries her, even when she has been widowed by husband number two. (In our literary-legal paradigm, it may be argued that the audience was aware that this law was contravened by David in 2 Sam. 3:12-16. Such an interpretation would add an extra dynamic to the scene of Paltiel crying after Michal as she is being led away. Accordingly, it is possible that Deut. 24:1-4 is an invented law for literary impact. Note that 2 Sam. 6:23 may suggest that David did not have sex with Michal after taking her away from her second husband, and thus probably did not contravene Deut. 24:1-4.) In contrast, ANE law does not have a prohibition on homosexuality (other than father-son, under the incest proscription, HL 190), and neither are there any laws preventing a man from remarrying his former wife after she has had a second husband.

If we examine Gen. 35:22 contextually with the narrative, Reuben's motives should be weighed in terms of his character. It may be argued that that Reuben's efforts to save Joseph in Genesis 37 and his appearance in the sexually laden mandrake scene (Gen. 30:14-16) set him up in the literary-legal framework as a compassionate person and a son who knew of the difficult sexual politics of his father's house. The saving of Joseph shows that of all the brothers, Reuben had a heart. Legally there is another subtext since Joseph, firstborn son of the loved wife, was Reuben's rival for his inheritance. It is not inconsistent with Reuben's character to suggest that he may have wished to rescue Bilhah from Jacob, thereby freeing her from performing intimate duties after her mistress had died (Lev. 19:20; 25:44-46), but this theory would presume anachronistic knowledge of the Mosaic law against incest. Since the text does not state that Reuben raped Bilhah, the situation may have been consensual (although in *Testament of Reuben* and *Jubilees*, Bilhah is raped by Reuben while she is asleep after Reuben has been aroused by the sight of her bathing).

PRIMOGENITURE AND SEXUAL TRANSGRESSION AS A LEGAL-LITERARY CATALYST

In sum, for the discourse on Gen. 35:22, the intersection of biblical narrative and law would mean that the audiences perceived that the various legal codes were implicit in certain scenes in Genesis. Since Reuben loses his inheritance rights because of his union with Bilhah (Gen. 49:4; 1 Chron. 5:1-2), it would appear that biblical laws were put into practice anachronistically. The Chronicler attributes the biblical prohibition of uncovering the father's skirt,

Lev. 18:8; 20:11; and Deut. 22:30; 23:1; 27:20, a euphemism for father-son incest (Phillips 2002, 245–50), as the reason for the loss of Reuben's inheritance. Conversely, Reuben's actions possibly would be permissible in biblical law (Lev. 19:20) and in the Hittite legal codes (HL 194) if Bilhah did not yet have the status of a free woman; and according to HL191, if she were free, because Jacob was in another land.

The audience, according to the legal-literary paradigm, may also have been familiar with the epic biblical theme of the younger taking the birthright of the older. Until this point, the loss of primogeniture was caused by murder (Cain and Abel), banishment (Ishmael and Isaac), or trickery (Esau and Jacob). The audience could have anticipated that something would happen to Reuben, the firstborn in the next generation. Yet no one killed Reuben, or displaced him, or tricked him out of his inheritance. The twist in Reuben's birthright was that he was the eldest son of the hated wife (Deut. 21:15-17), a law that was probably redacted or composed at the same time as Gen. 35:22 to work with the Genesis story, and I suggest that Reuben did not want such an inheritance. I posit that he ensured that his double portion would be transferred to Joseph, the eldest son of the favored wife, the rival wife. Thus Lev. 18:18 is the foundation of Deut. 21:15-17 and the background to Gen. 35:22. The narrative twist and drama completely intertwines with purpose-made biblical legal codes such as Lev. 19:20, and law codes that permitted such a liaison. The beauty of this drama is that due to the plethora of laws and the sympathetic appearance of Reuben in the narrative in relation to his family, there are many interpretations. An unwritten law is that each generation must see a loss of primogeniture; it is my submission that this was Reuben's method.

JUDAH AND TAMAR

In the same group of Hittite laws on sexual prohibitions and permission, HL 193ab states: "If a man has a wife, and the man dies, his brother shall take his widow as wife. If the brother dies, his father shall take her. . . . [HL 193c: When afterwards his father dies, his brother shall take the woman that he had]" (Roth 1997: 236)." That is an outline of the plot in Genesis 38 about Judah and Tamar. The biblical author poses the question of what is acceptable: should Levirate marriage really be permissible even where diagonal, cross-generational incest is involved?

The biblical law repudiates the Hittite law and, thereby, Judah's sexual encounter with Tamar (Gen. 38:16, 18).

- Lev. 18:15: "Do not uncover the nakedness of your daughter in law; she is your son's wife, you shall not uncover her nakedness."
- Lev. 20:12: "If a man lies with his daughter in law, both of them shall be put to death; they have committed incest, their blood guilt is upon them.

In addition, Tamar commits the crime of being a cult prostitute (for an alternative view, see Westenholz 1989), contravening Deut. 23:18. However, like Jacob's wedding night with Leah, Judah consorted with Tamar as a result of her being in disguise; hence, there were apparent extenuating circumstances for breaking the law. Genesis 38 condones this Levirate situation: Perez, Judah and Tamar's firstborn twin who usurped his brother in the womb, becomes the ancestor of David (Ruth 4:18), also through another Levirate marriage instigated by the widow Ruth. The crime of Judah—father-son incest through his daughter-in-law—is the mirror image of Reuben's son-father incest through his father's wife. Hence, circumstances are more important than the laws themselves, each case being judged on its merit.

Aside from the legal mirroring, there is a literary form-critical connection between the stories of Judah in Genesis 38 and Reuben. In the narrative, we learn of Reuben's unspoken intentions in Gen. 37:22d: he intends to return to the pit to rescue Joseph. Similarly, in Genesis 38 we hear Judah's thoughts as he schemes to keep Tamar from marrying Shelah (Gen. 38:11c). By contrast, Reuben saves Joseph; Judah sells Joseph, but Deut. 24:7, which views such a sale as a capital offense, is buried by the narrative.

There may be a didactic element to the number of laws created and broken in the Jacob-Reuben-Judah epicycle that are possibly associated with what seems to be a likely structural and intellectual link connecting the group of Hittite legal codes HL 190, 191, 193, 194; Lev. 18:15, 17, 18; and chapters 29, 30, 32, and 38 in Genesis. It is still possible to follow the story in its own right, as well as its echoes in Ruth, without being familiar with the possible influence of ANE laws on these narratives. This, I argue, is not so much the case with the storylines of Hagar and Ishmael.

HAGAR AND ISHMAEL

The story of Sarai/Sarah and Hagar may be a dramatization of several early Mesopotamian laws governing the relationship between the primary wife and the second, slave wife when the latter has a child before the primary wife. The legal documentary corpus includes inheritance laws in these situations, and the laws of adopting the slave's children for inheritance purposes. Corresponding laws in the Bible are absent, possibly because the relevant stories in Genesis are set in a bygone time and the practice of surrogacy had ceased.

In the Laws of Hammurabi, the preferred heir is the son of the first-ranking wife, and he has the right to choose his share before the children of a slave wife, even when the latter's children were adopted by the father (LH 170: Roth 1997: 113–14). Hagar's son was not Sarai's son, having been promised to Abram and Hagar separately in different annunciations (Gen. 15:18-21; 16:10-12; Frymer-Kensky 2002: 231–232). Ishmael's name was given by an angel (Gen. 16:11d) or by Abram (Gen. 16:15, according to redactions), not by Sarai, in contrast to the naming of Bilhah's and Zilpah's children by Rachel and Leah.

The harsh treatment meted out to Hagar by Sarai (Gen. 16:6b, 9) because she felt diminished in Hagar's eyes (Gen. 16:5) may have been drawn from LH 146 (Roth 1997: 109) as a source of inspiration. In this law, if a wife is a temple devotee not permitted to bear children (*nadītu*) (Roth 1997: 271; Seri 2011: 51n2) and the purchased slave wife aspires to equal status with the primary wife after she has borne children, the mistress "shall place upon her the slave-hairlock and she shall reckon her with the slave women."

Laws governing the fleeing of slaves, whether or not due to harsh treatment by their mistresses in particular, is well documented in ANE law (Seri 2011: 61); for example, in LH 15–20 (Roth 2011: 84–85), and reflected in the Bible (Gen. 16:6-9). From the literary viewpoint, the first conflict between Sarai and Hagar before Isaac is born (Genesis 16) gives the point of view of both women; Hagar's plight is presented sympathetically.

Documents from the practice of Nuzi Akkadian law on adoption[7] describe contracts that protect the second wife's children from being sent away by the primary wife (Meek 1992: 168–69). Sarah explicitly contravenes this code because she does not want Ishmael to be an heir with Isaac (Gen. 21:10). Such a conflict appears to be reflected in a letter from the Old Babylonian period (Seri 2011: 56; Veenhof 2005: 189). This text contains the line, "A father with sons does not adopt his slave son." Seri suggests the reference may allude to the fact that "the slave son whom the father in our letter adopted was born to a domestic slave who was the master's concubine." If so, one may infer that these resentments constituted real human dramas and provided the stuff of literature.

It may have been more common for the arrangement to work. There are ANE documents showing the opposite case: a papyrus record from Thebes during the later Egyptian New Kingdom period (twentieth dynasty, ca. 1104–1075 BCE) details that a man adopted his second wife as his daughter so that she could inherit his estate. After his death, she left the entire inheritance to the three children of the slave woman, two girls and a boy, presumed to have been fathered by her husband, by adopting them as well as the husband of the elder daughter, her own brother. She also emancipated them (Ashmolean Museum, AN1945.96).

Not only is it clear that women in Egypt were allowed to own and distribute property, but here Sarah certainly wields some power and influence over the matter of who should inherit Abraham's estate. In ancient Mesopotamia, if the slave wife's son was adopted by the husband, he was a joint heir with the primary wife's son, who had the privilege of taking first choice of the inheritance (LH 170: Roth 1997: 113–14). It is evident that Abraham had adopted Ishmael and that it was the intention that he would be an heir (Gen. 16:2), as the narrator refers to Ishmael as Abraham's recognized son (albeit not Sarai/Sarah's, 16:15; 21:11), a legal requirement for adoption and inheritance purposes (LH 170). If the father did not call his slave wife's offspring "My children"—that is, adopt them—those children were not entitled to a share of the estate (LH 171).

Where the slave's son is not adopted by the father in the Laws of Hammurabi, the primary wife's son becomes the rightful heir over the slave wife's son and the slave woman and her children are freed (LL[8] 25: Roth 1997: 31; LH 171: Roth 1997: 114). This rule may be reflected in the narrative of Hagar and Ishmael's release into the wilderness (Gen. 21:14). Although the legal-literary theory is speculative, we may hypothesize that audiences likely realized these legal customs were being referenced. This background knowledge adds depth to the narrative. As in the ANE codes, the slave women in the biblical narratives are servants of the mistress, not her husband; and it is their mistresses who control the slaves' conjugal situation. Also, as in the ANE codes, the children of the slaves such as those in the biblical stories can be adopted by the husband to share in the inheritance of his estate.

The significance of divine intervention in absolving Sarah of wrongdoing for Ishmael's disinheritance (Gen. 21:12) becomes meaningful: Sarah was asking for a situation that would mean a break of contract or established law. It would also appear that God was involved in a forced un-adoption of Ishmael so that Isaac was the sole heir, in accordance with Sarah's wishes. In this way, Hagar and Ishmael could be freed and Ishmael disinherited (Gen. 21:14; LH 171). The un-adoption of Ishmael may be evident in Abraham's distress in that the matter concerned "his son" (Gen. 21:11), but God assures him that his bloodline will continue through both Isaac and Ishmael (Gen. 21:12-13).

The scene of the Akedah in Genesis 22 underlines the idea that Abraham's faith is being tested, as he loses his first heir by un-adoption and is about to lose his next firstborn by his primary wife by sacrifice, in contrast to the promise of

Gen. 12:2. Isaac is described by God as Abraham's only son (Gen. 22:2, 12, 16); this is legally correct, since Ishmael would not inherit. Technically, Isaac has become Abraham's only heir, not his sole biological son. Without the familiarity of complex ANE adoption laws, these difficult scenes lose their underlying Mesopotamian references. The legal aspect is woven here with the literary text, which highlights Sarah's attitude, and feelings, toward the arrangement that Abraham had with Hagar.

Aside from the Nuzi law described, where the son of a surrogate mother is adopted when the primary wife is barren, the ANE laws do not distinguish inheritance rights between cases where the primary wife already has children (Leah: Gen. 29:32-35) before slave wives also bear offspring (Gen. 30:3-13), or after the slave wives bear children. In the biblical narrative, as in ANE law, the sons of the primary wives are the preferred heirs: for example, Gen. 35: 23-26 lists the sons in order of their mothers: Leah, Rachel, Bilhah, and Zilpah (see Jackson 2007: 48 n. 39).

In sum, the references to ANE law codes in the narratives of Hagar and Ishmael come from a variety of sources. Akkadian Nuzi law protects the son born to a surrogate mother, who is the rightful heir, from being sent away by the primary wife. Sarah breaches this law explicitly because she does not want Ishmael to share the inheritance with Isaac. It is likely that these scenes showed that her actions were unlawful, even though the feelings of both women are described by the writer; these are the elements of all good character drama. Abraham is distressed by the outcomes, as he has clearly adopted Ishmael. His humane response, showing his character, reveals that the situation is extremely uncomfortable for him. The literature and the underlying legal references work together to maintain the theme of the overturning of primogeniture. In LH 170, the son of the first-ranking wife is the preferred heir and takes his share first, but the estate is divided equally between the primary wife's son and the slave wife's son if the father has called the slave wives' children "My Son." This legal situation has developed in the narrative and becomes a problem for Sarai/Sarah; her tension is resolved by a contravention of law, an action that is supported by God.

CONCLUSION

It has been found that the narratives on sexually transgressive behavior in Genesis are mirrored in a group of relevant ANE laws and corresponding biblical laws (supporting the theses of Welch and Berman, mentioned above). I have further postulated that some biblical laws were actually created to work with these stories as part of the fiction, possibly authored at the same time, or consciously redacted, thereby adding another dimension to the scenes concerned. In some cases, particularly the case of Reuben and Bilhah, the intersection of ANE laws and biblical legislation make for a labyrinthine puzzle. My hypothesis posits not only that the biblical law codes are implicit in the narratives but also that literary characterization must also be considered in relation to the plethora of ANE legislation, contracts, and the way actual written laws affected people's lives—all rich material for drama.

The issue of the reversal of primogeniture, and sexual transgression as a means of manipulating the inheritance line, is illustrated with Reuben and Bilhah, and Judah and Tamar. These underlying themes are a central force driving the story lines forward within the long-term epic through the generations. By contrast, classical Greek drama, which may also use law as a centripetal force in the story lines, is more self-contained. In the case of Hagar and Ishmael, we should presume that the audience would be aware of the role of relevant ANE codes on slave wives in the narrative.

Without modern interpreters' aligning knowledge of ancient legal texts with the biblical narratives, the story lines lose their dramatic impact, significant layers of meaning, and possible legal and societal implications. The unfolding dramatic irony and literary conceit within some trajectories in Genesis—involving a supposed lack of anachronistic knowledge on the part of the players—not only segues with internal, literary narrative patterns, but also involves a relationship with external foreign law codes, biblical laws, and creatively revised ANE laws that loop back into the narrative. Once all these textual layers are appreciated in an interactive sense, the stories concerning the slave wives take on a different light.

Epilogue

I have suggested in this essay that Deut. 24:1-4 may be read as a theatrical piece of legislation that heightens the dramatic subtext in the David cycle. It has been used and continues to be used today as a law in rabbinical Judaism to prohibit a woman from filing for divorce. The phrase in question is in Deut. 24:1d, "and he writes a bill of divorcement and puts it into her hand and sends her from his house." This incidental piece of information in the legislation of Deut. 24:1-4 is interpreted to mean that only a husband can file for divorce, not the wife. In practice, that has meant that where a marriage breaks down and the man refuses to give his wife a bill of divorce, she becomes a "chained wife" (Heb. *'agunah*). The chained wife's second sexual union, if effected before the first husband agrees to a divorce, is in rabbinical law an adulterous union, and the children from that union and their descendants are *mamzerim*. They have a lower status in the community and cannot marry in a synagogue. The incompatible gap between biblical law and literature and institutional theology is a living issue today. And this is but one example.

The well-known rabbi mentioned in the prologue to this essay has said at another meeting I attended that the law on the "chained wife" cannot be changed because it emanates from the word of God. Yet all the biblical passages mentioned here involve different narratives of legal contraventions, circumventions, and redemption. The idea that institutional modern religion can adopt a brutal interpretation of an incidental phrase within a possibly fictitious and spurious Deuteronomic law, create a rule out of it, and implement it in such a fixed way so as to not leave any maneuver for a loophole whatsoever, appears to be in stark contrast to the practice of biblical case law on conjugal relationships, which is anything but straightforward.

Notes

1. The Laws of Hammurabi (LH) were compiled ca. 1750 BCE and were repeatedly copied over the centuries in Mesopotamian scribal centers. The references to these codes are from Roth 1997: 76–142. Background and description: Roth 1997: 71–76; Tetlow 2004: 53–72. For a comparative description of this law code with the other Mesopotamian codes, earlier and later, see Tetlow 2004: 205–20. Website for the Code of Hammurabi, translated by L. W. King (early twentieth century): http://www.ancienttexts.org/library/mesopotamian/hammurabi.html (retrieved March 6, 2012). I am grateful to Athalya Brenner and Sandra Jacobs for some useful references used in this article.

2. The earliest copies of the Hittite Laws (HL) date to the Old Hittite period (ca. 1650–1500 BCE), from their capital Hattusha, in present-day Turkey, and copies were made until 1150 BCE (Roth 2007: 217–47; translated and introduced by Harry A. Hoffner Jr., 215–17). Further commentary and summary: Tetlow 2004: 178–88.

3. A day after I put forward these observations at the ISBL session in London, July 2010, two papers were given in the SBL Biblical and Ancient Near Eastern and Biblical Law section expressing a similar theory. These were "A Structural Comparison of Hittite Laws 187–200, Leviticus 18:6–23, and Leviticus 20: 1–21," by J. W. Welch of Brigham Young University; and "Law Code as Story Line: Deuteronomy 24:16–25:10 and LH 1–5 as Literary Templates in Biblical and Mesopotamian Tradition," by J. Berman of Bar Ilan University. Also see Berman 2007: 22–38.

4. Plato, *Laws* 8.838A–B (Bury 1926; see also Ostwald 2009: 151).

5. The plotline of a woman having her husband killed apparently to be with her lover is a recurrent story in modern film, for example, *Double Indemnity*, *The Postman Never Rings Twice*, *Body Heat*, *The Last Seduction*, all with a final twist.

6. Translation: my modification of *JPS Hebrew-English Tanakh* (Philadelphia: Jewish Publication Society, 2003).

7. See Pritchard 1969: 219–20. Nuzi (formerly Gasur near Kirkuk) in northern Mesopotamia was taken over by the Hurrians in ca. 1800 BCE, and they changed its name to Nuzi. The tablets date from the middle of the second millennium BCE (Roux 1992: 234–35; Meek 1992, 167).

8. The Laws of Lipit-Ishtar (ca. 1930 BCE) were mainly found in Nippur in Lower Mesopotamia, as well as in Kish (Roth 1997: 24); translations: Roth 1997: 24–35; background: Tetlow 2004: 15–18.

The Notion of כפר in the Book of Leviticus and Chinese Popular Religion

Sonia K. Wong

INTRODUCTION

The term *Chinese popular religion*[1] has been much debated and problematized in religious studies and thus demands further elaboration[2] (Bell 1989; Fowler and Fowler 2008: 224–49).[3] First of all, I do not use the term in opposition to the so-called official/institutional/elite religions, whether in ancient or in modern China. The two categories, in spite of their noticeable differences, do not constitute a dichotomy. In fact, their relationship is much characterized by intricacy, complexity, and inextricable interpenetration.[4] Second, the word *religion* in the term should not be understood as a linguistic equivalent to "faith" or "belief system." Even though common beliefs and long-standing traditions are clearly present in many regional variants of Chinese popular religion, due to its eclectic nature, none of them should be regarded as immalleable, absolute, and definite. Rather than stressing "correct" beliefs, Chinese popular religion tends to accentuate the proper administration of rituals (*praxy*) in its worship, namely, in family and communal settings.

In accordance with the scholarly construct, the collective term *Chinese popular religion* is used here to designate the dynamic, multifarious, and diffused polytheistic religious phenomenon observable among different socioeconomic strata of the Chinese populace (thus the qualifier *popular*) in both the indigenous and diasporic localities. Although popular religious traditions may vary from one locality to another, the singular term is made possible because of the shared beliefs, values, and ritual traditions that buttress the phenomenon.

The idea of putting the book of Leviticus and the so-called Chinese popular religion into dialogue, without privileging either text, springs from two necessary grounds: my academic training and my cultural background.

Through the academic training that I am undergoing as a Hebrew Bible scholar, I have been exposed to various exegetical methods and have come to appreciate and be inspired by Asian biblical scholar Archie C. C. Lee's proposed approach of "cross-textual hermeneutics" as a creative way of intersecting the "text" of Asian cultures and the biblical texts without privileging either one (Lee 2000a, 2000b, 2002, 2008). This emphasis on an egalitarian and mutually illuminating approach to the interpretation of these two "texts" has its roots in the (post)colonial history of Asia. It is a truism that Christianity, widely seen as an accomplice of colonialism, has culturally colonized many Asian countries with the biblical texts, engendering a situation in which the classical scriptural texts of Asia (Text A) and the biblical text (Text B) are often put into an antagonistic position, making an irenic dialogue or syncretistic integration impossible. In acknowledgment of the significant roles that each of these two texts have played in cradling and shaping (post)colonial Asia, Lee considers it imperative that the two "texts" be read appreciatively yet critically and put into conversation, contestation, and/or complementation without imposing or presupposing the supremacy or hegemony of one over the other.

Although Lee, in his original conceptualization of cross-textual hermeneutics, limited his delineation of Text A to classical texts of scriptural (read "canonized") status, whether in written forms or in oral variants, he has subsequently expanded the concept of "Text A" to encompass all other Asian cultural contexts and coined the term "con/texts" for this all-embracing notion of "Text A" (Lee 2010). However, on the practical reading level, scriptural texts still dominate his Text A, and phenomenal contexts that embody the everyday socioreligiosity of the populace are not given their due attention. Inevitably, this tendency creates an inextricable link between cross-textual hermeneutics and institutional religions in Asia, which are predominantly responsible for the "scripturalization" of texts.

This essay more or less follows the cross-textual approach that Lee proposes, with which I, by and large, concur, but I also wish to revise and extend it in certain respects. While Lee's approach tills fertile ground for the constructive interaction between texts of different cultures and provides an alternative hermeneutical means that surpasses the traditional literary and historical-critical criticisms in the field of biblical studies, on its practical if not theoretical level it also marginalizes certain contexts, in particular the nonscripturalized, nonverbal, and phenomenal ones. One of these contexts is Chinese popular religion.

It is unfortunate that such a rich heritage as Chinese popular religion has often been neglected, marginalized, and deterritorialized in the academic discourse of comparative religious and biblical studies.[5] In ancient times, Chinese classics and scriptures, however great their influence on cradling Chinese civilization, were only accessible to a limited group of literate male elite. Even now, only a minority of intellectuals trained in reading Classical Chinese can fully appreciate or analyze these texts. However, the prominence and foundational importance of Chinese popular religion in Chinese communities have been largely recognized, and its visibility is ubiquitous in both their indigenous and diasporic contexts. Still, it is seldom a dialogical partner in comparative religious studies. One of the recognized reasons is that Chinese popular religion has often been dismissed as "primitive" and relegated to "superstition" (*mixin*), particularly after the arrival of colonialists and the adaptation of Marxist thought in China. Unlike many so-called world religions, Chinese popular religion does not follow certain scriptural authorities and is laity-based and ritual-focused. Thus, aside from historians, it has mainly attracted the interest of anthropologists and sociologists.[6] This essay is an attempt to approach this neglected phenomenal context with Lee's cross-textual hermeneutics, and also to counterbalance the logocentric inclination of such hermeneutical approaches.

The other cultivating ground is my cultural background as a Chinese Christian who grew up in colonial Hong Kong, where both the biblical texts and Chinese popular religion have always been an intimate part of my life. These contexts have exerted tremendous influence on the ongoing process of my identity formation. In the present study, the two contexts, the book of Leviticus and Chinese popular religion, are not chosen arbitrarily or out of convenience. Having been raised in the pluralistic religious setting of Hong Kong, where "indigenous" religions are constantly in conflicting and interpenetrating tension with "imported" religions both in terms of ideologies of and ritual practices, I inevitably interpret biblical texts as based on the experiences, pre-understanding, and prejudices that I, like many Asian Christians, have acquired and accumulated in my own cultural contexts. Thus I cannot read the Levitical rituals without having the comparable ritual practices of Chinese popular religion in mind.

The ethical nature and the legitimacy of the ransoming notion of the purification and reparation offerings in the book of Leviticus have often gone unchallenged in biblical scholarship. However, I, among many people who also belong to the same cultural and religious settings, have always found it problematic to make offerings to a deity in order to have faults forgiven. Why is it legitimate for YHWH to forgive the faults of guilty people through sacrificial rituals? Why must purification and reparation offerings be regarded as legitimate ransoms and not illegitimate bribes? In what ways can the legitimacy of the sacrificial rituals be justified in the book of Leviticus? These questions are not so easy for someone who grew up in the pluralistic setting of Chinese popular religion. In a way, these contexts are also my "intra-texts." They are two coexisting, multifarious, complex, and at times overlapping voices in my psyche, vacillating between polyphony, harmony, and cacophony.

This paper puts the book of Leviticus and Chinese popular religion into a fruitful dialogue, not merely a superficial comparison. As Lee writes, "Both Text A and Text B must be held in creative dialogue and interaction. One text has to be open to the claims and challenges of the other text in order for transformation to take place in a meaningful way" (Lee 2002: 249). With this critical aim, I seek to analyze how a reader presumably ingrained with the prominent presuppositions of Chinese popular religion would understand the ransoming notion of כפר (*k-p-r* Piel, often rendered as "atone" or "expiate") in the Levitical offerings for purification and reparation. I intend to show not only that a parallel notion of *k-p-r* cannot be found in Chinese popular religion but also that its absence reveals an issue of legitimacy for such a notion under the Chinese three-realm worldview, the imperial bureaucratic structure of the pantheon,[7] and the ambiguous moral nature of deities, ancestors, or ghosts. It is likely that those of us who are brought up in Chinese religious contexts, in particular those being unfamiliar with the Levitical presuppositions, would find the Levitical notion of *k-p-r* to be incomprehensible and even reprehensible. However, the legitimacy of the ransoming power in purification and reparation offerings seems to have been sustained within the internal logic of Leviticus. Toward the end of the essay, I will also explore the possible implications for Chinese popular religion of the lack of a parallel notion of *k-p-r* in sacrificial rituals.

THE LEVITICAL NOTION OF *K-P-R*

In the book of Leviticus, the verb כפר (*k-p-r* Piel) occurs only within the sacrificial context of חטאת (*hatta't*, "purification offering") and אשם ('*asham*, "reparation offering"), with detailed prescription in Lev. 4:1—6:7 [5:26]; 14:1—15:33, and the calendrical rite of atonement, which is referred as יום כפרים (*yom kippurim*, "Day of Atonement") in Lev. 23:27-28 (cf. Exod. 30:10), with detailed prescription in Leviticus 16. These offerings are prescribed to effect forgiveness on behalf of those who have committed expiable moral faults and physical ritual impurities (Lev. 4:20, 26, 31, 35; 5:10, 13, 16, 18; 6:7 [5:26]). In my pursuit, I will limit my scope to purification and reparation offerings

(Lev. 4:1—6:7 [5:26]). The two offerings follow the same ritual principle (Lev. 7:7) as part of the unified system of atonement rituals in Leviticus, which also includes the Day of Atonement.

K-p-r (Piel) occurs ninety-four times in the Hebrew Bible, with the majority (seventy-four times) found in the Priestly materials (P) of the Pentateuch (the Torah).[8] Although most English versions have predominately translated k-p-r (Piel) as "make atonement/expiation," particularly in the Priestly materials (for instance, Exod. 29:37; 32:30; Lev. 1:4; 4:20; Num. 5:8; 6:11), its meaning is still a moot question. Scholars debate the meaning of k-p-r (Piel). Various suggestions for its meaning include "to wipe off, to clean objects, to rub, to purify magically" (University of Chicago Oriental Institute and Gelb 1956: 178–79; cf. Milgrom 2007: 180), "to cover," "to purge, remove," and "to ransom."[9]

Jay Sklar (2005) has convincingly argued that k-p-r, as a key concept in sacrificial rituals, carries a dual meaning of ransoming (as the denominative of kopher, "ransom") and purging (see Milgrom 2007). This dual meaning of k-p-r conveys the dual function of the offerings prescribed for atonement. On the one hand, such an offering functions as a ransom payment presented by a guilty party, namely, the offerer, to the offended deity YHWH in order to avert or mitigate an impending punishment of greater severity.[10] On the other hand, It also serves to purge or to remove any impediments that hinder the divine-human relationship, including those caused by physical ritual impurities and the indirect defilement of the sanctuary by the Israelites' sins and transgressions (Lev. 16:16, 30).

When one accepts the meaning "to ransom" one also, implicitly, accepts k-p-r as the denominative of noun kopher.[11] The noun kopher and its variants occur seventeen times in the Hebrew Bible, of which thirteen times carry the meaning of "ransom," namely, a material or monetary payment intended for compensation, whether (il)legal or ritual (for instance, Exod. 21:30; 30:12. Even though kopher is used in most of these cases to designate a legitimate ransom, in five occasions, it is also used, either explicitly or arguably, to signify an illegitimate payment, namely, a "bribe" (Num. 35:31, 32; 1 Sam. 12:3; Job 36:18; Amos 5:12; see Sklar 2005: 56–61). I will put forth two explicit instances. First, in response to the demand of "all the elders of Israel" for kingship, Samuel establishes Saul to be the first king of the Israelites (1 Samuel 8–12). After the formal inauguration, Samuel delivers his "end-of-service" speech, in which he claims (in the form of a rhetorical question) that he has never taken any "bribe [kopher] to blind his eyes with it" (1 Sam. 12:3) during his term of judgeship. The second example comes from the prophetic literature. In one of Amos's prophetic indictments to Israel, he says, "For I know how many are your transgressions, and how great are your sins—you who afflict the righteous, who take a bribe [*kopher*], and push aside the needy in the gate" (Amos 5:12). In both of these instances, *kopher* is unequivocally used to mean an illegitimate payment. This raises a question of the legitimacy of the ransoming power of purification and reparation offerings.

An Overview of Chinese Popular Religion

Chinese popular religion has integrated many beliefs, values, and rituals of three so-called institutional (or elite) religions—Buddhism, Daoism, and Confucianism—whose equal orthodoxy was established in the Tang dynasty (618–907 CE).[12] To a certain extent, Chinese popular religion is a collective term for the local variants, appropriated and amalgamated versions, of these institutional religions. From a sociopolitical perspective, Chinese popular religion has often been manipulated to promote, reinforce, or support elite beliefs and values (Szonyi 2007; Watson 2004). Although Chinese popular religion does not rely on any scriptural or institutional authorities, the institutional religions have exerted great influence on its development. Chinese popular religion, just as its institutional counterparts, emerged from myths, folktales, and legends that have embodied many popular beliefs, social values, and moral precepts.

Ghosts, Deities, and Ancestors: Three Relative Concepts

A common belief in the coexistence of three realms—the divine, human, and ghost realms—is upheld in Chinese popular religion. The three realms are interconnected, interdependent, and influence each other. When a person dies, it is believed that she or he will enter from the human realm (*renzian* or *yangzian*) to the ghost realm (*guijie* or *yinzian*) to undergo retributive judgment and a purgatory process, and await further "reassignment." The duration of the purgatory process is subject to the amount of merits or evils that the person has done in his or her previous life and the intensity of his or her remorse. After the purgatory process, she or he is believed to be reincarnated as a human, another form of living being, or an immortal (a state of ultimate personal salvation that escapes the cycle of reincarnation).[13] In other words, people can become ghosts or deities. Conversely, it is also possible for a deity to be demoted to a lower rank or into human state if she or he makes serious mistakes during his or her divine office, such as offending a superior deity.

It is believed that the peaceful coexistence of these realms ensures universal harmony. Both the divine realm and the ghost realm mirror the human realm. Deities and ghosts have needs, such as food and clothes, just as humans have. However, ghosts cannot provide for their own needs, and thus they must rely on human provision through ritual offerings. People who die without descendants to attend their needs or people who suffer tragic deaths will become hungry ghosts (*egui*) or orphan souls (*guhun*). These spirits are believed to have the ability to roam around in the human realm and possibly cause illness, harm, and misfortune (Overmyer 1986: 26–27).

Some people believe that ghosts, particularly the hungry ones, have the power to grant wishes if they are attended. When a ghost's efficacy (*ling*)—his or her ability to grant wishes, heal disease, and perform miracles—is recognized, people would even build a shrine or a temple for the ghost and henceforth treat him or her as a deity (Harrell 1974: 193–206).[14] Most deities in Chinese popular religion were originally historical or historicized humans prior to their deification. They are installed as deities because their efficacy was recognized.[15] Thus deities and ghosts are not two discrete and unrelated concepts. Both are capable of benevolence and malevolence at various times. Even benevolent deities can make occasional mistakes, just like humans. There is a vast gray area regarding the ethical nature of deities and ghosts in Chinese popular religion. For instance, it is widely known among Hong Kong people that *Guandi*, also called *Guangong*, the god of the military and of commerce, has a history of being installed as a patron deity by both the law enforcers and the law-breaking mobsters. The god is renowned for his justness, loyalty, and trustworthiness—virtues that are typically valued by these two antagonistic parties.

What are ancestors? Are they deities or ghosts? The question cannot be answered unequivocally, especially when the concept of reincarnation is taken into consideration. They are generally viewed as ghosts awaiting rebirth and enjoying offerings from their descendants (see Scott 2007: 91–96; Wolf 1974: 131–82). Ancestral worship is commonly practiced in Chinese communities, but it is not necessary for ancestral worshipers to uphold a three-realm worldview. Ancestral worship has been practiced in China since the Shang period (c. 1500–1040 BCE), when the aforementioned three-realm worldview had not yet matured. Shang people believed that after their ancestors died, their souls go up to join *Tian* (heaven) and they become intermediaries between their descendants and *Tian*.[16] To many contemporary Chinese, ancestral worship has become primarily an act of filial piety. As Confucius puts it: "Thus they served the dead as they would have served them if they had been continued among them:—all this was the perfection of filial duty" (1967: 311). Offering incense, foodstuffs, clothes, spirit moneys, and other daily necessities is considered an act of filial piety, a family obligation in Chinese societies, irrespective of one's view on the afterlife. However, this is not to say that the belief in ancestors' benevolent or potentially malevolent power as family patron deities or ghosts is uncommon in Chinese popular religion. Ancestors are generally considered as protectors of their descendants; however, some also believe that ancestors could turn into troublemakers, inflicting their descendants if their proper care is neglected (Wolf 1974: 164–69).

BUREAUCRATIC AND NON-BUREAUCRATIC DEITIES

The Chinese pantheon is patterned after the human realm, with an imperial metaphor (Weller 1987: 37–59; Feuchtwang 2001; Goossaert 2005: 1619). Deities can generally be classified as bureaucratic and non-bureaucratic. Bureaucratic deities can further be divided into universal or local deities. Universal deities include the Jade Emperor (*Yuhuangdadi* or *Tiangong*), the head of the pantheon, and imperial ministerial deities, such as *Guandi*, and the chthonic deities whose divine duties concern the welfare of all. Local deities include magistrate deities like the city god (*Chenghuang*) and terrestrial gods like the locality god (*Tudi Gong*), whose jurisdiction is limited to a particular region. Titles of magistrate deities function more as administrative posts than deities' proper names. In theory, each city would have its own city god, usually a deceased local magistrate whose uprightness and impartiality have been well recognized. Similarly, each village or community would have its own locality god, usually one of their ancestors. A city god is superior in his jurisdiction to locality gods and other terrestrial gods. Bureaucratic deities are hierarchical officials responsible for different categories of social life. To illustrate the imperial structure of the Chinese pantheon, I will borrow a story told by Stephan Feuchtwang.

Feuchtwang (2001: 103–5) was informed of a local tale in Mountainstreet, Taiwan, about how a cashier named Ng Leto became the locality god of the region. The tale goes like this: Ng Leto was walking home on a hot day to celebrate his birthday with his wife. On the way home, he stopped by a river to swim. He hung his clothes on the locality god's shrine table and thus offended the deity. After Ng arrived home, he had a stomachache. His wife found out what had happened on his way home and suspected that the locality god might have caused the ailment. So she went and made an offer to the locality god and asked for forgiveness. Ng was infuriated by the locality god's act of inducing illness on him in order to extract offerings, an act of extortion in his view. Ng burned a yellow dispatch of accusation in order to bring the matter to the city god, who is the locality god's superior, and then went into a trance to go to court with the locality god. The locality god defended his act, insisting that he did not inflict the stomachache and that the offerings were made by Ng's wife according to her own wish, and healed Ng according to the sign of the divination block. The city god, knowing that a person who dares to accuse a god will be a great troublemaker in *Yinzian* after he has died, penalized Ng with forty strokes on his hips. Nonetheless, Ng persisted and appealed to the Great White and Golden Immortal (*Taibaijinren*), a higher-ranking deity who reports directly to Jade Emperor, and was able to bring the matter to his attention. Jade Emperor supported Ng and assigned the Day and Night Wandering Spirits (*Riyoushen* and *Yeyoushen*), two "secret-agent" deities, to follow up the case. Eventually, Ng was vindicated and the locality god was found guilty of extortion. Unfortunately, Ng, who had made good use of a money-yielding pearl given by the Jade Emperor to help the poor, was persecuted by the greedy local magistrate, who was going after his pearl. The story ends with the magistrate's bodyguards chased Ng and his wife to a big rock, where he jumped off and died. After his death, Ng was installed as the locality god in lieu of his corruptive predecessor, and his wife was also venerated as the spouse of the locality god (*Tudi Ma*).

This tale about the replacement of a locality god not only illustrates the bureaucratic structure of Chinese pantheon, but also demonstrates the potential fallibility and corruptibility of deities who are supposed to be the protectors and benefactors of humankind. Because deities are regarded as officials, the act of inflicting harm in order to receive gains is considered *extortion*. By the same token, making an offering to deities in order to avert punishment or harm is considered a *bribe*. Offerings to deities are regarded as legitimate only if they are *gifts* of obeisance or gratitude presented at the worshiper's own wish.

THE ABSENCE OF A PARALLEL NOTION OF *K-P-R* IN CHINESE POPULAR RELIGION

The notions of punitive spirits (deities, ancestors, and ghosts), sins and impurities (as offenses against spirits), punishment as consequence of offenses, and seeking forgiveness/appeasement are not lacking in Chinese popular religion. However, the presence of these notions does not converge to a parallel notion of *k-p-r* that carries a dual meaning of ransoming and purging.

DIFFERENT VIEWS ON THE DIVINE AND SACRIFICIAL RITUALS

The absence of a parallel notion can partly be attributed to the different views on divine and sacrificial rituals between the Levitical traditions and Chinese popular religion. First, in the polytheistic context of Chinese popular religion, pledged loyalty to a single deity by an individual worshiper is not required, nor is there a covenantal relationship between a particular deity and a community, as in the Levitical traditions. A devotee is free to worship multiple deities; ritual attendance is regarded as obligatory only in the case of ancestors.

Second, unlike YHWH, deities in Chinese popular religion do not hold a set of fixed evaluative ethical standards of their own. Thus their adherents have no statutes, rules, or laws by which they must abide. Even though the Chinese pantheon is structured after an imperial metaphor and bureaucratic deities are deemed protectors of "public morality" (Wolf 1974: 168), a breach of public morality does not constitute a direct offense against deities. Only matters of personal insults are regarded as offenses against deities. Failure to observe preparatory rituals (such as ablution, vegetarian diet, and sexual abstinence) before major rites is considered a personal insult against the deities and is subject to divine punishment. For instance, a man who suffered a severe burn from fire-walking attributed his burn to his failure to keep the three-day sexual abstinence before the ritual event (Wolf 1974:162). As for the ancestors, improper care or negligence is a serious offense, which, as some people believe, can cause harm and misfortune to befall descendants. Thus, while the concept of divine/ancestral punishment is present, punishments are not given on the ground of breaching a set of evaluative standards.

Third, in Chinese popular religion, when a deity rightfully punishes a human, no evasion whatsoever can be made. Because the pantheon is structured into an imperial hierarchy and bureaucratic deities are officials, their verdicts have binding force. In case a deity wrongly punishes, vindication can be sought by appealing to a higher-ranking deity. It is possible for deities to wrongly mete out punishment, because they are potentially fallible and corruptible, as I have illustrated above with the Taiwanese tale. By contrast, in the Levitical traditions, while YHWH is infallible and incorruptible, his punishment does not appear to be absolute. At least in the case of expiable moral faults and ritual impurities, the offenders could avert divine punishment through the ransoming power of purification and reparation offerings.

Fourth, in the case of ancestors, their punitive acts are often interpreted as a way of demanding afterlife prerogatives, adequate attention, or proper care from their descendants. In this case, offerings may not be able to solve the problem. Shamans are to be consulted to find out what exactly the ancestors demand. Genuine repentance of the descendants is a nonissue here. The real issue is setting things right according to the demand of the ancestors. Even if the anger of an offended ancestor can be placated with offerings, the sacrificial ritual does not bear any sense of the biblical notion of *k-p-r*. Unlike purification and reparation offerings, in which the offerers are the beneficiaries of the rituals, in ancestral worship the ancestors who rely on human provision are regarded as the beneficiaries.

Fifth, the emphasis on "blood consciousness" (see Abusch 2002: 44), the efficaciousness of blood as an active agent in *k-p-r* offerings (Lev. 17:11), is lacking in Chinese sacrificial rituals, where blood in fact has no significance. The ransoming and purging power of blood in offerings is foreign to Chinese popular religion. When meats are offered, they are usually cooked. In short, there is no concept of a ransoming agent in the sacrificial rituals of Chinese popular religion.

Finally, there is no ordained priesthood in Chinese popular religion. Ritual practices and shared beliefs are transmitted as family and communal heritage. Usually, worship is carried out in a domestic setting, through a family altar that enshrines icons of deities and/or tablets of the ancestors. Temples are founded and maintained by self-governing, self-financed, and voluntary groups. The day-to-day operations of temples and ritual practices are carried out mainly by laity. Daoist priests and Buddhist monks are hired only occasionally for special rites, such as communal sacrifices (*jiao*), death rituals (*zhaiyi*), and deities' birthday processions (*shengdan*). In Chinese popular religion, professional clergy enjoys little centrality; whereas in the Levitical rituals, the officiating priests play a central role in the ritual process, and their ritual misconduct can bring forth divine wrath on the whole community (Lev. 10:1-6). They also actively participate in the *k-p-r* offerings by bearing the culpability of the offerers (10:17). Such an important role of professional clergy as a divine agent is not seen in the laity-based sacrificial rituals of Chinese popular religion.

THE IMPERIAL METAPHOR AND THE ILLEGITIMACY OF RANSOMING OFFERINGS

Another factor that contributes to the absence of a parallel notion in Chinese popular religion is the imperial hierarchy of the Chinese pantheon. As I have mentioned, only volitional gifts are considered proper ritual offerings. Gifts that are paid as ransoms to avert divine punishment would be interpreted as either a bribe or else extortion. The inevitability of this interpretation is primarily caused by the imperial metaphor on which the bureaucratic pantheon is built. The deities are adorned in imperial official garments, and their temples are decorated as magistrate courts. Some non-bureaucratic deities that are integrated into the pantheon are often endowed with imperial titles. Matters of different natures—personal, social, or legal—are brought to bureaucratic (and often non-bureaucratic) deities. These enforcers of public morality "punish people for crimes against society at large" (Wolf 1974: 168). Their primary tasks are to maintain social order and look after the welfare of the community. While social disputes and legal cases are brought to the bureaucratic deities' attention, such cases do not constitute offenses against the deities. A direct offense against a deity, as mentioned, is in matters of personal insult.

The ethical nature of non-bureaucratic deities, although these deities usually embody traditional virtues, remains ambiguous, their morality varying from one deity to another. The kaleidoscopic ethical positions of non-bureaucratic deities create a free market of religious adherence in Chinese popular religion. Irrespective of one's socioeconomic status and moral inclination, there is always a *right* deity for everyone. As for bureaucratic deities, their morality is also subject to divine fallibility and corruptibility. The moral ambiguity of non-bureaucratic deities allows no room for the notion of *k-p-r*. One of the underlying assumptions behind the notion of *k-p-r* is a retributive deity with evaluative ethical standards, which is precisely what is lacking in Chinese popular religion.

A DIFFERENT NOTION OF ATONEMENT IN CHINESE POPULAR RELIGION

A different notion of atonement can be found in the ritual offerings to ghosts. During the Hungry Ghost Festival, also called Middle Origin Festival (*Zhong Yuan Jie*), in the seventh lunar month, it is said that the gate of purgatory is opened and ghosts are released to the human realm. Many families and religious institutions offer foodstuffs to ghosts; at the same time, Scriptures are read and operatic plays are performed to foster the remorseful feelings of hungry ghosts, hoping to purge their bad conscience and thus to shorten their purgatory process (Lai 2003; cf. Goossaert 2005: 1618–29; Fowler and Fowler 2008: 240–47). Remorse is considered a prerequisite for rebirth. These rituals are parts of a ritual system, called the Universal Purification (*Pudu*).

Generally, offering to hungry ghosts in the Hungry Ghost Festival is given in keeping with long-standing tradition, but offerers are often motivated by compassion and/or fear. Some people believe that hungry ghosts in general are pitiful, unattended, and harmless souls; others believe that if hungry ghosts are neglected, they could "wreak havoc" (Fowler and Fowler 2008: 225); still others believe that hungry ghosts are potentially powerful spirits and they would "support anyone who feeds them without principle" (Feuchtwang 2001: 105).

Offering to hungry ghosts is considered a merit; by doing so, the offerers would gain credits toward their own personal salvation. In theory, this is a win–win situation for both parties. From a religious-communal point of view, offering to hungry ghosts serves to reduce the number of roaming spirits in the human realm, thus promoting balance and harmony between the two realms.

Daoist funeral rites, also called purification or purgation rites (*dajai*), have the same function (Tong 2004; Lai 2005). The obvious difference is that there is only one beneficiary in every funerary performance. It is believed that the deceased could receive merit donations from the ritual participants through the purification rites.

Both the universal and individual purification rites reflect great concern over one's afterlife. Similarly, the concern over one's ancestral status after death also produces anxiety toward the afterlife. Successful installation as an ancestor means that one's afterlife provision will be taken care of by one's descendants, and thus the fate of becoming hungry ghosts or orphan souls can be averted. In turn, the purgatory process can be shortened. In Chinese popular religion, there is a clear notion of atonement in the offerings to ghosts. It has the components of averting or mitigating punishment (shortening the purgatory process), transferability of merit (from humans to ghosts), and purging of souls (removing bad conscience from the ghosts). Purging a bad conscience is equivalent to removing an impediment that hinders the path toward personal salvation. Atonement in this sense can be understood as purgation. However, the notion of ransom is still nowhere to be found. In fact, the relationship between the guilty party and the offended party could well be reversed in the ritual offerings to ghosts. The offerers are the offended party, which is subject to the havoc of the roaming, troubled ghosts; whereas the ghosts are the guilty party, which benefits from the purification rite. The rituals are performed to appease the guilty party, to foster their feelings of remorse, and to maintain the state of harmony between the human and ghost realms. While a notion of atonement as purgation is present in Chinese popular religion, it is in many aspects different from the Levitical notion of k-p-r.

A Chinese Religious Perspective on Purification and Reparation Offerings

Under the bureaucratic metaphor, in which deities are morally fallible and corruptible, offering to deities in order to avert or mitigate punishment is inevitably conceived as either an act of bribery or of extortion. Having come to this point, an interesting question arises: How can the legitimacy of purification and reparation offerings as ransom be justified? Persons who are brought up in the Chinese cultures are likely to challenge the legitimacy of such offerings, since similar practices would have been regarded as an act of bribery or extortion in their (or, shall I say, "our") religious contexts. As I have pointed out, k-p-r is a denominative of kopher, "ransom," which is used to denote an illegal payment rendered to avert a more severe impending consequence. Since the efficacy of purification and reparation offerings lies partly on their ransoming power, efficacious legitimation cannot be taken for granted. Hereafter, I will look into several important Levitical presuppositions that undergird purification and reparation offerings and that thus serve to safeguard the legitimacy of the ransoming notion of k-p-r within the Levitical ritual system of atonement.

THE LEGITIMACY OF PURIFICATION AND REPARATION OFFERINGS

First, according to Leviticus, punishments are avertable through purification and reparation offerings under the following conditions. (1) Sins or impurities must be expiable. Not all sins are expiable. Roy Gane (2005: 198–213) has aptly observed that a gradation of sins with regard to intentionality and gravity is clearly operative in Leviticus. Noncalendrical purification and reparation offerings are only prescribed for inadvertent sins, some expiable intentional sins, and physical ritual impurities (Leviticus 4–6; 14–15). Failure to undergo prescribed purification for ritual impurities and expiable moral faults, irrevocable moral faults, and defiant sins are inexpiable by these noncalendrical offerings (Gane 2005: 198–202). (2) The offender must demonstrate genuine repentance (Lev. 4:13, 22, 27; 5:2-5, 17; 6:4 [5:23]). The lexeme ואשם, ve'ashem, "and incurs guilt," occurs numerous times as a descriptive of the offerer's psychological state, indicating that genuine repentance is a prerequisite to the efficacy of purification and reparation offerings. (3) Compensation must be made by the guilty party where an injured human party is involved, prior to the administration of the ritual (Lev. 5:16). This suggests the willingness of the guilty party to set things right and to express remorse to both the community and the deity through the prescribed offerings. The gradation of sins, the prerequisite of genuine repentance, and the need for compensation prior to administering the ritual preclude the guilty party's deliberate premeditation to avoid the consequence or liability of her or his fault through offerings, possibly also of a deceptive motivation on YHWH's part to extort ritual gifts for his own benefit.

Second, there are clear administrative guidelines for purification and reparation offerings. The prescription has taken the financial situation of the offerer into consideration. The practical concern over the offerer's financial ability even overrides the significance of "blood consciousness" in individual purification offerings. If an offerer cannot afford the minimal slaughtering of two turtledoves or pigeons, a grain offering is an acceptable substitute (Lev. 5:11). This concern over the offerer's financial situation and graded requirements are incompatible with an interpretation of these offerings as extortions. The clear ritual guidelines ensure the proper administration of these offerings, preventing the priests from exercising corruptibility on the deity's behalf.

Third, contrary to deities in Chinese popular religion, the Levitical YHWH does not rely on human provision. In Levitical traditions, YHWH is portrayed as self-sufficient. Hence, he has no reason to extort offerings for his own gratification.

Finally, as pointed out earlier, deities' moral ambiguity, fallibility, and corruptibility are the main barriers to a parallel notion of atonement as ransom in Chinese popular religion. In the Levitical traditions, YHWH is portrayed as infallible, incorruptible, and morally superior to humans. In short, the conditions for purification and reparation offerings, their clear administrative guidelines, and YHWH's self-sufficiency have precluded these offerings from becoming illegal ransoms and have thus safeguarded the legitimacy of their ransoming power within their ritual context.

THE NOTION OF K-P-R AND THE NOTION OF GUILT COMPLEX

Guilt complex is a fundamental and universal problem in human psychology. Before the invention of psychotherapy or counseling, religious practices might have already been providing channels for the resolution of guilt. The ritual goal of purification and reparation offerings is to effect forgiveness (Lev. 4:20, 26, 31, 35; 5:10, 13, 16, 18; 6:7 [5:26]). Sklar (2005) interprets "forgiveness" as an aversion of punishment; however, the lexeme ונסלח, *we-nislakh*, "and he is forgiven," can also be interpreted as the subjective experience of the offerer. Through purification and reparation offerings, the offerer experiences the absolution of sin and the resolution of guilt through the ransoming and purging power of these offerings. In the act of offering, the offerer has indeed paid a price, in terms of sacrificial animal(s) or a measure of semolina. The complex and elaborated rituals can serve to satisfy any psychological need of the offerer to experience a concrete form of divine punishment and publicly confess his or her offense. In a sense, purification and reparation offerings function like some sort of penance, an important process for people who are genuinely remorseful. Moreover, as public confession, the rituals provide an opportunity for the community to accept and reintegrate those who have committed expiable offenses. The ritual logic is that if the guilty party's transgression is forgiven by the deity through a prescribed offering, then the community that has established a covenantal relationship with that deity must accept the guilty party. In a way, the ritual contributes to social order and communal harmony by providing a channel for those who have committed offences of lesser severity, but still detrimental to the community's well being, to reenter that community.

In Chinese popular religion, ritual offerings to deities cannot function as a channel for the absolution of sins or the resolution of guilt because of the bureaucratic metaphor and the ambiguous morality of deities, as already expounded. The questions are: What kind of religious resource is available in Chinese popular religion for the resolution of guilt? Are there any rituals that can address the need of guilt resolution and sin absolution? Not only does Chinese popular religion provide no channels for the resolution of guilt, but, by contrast, there seems to be an emphasis on the cultivation of guilty feelings and fear for lack of remorse. The universal and individual purification rites are aimed at nurturing the remorseful feelings of ghosts in order to shorten their chthonic suffering and to expedite their rebirths. As for the living, the focus tends to be on self-cultivation and accumulation of merit points (however "merit" is defined). In Chinese popular religion, there is no tangible and elaborated way for worshipers to experience the absolution of sins, the resolution of guilt, and communal reacceptance.

CONCLUSION

There is no parallel notion of k-p-r in the sacrificial rituals of Chinese popular religion. In fact, in Chinese popular religion, making an offering to an offended deity for the purpose of appeasing the deity and averting or mitigating punishment is regarded as an act of bribery or extortion. The notion of k-p-r is incompatible with the three-realm worldview, the imperial metaphor of the Chinese pantheon, and the ambiguous moral nature of deities in Chinese popular religion. Deities, ancestors, and ghosts, who rely on human provision, are capable of extortion. They are like humans: fallible, corruptible, and each with her or his unique temperament and moral inclination. Although most of them are regarded as protectors of public morality and benefactors to humankind, they do not guarantee the fair judgment that their devotees expect from them, and they take personal insults seriously. Their "official" status makes offerings that are intended to avert or mitigate just punishments illegitimate.

The notion of *k-p-r* inevitably would have been regarded as illegitimate in Chinese religious contexts.

On the other hand, in Leviticus the legitimacy of the ransoming power of purification and reparation offerings is safeguarded by the gradation of evils; the consideration about the intentionality of the offenders; the gravity, compensability, and revocability of offenses; the clear guidelines for ritual administration; and by YHWH's own self-sufficiency, infallibility, and moral supremacy. By putting the notion of *k-p-r* into dialogue with Chinese popular religion, the legitimacy of the notion of *k-p-r* in purification and reparation offerings, which has been taken for granted, is elucidated. Due to the incompatibility of the notion of *k-p-r* with various concepts in Chinese popular religion, purification and reparation offerings are still highly likely to be regarded as acts of bribery or extortion by those of us who have been immersed and acculturated in Chinese religious contexts. To us, the notion of *k-p-r* can be puzzling, highly incomprehensible, and even reprehensible. How can a person make an offering in order to avert or mitigate punishment? How can a deity that is supposedly just and fair accept such offerings? In Chinese religious contexts, these questions are not easy to answer.

As I have pointed out, the cathartic power of purification and reparation offerings is absent in Chinese popular religion. The complex and elaborated rituals in Leviticus function as a kind of penance and passage to the reintegration of the guilty party into the community. In contrast, in Chinese popular religion, ritual offerings are not efficacious: they do not contribute to the absolution of sins and the resolution of guilt. Rather, there seems to be a concern over the lack of remorse and an emphasis on self-cultivation and accumulation of personal merit, which can be clearly seen in the purification rites for ghosts. In my opinion, the lack of guilt-resolving rituals for worshipers constitutes a loophole in Chinese popular religion and invites other social or religious groups to infiltrate and supplement this lack. When there is such great emphasis on personal merit and afterlife retributive judgment, guilt is indeed an issue.

Notes

1. For a succinct introductory book on Chinese popular religion, see the work by Goossaert 2005 or Fowler and Fowler 2008.

2. Because the term *Chinese popular religion* has been problematized, some scholars choose not to use it at all. For instance, Tik-sang Liu (2003) calls the phenomenon "a nameless but active religion." My own position is that for the sake of academic engagement, we need some kind of designation for the phenomenon. The term *Chinese popular religion* is an adequate candidate, since

it does convey some fundamental characteristics of the phenomenon. However, to clear the clouds of confusion, the term must be used with qualifiers.

3. I would like to thank Professors Douglas Knight and Jack Sasson (both at Vanderbilt University) for reviewing and commenting on various drafts of this essay.

4. Catherine Bell (1989) provides a succinct review on the research history of Chinese popular religion and the problems that have arisen in approaching and naming this phenomenon. She has assessed three main approaches to "Chinese popular religion," from the first-stage elite-folk dichotomy, which contrasts the religious practices of the Chinese populace with the institutional religions of the elite, to the second-stage search for unity and commonality between the two; then to a more historically conscious third-stage approach of depicting the inextricable interpenetration between the religious popular cultures and the three institutional religions—namely, Daoism, Buddhism, and Confucianism—within the Chinese historical, social, economic, and cultural contexts.

5. Note that Paper 1995 is comparative in terms of different chronological periods within Chinese culture.

6. For instance, recently (in English) Feuchtwang 2001; Sangren 1987, 2000; Stewart and Strathern 2007.

7. The Chinese pantheon is an open system and varies among traditions and localities. Theoretically, new deities can emerge and be canonized into the existing pantheon at any time.

8. There are only four occurrences of k-p-r (Piel) in the Pentateuch that do not belong to the Priestly strand (Gen. 32:20 [Yahwist, J]; Exod. 32:30 [traditionally assigned to Elohist, E]; Deut. 21:8 and 32:4 [Deuteronomist, D]).

9. Thus it is not a surprise to find that there are variant renderings of k-p-r (Piel) even in the same English version. For instance, in the NRSV it is rendered as "make atonement" (Exod. 29:37), "appease" (Gen. 32:21), "absolve" (Deut. 21:8), "cleanse" (Deut. 32:43), "cover" (Ps. 65:4), "forgive" (Ps. 78:38), "pacify" (Prov. 16:14), "purify" (Ezek. 43:26).

10. Regarding the punishment of expiable sins, Sklar argues that even though it is not explicitly stated in the prescription of purification and reparation offerings, one can "safely" assume that all sins lead to the death penalty. He also attributes the reason of the nonmention of punishment to the expected efficacy of the rites to avert punishment (Sklar 2005: 11–43). I concur with Sklar that all sins are punishable and the ransoming power of purification and reparation offerings to effect forgiveness implies a mitigation of punishment. However, I find problematic his thesis that divine punishment is limited to the death penalty. The notion of uniform punishment for sins contradicts the gradation of sins that is explicitly set forth in the prescription of the atoning rituals. The nonmention of punishment can be interpreted as an "indication" that the aversion of punishment, though an anticipated effect of the rituals, should not be the focus of purification and reparation offerings or the motive of the offerer. The nonmention of punishment suggests that these offerings should not be presented out of fear for punishment. Also, notably, whenever the punishment of sins is stated or executed (whether by YHWH or by the community) in Leviticus, it serves a purpose of *deterrence*. Deterrence is unnecessary and irrelevant in the prescription of these offerings if the inadvertency of the expiable sins and genuine repentance of the guilty party are already assumed. Moreover, death penalty for the purpose of deterrence is unnecessary because of the lesser gravity and compensability of the faults.

11. The argument for k-p-r (Piel) as the denominative of *kopher* is a major part of Sklar's thesis in *Sin, Impurity, Sacrifice, Atonement* (2005). Milgrom also acknowledges the connection between k-p-r (Piel) and *kopher* and admits that this connotation of ransoming is clearly operative at least partly in the 'Azaz'el ritual, where the Israelites, the guilty party, pacify the wrath of YHWH, the offended party, and thus avert the death penalty (Lev. 16:7-10). However, Milgrom's interpretation raises a question on why the living goat is designated to 'Azaz'el rather than to the offended party, YHWH (Milgrom 2007: 181; 1991: 1082).

12. Interpenetration, commonly referred as "syncretism," among these three institutional religions is undeniable. The recognition of their equal orthodoxies in the Tang dynasty can in no way lead to the conclusion that there existed three independent, pristine religious traditions. While

there are distinguishable characteristics among these religious systems, they are nonetheless inextricably related to each other. Their intricate relationship also blurs the line between orthodoxy and heterodoxy. Furthermore, it has been argued that humane ideals, ethical principles, and moral precepts of Confucianism have permeated all dimensions and all forms of Chinese culture; thus cultural extraction of Confucian elements is simply impossible. This argument also goes well with the Daoist and Buddhist traditions in Chinese communities (Fowler and Fowler 2008: 254; Goossaert 2005: 1614–15).

13. Contrary to Jochim's view that individual salvation is not important in Chinese popular religion and what matter are "(1) passing from this world into an ancestral realm . . . (2) the interactions between living persons and their ancestors" (Jochim 2003: 158), I see that ancestral worship is much related to the obtainment of personal salvation. To avoid becoming a hungry ghost assures a successful passing in purgatory, and this could be regarded as an intermediate salvation. However, it is true that self-cultivation toward personal salvation in terms of meditation, nurturing of vitality (*qigong*), or ritual diet (as in Daoist or Buddhist concepts) has little significance in Chinese popular religion.

14. Here I have rendered a unilateral representation of *ling*, "efficacy." The concept is actually more multifarious. As Sangren (2000: 99–103) points out from an anthropological point of view, the concept of *ling* involves the reputation of the deity, state sanction, and relation to ancestral temple; it is a result of collective and individual cultural production through ritual participation (see Feuchtwang 2001: 84–89).

15. For instance, Mazu, a popular goddess along the South China Sea, was a historical figure in the tenth century ce (Bosco and Ho 1999; Nyitray 2000); and the deified Lü Dongbin was a Daoist priest in the ninth century ce (Lai 2003: 460–63).

16. Heaven (*Tian*) is a major motif in Chinese cosmology and is a complicated, dynamic, and evolving concept in Chinese religious history. *Tian* has multiple meanings, and its definition has also undergone a series of transformations. Zhang Huaicheng (1998: 48–49) lists four possible traditional interpretations of *Tian*: (1) the sky, (2) the High/Supreme Lord/Emperor (*Shangdi*), (3) destiny (an invariable objective necessity), and (4) nature.

Golden Do's and Don'ts

Leviticus 19:1-17 from a Human-Rights-Based Approach (HRBA)

Carole R. Fontaine

Preface: Tortured Textualities

In a recent seminary course where we discussed the ethical values of the Hebrew Bible, the New Testament, and the Qur'an, students compared the guiding ethical principles of these scriptures to the principles and values coded in the United Nations Declaration of Universal Human Rights (UNDUHR),[1] the foundational document for the international laws governing human rights. Students were quite dismayed to discover that we would indeed be considering legal texts from the Hebrew Bible, and that the Ten Commandments, so popular in United States' religious discourse on values and legal foundations, might not be the be-all and end-all legacy for human rights that they had been taught to expect by their church affiliations and seminary training. They saw very little support of the intrinsic worth and dignity of gay and lesbian persons in any of the documents we were studying. This was a matter of considerable concern, and that was even before we began to consider the situation with respect to legal warrants for protecting human rights found in the church fathers, or rabbis of classical Judaism, much less in the Qur'an, or shari'a law derived from various interpretations of the Qur'an, all sources developed in a patriarchal context and in opposition to more dominant cultures. In our local setting, it was important to the students to affirm all religious points of view as equally valid; but when they came to *their* key issue, sexual orientation, they were completely at a loss to discover that religions of antiquity did not affirm that to which they so firmly adhered or the issues to which their diverse ministries would be directed. (The issue of gender had been labeled by this class as clearly heterosexist, and hence invalid, so they were not especially troubled by the treatment of straight women in our texts, nor did those who were not African American detect any particular issues of race and ethnicity as a difficulty in the Scriptures surveyed.) Most of the students embraced a liberal philosophy, which caused them to assess the rabbinic writers of the *Sayings of the Fathers* as a wee bit narrow in their focus on only one community—their own—to the exclusion of universal concerns in evidence in the New Testament transformation of Judaism.[2] In the absence of explicit focus on students' personal issues in what we read, only a couple of diehard Jesus-loving conservatives wanted to argue that biblical laws or ethics had much use in today's world. Hearing my discussion of ethics in Q and their reformulation in the books of Matthew and Luke in the Sermon on the Mount (Horsley 2008), one of my Jesus people asked plaintively which text I would take if I could only take one to found a new civilization on a desert island somewhere: the Hebrew Bible, the New Testament, the Qur'an, the US Constitution, or the UNDUHR.

I answered firmly that if only one text were available to me, it would have to be the UNDUHR, despite the well-known critiques of its focus on individual rights and the neglect of reasonable and legitimate group values, among other things. But I also noted at the same time that although the three Scriptures in question were held captive by the cultures of their time (especially in regard to slave ownership, patriarchal views of women and children, xenophobic attitudes toward the other, hierarchical and stratified views of social organization in economics, and purity fetishes), I retained a soft spot for each Scripture, despite many difficulties. The Sermon on the Mount, I told them, presented a radical protest against Roman occupation, and it could never have existed without Leviticus 19, its partial *Vorlage*. Further, the Qur'an did the best job inscribing intrinsic human worth and dignity for slaves, and better encoded the equality of the sexes in rationality and responsibility, so ought not to be dismissed out of hand. The U.S. Constitution outlines a republic, not a true democracy and even with the Bill of Rights is primarily concerned with how creditors might receive payment across sovereign state lines. The students were deeply horrified by my praise of Leviticus, and the class as a whole never recovered from my statement in favor of partial affirmation of scriptural texts. (Perhaps my subject status as a middle-class, white, married woman in charge of their grades formed a basis for some of their discontent.)

In retrospect, I realize that in the world of my students, Leviticus has been repeatedly designated as one of the horrifying "clobber texts" routinely used by fundamentalist Christians in the United States to damn all so-called sexually deviant sinners to eternal hell[3] (Weldon; McNeill 2010). Oddly, the

New Testament letters, similarly disparaging to homosexuals, received far less disparagement from my students, although they could not explain to me why this was the case. "But the Great Commandment," I said in reply to their objections, "is the foundation of all Christian ethics, and it was a direct reference to Leviticus 19:18!" But, no: good Samaritan or not, the many nascent human rights affirmations made in the Holiness Code all fell before its imputed mistreatment of lesbians, witches, and the code's mixing of ritual and ethical elements. Taken together, these features were enough to cause any modern reader (at least in my class) to dismiss the whole of biblical law as irrelevant at best and profoundly damaging at worst.

I was deeply troubled, and not in the least because I foresaw (rightly so, as it turned out) the flurry of negative course evaluations that would come my way for having defended an unpopular text. Parts of the discussion clearly smacked to me of a supersessionist Christianity that disparages the Hebrew Bible in order to elevate Jesus' purported objection to "the law" (Amy-Jill Levine 2006; Daniel Boyarin 2012). I suspected that while any substantive critique of Judaism was impossible for my students due to their social locations, they had learned to achieve the same effect by their treatment of Jesus as someone who spoke only in contradiction of his inherited faith. Problem solved.

However, as a Bible scholar who has worked for over a decade in human rights work with respect to the analysis of the role of religion on the rights of women and girls worldwide, I found my students' dismissal of the texts to be a source of many problems for ever bringing about change from within religious communities holding these texts as "Scripture." My agenda as an activist is simple: wherever the cultural values of biblical religion and its monotheistic siblings of the book are used to curtail rights and become part of the problem in solving global crises, I seek to dismantle the texts that undergird restrictive use by people of faith. To do this, I seek to better understand the way religious sources are appropriated and applied to modern issues, and hope to offer, where possible, different texts and processes that allow the human community to better achieve an equal and flourishing movement into the future of a precious and dying planet. Popular liberalism has failed the modern church communities of Christianity when it does not distinguish between cultural relativism and openness to diversity: the simple inclusion of formerly silenced voices does not, in itself, guarantee the deconstruction of a terrifying status quo where women, girl children, and others are concerned (Lopez: 2011). In this vein, I find even the technical and extremely dry studies of the disciplines of biblical scholarship to be worthy and necessary projects for the concerned professional. Study has shown the role of the Bible and other Scriptures around the world to be one of the arenas in which human rights finds its most problematic application. Faced with the need to uphold freedom of choice of religion and the values of affiliation and freedom of practice of religion, governments, societies, and other groups are more than willing to throw the human rights of women and girls under the bus with alarming regularity. In fact, this trend has been so well documented that I will simply refer to the many studies and releases on the topic by the United Nations available online, and I suggest a stiff drink to accompany your reading. From the estimated 2000 women and children in Ghana held captive and subjected to daily violence in the so-called witch camps set aside for those accused of witchcraft by tribal and religious officials, to the role of evangelical churches in Zimbabwe of making sure that Christian congregations do not actively confront the scourge of AIDS among married women, the news is bleak with respect to how Scripture is interpreted out of context and applied to justify what can only be considered crimes against humanity (Alston 2009; Meyer 2004; Okeke 2010; Marshall and Taylor 2006). To speak against these abuses, one must know the text, and know it well, even though the state of scholarship makes it impossible to speak with certainty of many things—authorship, first community of reception, and even the way in which ancient audiences made sense of what may or may not have seemed self-evident (Rendtorff 1996; Gutzwiller 1996). Nevertheless, considerations other than those of difficulty remain before us.

In my dual role of scholar and activist, I do not deny the many problems that exist in the Holiness Code, but I continue to insist—now in writing—that the text of Leviticus and other legal treatises from the Hebrew Bible have much to offer those who seek to understand and guarantee the rights of individuals and groups in the modern world. In a world in which Christians in developing nations seek to kill homosexuals and witches as a response to the AIDS epidemic (Okeke 2010; Alston 2009; Harrison 2008),[4] we require more than a rejection of biblical texts to defend the lives and dignity of those castigated by the laws of antiquity; we must pursue deeper understanding (followed by rejection at times, of course) instead. In the face of these views, let me explain why I find Leviticus useful.

HUMAN RIGHTS AND HUMAN FLOURISHING: SOME BASIC OBSERVATIONS

I have written elsewhere about basic concepts of human rights and the epistemological difficulties for founding such rights, either within Western philosophy or in inherited religious texts (Fontaine 2008). Such difficulties are legion, and complicate any attempt to secure international consensus on the defense of human rights and personal liberty. Much can be explained by reference to the cultural currents in the modern period, during which various human rights documents were proposed by their adherents after World War II: Communist nations were unwilling to grant the notion of religious freedom as an important basic right, while leaders from the South in the United States would not consent to regulations concerning intermarriage or equal rights to education, as this contradicted the long-held biases inscribed during the period of slavery in North America. Muslim countries struggled with the notion of equality in inheritance rights and marriage as well as the situation with respect to equal rights for various minorities, be they religious or ethnic. With the rise of nationalism and later Islamic fundamentalism in some countries whose religion was predominantly Muslim, the issue of Western nation states or Western philosophical groundings for international law came to the fore, even though Muslim contributors to the UNDUHR had had no trouble presenting vigorous defense of human rights during the formulation of that document, often serving as a bulwark against the ideology of Communism and the racism of the United States (Mayer 2007: 13–16). Leaving aside the philosophical difficulties in an epistemology that does not ground human rights in any sort of religious context, one of the pressing issues of the UNDUHR, which still continues to dog the work of many good people, is the premise that the nation state serves as the guarantor of human rights. In a world where many developing nations can barely feed and house their citizens, the presupposition that there are resources and interests for securing the human rights of all their citizens is preposterous, to say the least; nor is there any lack of avoidance of human rights issues in the supposedly civilized countries of the world. Despite wonderful work being done around the world by some nations and NGOs, along with sustained discussion by experts as well as nations, human rights enforcement by nation states, or even the United Nations, remains the great unfunded and unenforceable mandate. Instead, treaties are drafted and signed that urge, but cannot require, member states of the United Nations to support human rights for all. Some countries faced with the prospect of enforcing equal rights even refuse to draft a constitution. Meanwhile, people perish in droves as the world looks on, and women and girls are among the forefront of those at risk.

All these problems notwithstanding, those engaged in the work of humanizing the world continue to press their agendas, if not on abstract levels, at least in the concrete instances that require immediate attention. This has led to the so-called human–rights–based approach (HRBA) to problems within and between countries and regions, especially in development work in light of the failures of the nations of the world to meet the United Nations Millennium Development Goals (MDG). Beijing (Fourth World Conference on Women, 1995) has come and gone; yet women and children still starve at a greater rate than their adult male counterparts. The West continues to enjoy a gross national product and concomitant lifestyle that dwarfs that of other regions of the world, even in the midst of recessions and financial crises. Various regions still engage in military arms races that beggar their treasuries and take focus away from national projects promising real progress to their people. Where the will to turn away from violence and greed is weaker than the desire to provide a baseline for human dignity and empowerment, activists have begun to speak of elimination of poverty, disease, and other scourges of humankind under the framework of international human rights law in their attempt to mobilize advancements of whole populations. This movement, then, serves as the foundation for the HRBA (London 2008).

Human rights specifics are developed from a basic axiom: there are some things that, simply because they *are* human, ought *never* to be done to human beings; conversely, there are other things that ought *always* to be done for human beings as part of their birthright of existence. Put this way, human rights are either a floor beneath which no human being ought ever to exist, or they represent a threshold that all human beings must cross in order to fulfill their full capacities as humans. The latter formulation—that of capacities—is a newer epistemic category, devised in order to speak more broadly of all those things that must be present for human beings to flourish. Such a "capacities approach" seeks to advance real progress in achievement of rights without falling into many of the philosophical difficulties or presuming that there is broad consensus on those difficulties. This approach to thinking about rights has been pioneered by Amartya Sen and liberal philosopher Martha Nussbaum, and aims to establish a concrete moral basis for resisting the utility-based solutions and choices of nations and transnational corporations in a period of increasing globalization (Nussbaum 1997; 2000: 34–110). Human flourishing via honoring the capacities approach allows the blending of so-called first-generation rights (civil and political) and second-generation rights (economic and social), and makes the claim that some capabilities are so essential to human flourishing that they must be understood as "freestanding moral ideas" that do not rely on a particular religious point of view, or a philosophical or utility-based ideal, for justification to act (Nussbaum 2000: 83). Capabilities act as social goals that are prerequisites for full human life and may be divided into basic, internal or combined capacities, all necessary prerequisites to a human's functioning as a whole person. Nussbaum cites the following list of human functional capabilities: life; bodily health; bodily integrity; senses, imagination, and thought; emotions; practical reason; affiliation; other species; play; and control over one's environment, political and material (Nussbaum 2000: 78–83).

By speaking of functional capabilities, Nussbaum is able to distinguish particular situations of various groups: for example, women may have rights technically granted "on paper," as it were, but in reality are unable to exercise the enjoyment of those rights based on a gender code that disadvantages them in most areas of social, economic, and political life. Similarly, speaking of combined human capabilities allows one to distinguish the level of human functioning even in the presence of a typical widely used but flawed measure like gross national product: in places like the United States with a high GNP, it would be wrong to conclude that this widely used measurement of wealth represents a true measure of the flourishing of immigrant communities or the children of the poor. Where freedom to choose and practice religion are concerned, we are operating within a complex set of capacities: imagination and thought, emotions, affiliation, and control over one's environment, since religion straddles and pervades all these areas of concern—a fact of which ancient Scriptures are aware, however much this may unsettle liberals of the modern secular state (Hackett 2005: 74–75; Batson et al. 1999; United Nations Document Reference A/CONF.177/20/Rev.1 1996).

DEFENDING LEVITICUS: SOME OBSERVATIONS

With these thoughts about human capabilities in mind, I turn now to a HRBA approach to the Holiness Code in the book of Leviticus, with particular attention to Leviticus 19, which makes some quite astounding—at least to modern sensibilities—legislative moves. Although biblical legal documents are addressed to the elite males of the community, with particular focus on in-group males, if we promote all human beings—women, children, foreigners, elderly, the disabled, and other inferiors and outcasts—to the ideal level occupied by the elite males of the designated group receiving the texts, it is possible to establish a universal ethic, one that represents the highest ideal of the text itself (Fontaine 2008). In such a way, the text itself answers at least part of the charge of exclusivity and irrelevance that offends so many, such that it may function as a traditional resource for considering the whole question of human rights and the desired goal of the flourishing of individuals and groups. Similarly, where we find a text that forbids certain actions from being applied to in-group male elites, we take those actions as unacceptable in application to any member of the human family. So, on this basis, we have a clear dividing line between those texts we might reject and those we might wish to retain. There will, of course, be other circumstances of advised actions to perform or from which to refrain within the text that may well require more sophisticated adjudication: What are we to do with the deaths of Aaron's sons, Abihu and Nadab, on ritual grounds (Lev. 10:1-3),[5] or the zeal of Aaron's grandson Phinehas, who takes it upon himself to kill a married couple either for their mixed marriage or because they have intruded into a greater zone of holiness forbidden to them (Num. 25:7-8, 10-12)?[6] In both those cases, Aaron and Moses are silent, but God is not. No wonder modern U.S. white supremacists proudly brandish the book of Numbers as their warrant for racist and genocidal murder.[7]

CONCEPTUAL CONFUSIONS: JESUS, THE SACRED, AND THE ORDINARY

One of the purported problems with Leviticus and its concept of holiness in its application to the modern context is its complex blending of ritual, moral, and criminal laws, which are usually juxtaposed to the supposedly pure ethical concerns of Jesus of Nazareth. It is customary, especially for Christians, to exclude all but their favorite clobber texts from consideration in their applications of biblical law because Jesus supposedly rejected the ritual and cultic regulations of his people. Why would he have done this? Ah, because of his inherent anti-Judaism, or because, like modern Christians, he mainly views religion as a matter of personal faith between God and the individual. This view of course only holds when fundamentalist and extremist Christians are dealing with a text they do not care to take seriously, such as dietary laws or directions for Christians to sell all of their belongings and give to the poor. However, when such groups wish to employ ritual or cultic laws that engage the group to protect purity, they are glad to cite sexual regulations while simultaneously dismissing other equally difficult legal enjoinments. When questioned, these groups cannot produce a logical hermeneutic which permits them to distinguish between regulations for the preservation of purity and Holiness in their own communities, and those laws which they discard. Let us take some of these difficulties, in turn.

JESUS AND THE LAW

Objections to Leviticus on the basis of its rejection by Jesus of Nazareth turn out to be unsubstantiated by a close reading of the New Testament Gospels (Watson 1996). Jesus in fact assumes that one would obey the ritual and cultic regulations of his inherited religion. The point at issue comes to the fore when an ethical demand and a ritual demand compete for immediate attention; in such a case, Jesus promotes the ethical demand to the level of that which must first be met, but assumes that the actor will subsequently return and meet the ritual/cultic regulation after the ethical act has concluded (Matt. 5:21-24). Like his forebears, Jesus assumes that devotion to God permeates all realms of life and is not just a private matter of conscience or affection, and the New Testament continues to hold this point of view concerning the lack of separation between what moderns might call secular versus religious spheres of action (Kaminsky 2008: 125; Amy-Jill Levine 2006; Daniel Boyarin 2012).

CONFUSED CATEGORIES

Similarly, the blending of different kinds of regulations that guard and enforce holiness in Leviticus and elsewhere supposedly creates a logical confusion that renders the text unusable. This supposition is actually untenable as a hermeneutic of rejection. As writers on holiness have shown, the authors of the Holiness Code understand holiness to be a blended state of being, covering all aspects of human life in proximity to the covenant Lord (Kaminsky 1995; 2008: 126; Gammie 1989), such that even cultic and ritual laws relate systemically to ethical demands on the community. The work of Jacob Milgrom and Mary Douglas has persuasively demonstrated that such laws, usually so offensive to Christians, are in fact ethical at their heart, enjoin a higher level of moral functioning in daily life by limiting violence against even nature, and maintain certain separations based on understandings of dominant characteristics of different classes. In this world, the mother and her children cannot be slaughtered at the same time; the predatory bird has committed violence, and ought not to be eaten. Asking humans who are usually so ready to act on their inclination to violence to remember that they are not alone in nature as a focus of God's concern is no trivial matter. By holding humans to a higher standard of ethics in their relationship to creation, the laws seek to inculcate the divine image in a practical way that keeps God as near as the beating of blood in the jugular vein: as the text says again and again, "You shall be holy, for I am Holy" (Milgrom 1976; Douglas 2002 [1966]).

From the point of view of a HRBA to Leviticus, it is a major point to note that in much of the developing world we meet exactly the same worldview that we find in Leviticus and in the New Testament. Law and right living are not the province of the latecomer nation states of colonial making that try to reach down into the level of the village to inform right action based on an ethic alien to the community being regulated but that benefits the colonial overlord. Rather, it is the multifaceted world of religion and faith that informs the basic matrix out of which daily individual, ethical, and social action is fabricated. To be able to point to the Western inheritance of such a holistic worldview forms a point of contact for those who seek to make allies out of religious people around the world, rather than first insulting their belief system, their daily attitudes, and their most personal commitments at the outset, in the hopes of converting them to some bloodless and alien philosophy that cannot successfully explain itself in the context of their daily life (Nussbaum 2000: 178–81). One member of the United Nations Human Rights Council often tells the story of what would happen in her work with women in Pakistan if she arrived and proclaimed, "I bring you women's rights in the name of the United Nations!" as her first move in establishing a woman's right not to be beaten: nothing but suspicion of the West. However, if her first encounter with village women begins by asking them, "Who is Allah?" she knows they will answer that Allah is the Most Merciful and Most Compassionate One. When she asks as the follow-up question of whether or not the Most Merciful, Most Compassionate thinks that women ought to be beaten, eyes light up, backbones stand a little straighter, and women and girls lean closer to hear what she will say next. All aid workers and human rights NGOs could learn much from this lived parable that takes place in the real world on a regular basis. That this approach deconstructs culturally and religiously sanctioned violence from within, even when a religion is understood very traditionally in its modern context, is witnessed by the fact that this U.N. representative is a wanted woman with many death sentences pronounced upon her. (Her name is withheld here for just that reason.) Such is the power of an ancient text well understood and deftly employed.

A FINAL QUIBBLE WITH PURITY

As much as this scholar-activist lives by and believes that the sacred is a genuine human perception of a deeper dimension of our common life and that acknowledgment or encounter with it can be formative experience underlying much of what we call religion (or physics or metaphysics or artistic inspiration, and so on; Otto 1928; Eliade 1963), there are genuine negative issues that must be explored. When holiness is viewed as a scarce, "unnatural resource" to which some have access by accidents of gender, birth, ability, race, or history, and others do not, it is easy to see how a "holy city" or "holy people" could become a pretext for violent competition and a casus belli that no international human rights approach can endorse (Avalos 2007). Most cultures see themselves as the center of the world, whose exceptional status must be defended against all other claims—which is one of the reasons why cultural relativism as the program of liberal philosophy falls into circular reasoning where religion is concerned. While endorsing the freedom to choose and practice a religion, one also winds up having to accept religions that are anything *but* inclusive or rights-affirming, since all foreground their exclusive claims to truth and attendant practice (Nussbaum 2000:46–49). This provides yet another reason why the capacities approach to the discourse of human rights offers a nuanced chance to avoid collapsing into a tangle of epistemic dilemmas: we may not be able to adjudicate claims of who has the axis mundi in their territory, but we *can* judge how well a religious ideology advances concrete human individuals in the achievement of flourishing in their own particularized circumstances.

While holiness is generally misunderstood when taken out of context of its practicing culture (Harrington 1996), or perceived only as a category of exclusive separation, we must not, in postcolonial analysis, underestimate the role of a priestly ideology as a form of resistance against a dominant power seeking to render all subjects into neutral, interchangeable resources of an empire (or transnational corporation). Indeed, the identity of the colonized can be preserved by scrupulous adherence to ritual and cultic matters, but this may often be at the price of the poor or otherwise marginalized (like women who are forbidden certain religious, social, and economic rights), and who do not have the wherewithal to follow such regulations successfully. In a similar vein, we might also see holiness as a self-serving attempt at maintenance of personal or group power by a privileged male class that collaborates with its captors by maintaining order within the captive population. Such descriptions of Jesus' attitudes toward the leading religious elites in Jerusalem, who pander to Rome, while Romanization in Galilee rendered the life of the poor even more hideous than it was, have much to teach us (Horsley 2004). So, we must not be guilty of ignoring the uses to which holiness might be put by those who would maintain their power, even when it savages the poor of their own group and serves the empire.

We should also note that in many ways the notion of bodily purity, at least, is an illusion and too easily becomes a fetish of those who are able to think of themselves as whole and complete. Those with a blemish, a disability, discharges relating to sexuality, or many other permanent or fugue states of the body know full well that the body and its purity can never truly be maintained. When such ideas of purity in the body and in society become encoded in law, we are only a step away from eliminating any rights at all among those who bear their impurity in a more public way. The goal of creating a perfect race, a perfect body, and a perfect cult must always be regarded with suspicion. We will do better to speak of bodily integrity, which can reflect the actual circumstances of all of us, even if it must be defined differently based on the circumstances in which any particular body finds itself. The worth of the body cannot be based on its beauty, its inviolability, or its functioning: there are many who fail to meet these basic criteria, but possess rights to a decent attempt at flourishing, no matter their condition (see Lev. 19:14, 32; Avalos et al. 2007; Fontaine 2008).

WHOSE RIGHTS? WHOSE RESPONSIBILITY?

One of the things we gain by taking Leviticus seriously, and indeed all of the rabbinic reflections on legal texts, is a clear indication that rights create reciprocal responsibilities (Steinberg 1991). Similarly, by the text's and rabbis' obvious assumption that such reciprocal responsibilities bind both the native and the alien (who is provided with a way to convert and become one with the covenant community; Kaminsky 2008), we avoid the conundrum at the international level of legal thinking about who exactly is required to enforce the laws and demands of human rights. By being granted a right, one also undertakes the responsibilities not only of conforming one's own action in adherence to what has been granted but also of guaranteeing the enjoyment of that right by the rest of the group—and the group is by no means limited to one's own chosen preferences or affections. In the world of Leviticus, to be a "rights-holder" is to become a "duty-bearer"; and even nature holds rights, and acts out of the duty of its character and must be guaranteed protection by the human community (Berman 1992). This is indeed a welcome and useful observation of the unity of rights and responsibilities for anyone who watches the machinations of the United Nations Council on Human Rights when member states likes Sudan and Iran join the discussion, or when the U.N. Security Council's refusal to *act* on the slaughter of civilians in Syria is compromised by the political goals of China and Russia, leaving it to Al Qaeda to act on behalf of the wretched populace of "the blood-soaked epicenter of the Arab spring" (Rajavi 2012).

A HUMAN-RIGHTS-BASED APPROACH TO LEVITICUS 19:
A MAGNIFICENT MELANGE

Human rights theorists are not yet sure that every right potentially held by an individual or group creates an inherent "duty-bearer" with the responsibility to guarantee that right, or at the very least, not hinder its enjoyment. The Holiness Code of Leviticus has no doubt, however, that individuals are responsible to one another within the community, and that such responsibilities may well have implications for other groups existing beyond their boundaries. Covenant with God and each other clearly creates a set of obligations—responsibilities, if you will—for adherence to the demands of human decency in daily life on this earth. Indeed, when Israel adheres to these demands, even the rest of the peoples of the earth benefit (Gen. 9:1-17; 12:3; Kaminsky 2008: 125). Leviticus 19, the center of the Holiness Code, is a bundle of regulations aimed at encoding and preserving the well being of the individual, the body politic, and perhaps even God's sanity and composure as well—the Hebrew Bible is filled with places where a break in covenant observances causes grief, anguish, anger, disgust, and regret to the divine partner.

CAPABILITIES IN LEVITICUS

In the world of our text, it is not just the restatement of the Ten Commandments, the stipulations of a suzerain treaty between God and Israel, in Lev. 19:3-4, 11-13, and 16 that lend credence to this solemn, holistic approach to everyday ethical life; the whole bundle, with all its different parts, creates a hologram of a properly functioning community ethic "on the ground." We find all of Nussbaum's capabilities listed within Leviticus 19, with the possible exception of "play" (which may in fact be represented if we take vv. 3b and 30 in reference to keeping the Sabbath as a binary opposite of the work times during the rest of the week):

- Life: 13b, 16, 20, 32, 33
- Bodily health: 9-10, 16
- Bodily integrity: 14, 20, 23-24
- Senses: 5
- Imagination and thought: 15, 34, 16a
- Emotions: 17-18, 26, 34
- Practical reason: 11-12, 15, 17, 29, 35
- Affiliation: 3, 4 , 5, 11-12, 13, 18, 28-29, 31
- Other species: 19, 23-24
- Control over one's environment (political and material): 5-7, 9-10, 13b,19, 23-24, 26, 28, 29, 35

A FOCUS ON THE VULNERABLE

The poor, the alien, the daughter, and the female slave are called out as especially vulnerable entities that come in for special protection (vv. 9-10, 13, 21, 29, 33-34). This specification in the laws also acts as a pretext for questioning the underlying assumptions of a society in which persons of these classes perpetually find themselves at risk, allowing for metaphysical and legal amelioration of those conditions under a divine stamp of authenticity.

The old and the disabled also come in for their fair share of affirmation of intrinsic worth in vv. 14 and 32, setting up obligations to them by the majority that many "civilized" Western nations have yet to implement, even in part. (Just try climbing the stairs in the city of Amsterdam, visiting the House of Lords in London, or entering the Congressional building in the United States.) Even nature, as experienced by an agricultural people living in a region with many micro climates, receives protection: fruit trees are allowed to reach maturity before harvesting (vv. 23-25); farm animals are not to be abused by linking ones with different sizes and abilities together, such that they experience distress (v. 19);[8] nor does one kind of seed get sown in a micro zone where it cannot flourish, even though another type of crop might do just fine there and double-sowing might be more convenient for the farmer. These agrarian practices come from the basic insight that the human worker, charged with preserving and observing the "ordinances" of the garden and the field, knows perfectly well that some plants must be sown in the valley, lest they die on the water-starved terraces, where vines routinely flourish (Davis 2009). Even the curious injunction not to spin together two different kinds of thread into the same garment makes perfect sense to both the gifted high-end couture *and* the humblest mother mending a beloved item for the umpteenth time: one will pull against the other, and rips will only increase. Exploding wine skins are another example of this close observation of the way of things—their character, if you will—which affects their performance and their preferences. The wise person observes such things and acts accordingly.

Ritual regulations that protect the exclusivity of faith in the Lord and communal practice are present as well. The precise reason an offering may not be eaten on or after the third day is not entirely clear: it may represent the difference between the *shelamim* ("whole") offering versus the *todah* ("thanksgiving"; and hence the unsuitability of blending them), both discussed also in Lev. 7:11-14, and of which Lev. 19:5-8 may represent an earlier tradition. The *piggul* ("disgusting stuff," "abomination") that the delayed offering becomes in our text is used in Ezek. 4:14 to refer to a carcass torn by predators, and in Isa. 55:4 to refer to sacrifices made to idols, either one of which would violate the spirit of holiness that the book of Leviticus connects to the Lord alone. However, the meaning of *piggul* here is not precisely known, according to Baruch Levine (1989: 44, 126), but Jacob Milgrom argues that the issue is the continued holiness of the meat sacrifice once it has been consecrated: the presumption is that the one who offers the sacrifice must hold a family feast of the sacred meat at or near the sanctuary in a timely way. An attempt to use the meat after a regularized period (three days) means that a sacred item is out and about, putting everything it touches at risk for violating the contagion of its holiness (Milgrom 2004: 222–23), thus terminating the effectiveness of the offering.

Weird though this regulation may seem to the modern reader, since it is mixed in with clearly ethical and moral precepts, there is actually an attenuated application in human rights practice in the use of funds (sacrifices) contributed for humanitarian purposes by grateful donors, conscious of their own well being in general, or of deliverance from some evil in their own place. Glad that the hurricane passed them by, or that the tsunami did not wreak untold tragedy in their own region, and conscious of deep global empathy, many donate freely to causes that seek to aid those devastated by natural disasters, wars, and global famines. Leviticus might apply here by noting that donors *must* fulfill their pledges, or their humanitarian glow will have been all for show—and hence a sham that salved their own consciences and made them feel worthy of their own better fortune. Once the pledge has been fulfilled, that sacrifice (donation) must be delivered to those for whom it was meant, for the purposes for which it was given, in a timely way. The rescue agency cannot hold back the money to Haiti, Bandeh Aceh, or Japan in order to let interest on it grow and swell their accounts, nor should they divert it for administrative costs over and above what it actually takes to deliver the aid. Gratitude offerings are required to be timely, appropriate, and effective: when they are not, all human rights organizations are tarred with the same brush, and the caring public becomes cynical and less likely to open their coffers when the next disaster inevitably hits. While this is obviously a metaphorical application, it speaks again to cohesion of intent, means, and goal: they must work harmoniously together to be efficacious in alleviating the suffering of the innocent, especially as global climate change and robber-baron corporate decisions worsen the conditions of the poor around the world.

Regulations in Leviticus 19 also address foreign worship—worship generally conducted by states or regions the biblical authors considered "unholy" for a variety of practices, few of them sexual, and that were forbidden to Israel, the people who believed they had once escaped enslavement and returned from harsh exile. The worship of "other gods," then, is forbidden for a variety of reasons: only the Lord had acted on Israel's behalf (Leviticus 11; 18–19; 22–26), and so deserves their exclusive devotion; and "foreign gods" in the form of molten images and idols were associated with states and empires whose treatment of the poor enslaved Israel was thought to have experienced directly. Such items also represented a level of elite culture in the use of metalworking, the lot of slaves put to use in mining, the least desirable of all slave occupations in the ancient world. Such groups' forms of malign control over events in the form of consultation of sorcerers and soothsayers—the former always at a price and always malicious in intent[9]—violated basic norms of straight dealing inside a community, and suggested that some power other than the Lord was at work in Israel's world. Even affecting the particular styles of adornment of such nations, in the form of treatment of body hair or permanent decoration, conjures up the treatment of slaves and condemned criminals, whose heads were shaved and bodies tattooed for punishment and identification should they escape (Fontaine 2008). No such behaviors were allowed for the freed and those who held the captive, the slave, and the criminal in their empathetic view. Viewed in this way, the stipulations in Lev. 19:16-28, 31 are not so far removed from the ethical considerations elsewhere in the chapter as the modern reader might think.

For this reader, however, the most astonishing part of Leviticus 19, from the perspective of legal regulations for human rights usage, is Leviticus 19:16, important enough to quote here:

לא תלך רכיל בעמיך לא תעמד על דם רעך אני יהוה

The text (of course!) is difficult, and rendered variously. Standard translations include:

- KJV: Thou shalt not go up and down [as] a talebearer among thy people: neither shalt thou stand against the blood of thy neighbour: I [am] the Lord.
- Luther: Du sollst kein Verleumder sein unter deinem Volk. Du sollst auch nicht stehen wider deines Nächsten Blut; denn ich bin der HERR.
- Darby: Thou shalt not go about as a talebearer among thy people; thou shalt not stand up against the life of thy neighbour: I am Jehovah.
- BBE: Do not go about saying untrue things among your people, or take away the life of your neighbour by false witness: I am the Lord.
- ASV: Thou shalt not go up and down as a talebearer among thy people: neither shalt thou stand against the blood of thy neighbor: I am Jehovah.
- Webster: Thou shalt not go up and down [as] a tale-bearer among thy people; neither shalt thou stand against the blood of thy neighbor; I [am] the Lord.
- NRSV: You shall not go around as a slanderer among your people, and you shall not profit by the blood of your neighbor: I am the Lord.
- RSV: You shall not go up and down as a slanderer among your people, and you shall not stand forth against the life of your neighbor: I am the Lord.

- GWT: Never gossip. Never endanger your neighbor's life. I am the Lord.
- Vulgate: non eris criminator et susurro in populis non stabis contra sanguinem proximi tui ego Dominus.

While all translations agree on the first half of the verse, which states that gossip within the community sets up conditions for all sorts of legal violation, revenge, and other disruptions, the second half of the verse remains an issue. The Hebrew reads quite clearly. Literally, "You shall not stand upon/concerning/against the blood of your companion/neighbor." But what exactly does this mean? While there is no problem with understanding the word "blood" to signify life in toto, precisely what is the meaning of the verb in the imperfect, תעמד, when used in conjunction with the preposition על (together, *ta'amod 'al*)? James Kugel (1987) argues, based on his reading of early sources, that whatever one takes the second clause to mean, it was meant to be interpreted within the context of legal proceedings and relates to the verse about loving one's neighbor and refraining from hating that neighbor in one's heart (vv. 17-18). Gossip and hidden enmity set up a context in which legal actions that ought to be taken, such as testimony that corroborates an enemy's version of some contested issue, or where unfair litigation against one's enemy, spurred on by gossip, might cause a person to refrain from giving exonerating testimony, or worse, giving perjuring testimony. Either way, the injunction to love one's neighbor as oneself (v. 18b) has legal implications when court proceedings come into play: evil talk can lead to evil deeds; evil thoughts can lead to questionable deeds in the courtroom. Both circumstances are of concern to the authors of Leviticus 19, and both must be avoided. While this reading may be considered the most authentic, based on interpretations of early writers who themselves must have found the regulation somewhat ambiguous, I am happy to say that this verse has taken on a much bigger meaning, a meaning welcome to any feminist, human rights activist, or a person operating from secular views of fairness and decency. One need only consult Google Scholar to discover the role this verse has had in jurisprudence, medical ethics, environmental studies, and the life of the Jewish people and those who hold their philosophical and legal traditions dear and valuable.

Almost without precedent in the legal traditions of planet earth, the broader interpretation of this verse would go something like this: *You shall not stand idly by while your neighbor bleeds.* Inside the law court or out, within ancient history or the present, at the policy meeting or in the rescue shelter in New York City on September 12, 2001 (*Objects and Memory* 2008), this verse legislates *against apathy*. It is not enough to refrain from doing evil, according to those who read Leviticus broadly; one must in fact go beyond the duty *not* to disobey the laws of decency; one must actually act in the protection and defense of life.

In an HRBA, both halves of Lev. 19:16 have direct relevance. One of the first ways offenders seek to discount the reports of abuses is to claim that such information is anything from gossip to deliberate misinformation, all aimed at slandering the group or person who is charged with human rights violations. Denial, often accompanied by laughter or feigned surprise and lack of information, is the first form of response to allegations. For this reason, the role of documentation is critical for activists: the collection of testimony by survivors, witnesses, and those informed on the matter is crucial, since we are so often operating in a legal world where proof is required before any action is considered. The next step taken by abuser states, groups, and persons is to discount the reliability of witnesses, and this too must be countered by evidence, which might be anything from a thorough medical examination to a close application of forensic accounting, since abuse never occurs without some sort of material benefit to those committing it. Even dead bodies have a story to tell in confirming the incidence of crimes against humanity, and religious groups should consider this role, the "silent witness" of the corpse, before automatically forbidding exhumations and autopsies. Finally, when admission of the existence of abuses can no longer be denied (social media and mobile phones with cameras have been key here), the guilty parties try a spirited defense—economic, social, and cultural—of their actions as legal and seek to suborn international law by appeal to local proceedings. Again, these must be dismantled systematically, until all that is left is clear proof that the *jus cogens* of universal human worth and bodily integrity have been violated—but hopefully, not with impunity. Amnesty International (AI) does not engage in slander, and through their excellent establishment of credibility through clear and rigorous methodology of documentation, no one can claim otherwise, and the guilty have cause to fear when they see the logo of AI on a flood of letters arriving in their mailbox. In such ways, lives are saved each and every day.

In a globalized world, Lev. 19:6 invites us to use our reason and our empathy together: we cannot know if our neighbor is bleeding, wrongly accused, or dragged into court to silence whistle-blowing if we are not paying attention. The text demands that we ask again as the New Testament does, "Who then is my neighbor?" These days the answer must be "Everyone," for what happens in one country, in one neighborhood, can be instantly known around the planet, and its effects can be dramatic, even if they take a long time to unfold (Batson et al. 1999). It is no longer enough to attend only to one's own family; everyone's family is at risk when supplies of pure water are in the hands of transnational corporations. It is not enough to feel justified in one's own country and its legal systems and economic or foreign policy: the nuclear accident spreads far beyond the power plant in a single nation. The same drones that are used so successfully in the fight against terrorism may also be used to kill U.S. citizens from space, without warning, charges against the guilty, or legal review. Ignorance is bliss no longer; now it is a dangerous failure to think morally as a global citizen. We must know what is happening with our neighbors if we are to obey the positive law of intervening for the protection of life. A tall order perhaps, but one made easier by the technologies and growing awareness that have cast us all together as a species hoping to adapt successfully to the new conditions we have created.

The call to action in our verse represents the best of the human heart and codifies empathy, even in the face of inconvenience, difference, and other common divisions. No other people have given us a law that so clearly targets apathetic or willful dismissal of human suffering. This is something by which any person could live and present themselves before the bar of heaven or a human court of law and feel justified. Dismiss Leviticus? Never! The inspiration that this law infuses into the Sermon on the Mount and the ethical teachings of the prophet Mohammed continues to draw the human family together in something more than violent competition over scarce resources, ethnic hatred, or any of the other issue that divide us. Jewish contributions to public health, psychotherapy, legal foundations for overturning bigotry, the need to regulate things like treatment of AIDS, studies on human cloning, and environmental deprivation by greedy corporations (Steinberg 1991; Saul Berman 1992; Pearce 1995; Dorff 1996; Samuel Levine 1998) do indeed bless the whole world that heeds them. If anyone broadly interested in the world of human rights or biblical law is listening, they had better pay attention.[10] If I could only have one verse from the Bible to place within a capsule sent into space to testify for the human species on planet Earth, it would be Lev. 19:16.

Concluding Postscript

It is easy to see how affection and a close, empathetic reading of a favorite text can lead even the best of us astray. In a world where everyone from Nigerian evangelists (Harrison 2008) to U.S. elected representatives pulls Leviticus out of their backpack to place stumbling blocks in the way of the world's dispossessed and outcast, the unreserved profession of the goodness of Leviticus can only lead to trouble. Even one two-year-old child accused of witchcraft and shot in the head is one too many. Even one bullied gay teenager driven to suicide based on the readings of Leviticus's abominable abominations is unacceptable. Human rights abuses of human dignity and bodily integrity are unacceptable no matter what their bases, even religious ones. One of the salient benefits of reading biblical texts and scholarly research from within a variety of contexts is that it acts as a fence around our customary desire to make a text sensible and welcome, perhaps even binding. Love of texts can never replace love of life, and the text itself requires the defense of life, even when that defense casts the authority or content of our texts into question. When zeal for the house of the law threatens to consume us, we must be ready to seek other lodgings (Ps. 69:6; 1 Macc. 2:26; John 2:17)—how else shall we look on Cozbi's face (Numbers 25), or give account of our choices to Aaron's wife (Numbers 3), much less consider the little ones dead at the hands of religion, with the full complicity of the faithful? In the end, we are all like Job, turning for confirmation of our just actions to the very deity whose imputed theology has made us into guilty blasphemers. How does a Christian even respond to the use of the Bible in the name of a purity that kills, a holiness that allows us to act with impunity, so long as we name our actions "biblical"? Like the Hollywood exorcist (so habitually portrayed as ineffectual against evil), I can only say, "The Power of Christ compels you!" You *cannot* stand idly by.

In another of my classes, when my students were working assiduously on redeeming the "other" and God through their readings of Ruth, Jonah, Esther, and the Song of Songs, I suggested that they try an art project to bring their insights to congregations they were serving. So I told them, "Nobody wants to read your paper!"[11] Their crafty outpourings made those texts into a stand-up, "pop-up" Bible that astounded them and delighted me, and even brought a dean to our exhibit. What was true for the seminary class and congregation "goes double" for the human rights event and the suffering that demands it: nobody wants to read or hear my paper on Leviticus.

So, I bow to the will of my people, and conclude here with the distilled anger, anguish, and hope that research spawns in me, hoping to present a fish instead of a snake.[12]

Leviticus in Africa and Washington, D.C.: A Human-Rights-Based Approach

(UN Special Rapporteur on Extrajudicial, Summary Or Arbitrary Executions, Philip Alston, reports that two thousand women and children are held captive and daily subjected to violence and threat of death in "witchcamps" in Ghana, based on their identification as "heathen" witches, usually by Christian leaders.

On May 10, 2012, an excerpt of the book of Leviticus was read on the floor of the House of Representatives in defense of removing economic, social, and cultural rights from gay couples seeking to marry, to which a southern, white, male Congressman replied, "That's the *Old* Testament!" Poetry ensued.)

Purity is an illusion,
Holiness is just a scam
of little men with trembling hearts
who claim to tame the Great "I Am."
  They feast themselves on sacrifice
as they count up the emperor's money,
and wring out every widow's mite
from the land of milk and honey.
Such faith is just a neat contagion
whose dread they fear they can't maintain,
so dine from people's gifts of wholeness
but bid the starving to refrain.
Perhaps they carve what power they can
out of a world they can't respect,
reweaving frayed identity
with Empire's boot upon their neck.
  But *whose* laws make the widow poor,
the maid a slut, the strangers' stain?
And whose astute collaboration
stifles the desire for change?
  Alleging strange fire does the murder,
they say that God enacts these deeds,
but *they* construct the world of laws,
declaring some must surely bleed.
The Laws of Men on Blood of Women,
reversed by Holiness decreed,
Forever hang a woeful curtain
twixt suffering and those in need.
  Is *this* God's will? Who can believe it?
No, this is mere Utility,
to legislate the witchchild's death
on grounds of Pure Theology!
Who says the queer are always guilty,

outlawed in God's economy?
Who says the Stranger is inhuman?
Not friends of Life, and no, not me.
    Don't blame the Jews; don't blame the Christians,
the Qur'an, or Nature's Natural Law:
when every State supports the greedy,
Religion is their corporate maw.

Notes

1. United Nations Office of the High Commissioner for Human Rights, "Universal Declaration of Human Rights," http://www.ohchr.org/EN/UDHR/Pages/ Language.aspx?LangID=eng; for other documents, see Brownlie 2010.

2. To be sure, assessments of Jesus whose relationship to Judaism and its laws is a hotly contested issue among scholars and people of faith.

3. For a balanced discussion of some interpretive issues surrounding the Bible's view and regulations concerning sex, see Countryman 2008. Having been called a "pornographer" for my work on *Shir haShirim* (Song of Songs) on Internet religious blogs, I fall in this category myself, so disclose my interest in disputing all these categories. However, if the views of Christian and Muslim fundamentalists turn out to be true, I am well content with my eternal disposition: hell sounds a much more interesting place to bed down. All my friends and mentors will be there.

4. Alston's report confirms that accusations of witchcraft against women, the old, the disabled, and the different, as well as children, are not confined only to Africa, nor are they committed only in Christian communities.

5. See Shemesh's essay in this volume.

6. See the essays by Dor, Gafney, Rees, and Vaka'uta in this volume.

7. E.g., those Christian white supremacists who believe themselves "called" to the "Phinehas Priesthood" base their ideology of violent action entirely on Numbers 25.

8. What alert human with animal companions does not zealously make sure that the large dog does not eat the kitten's special food? What sane person expects the parakeet to flourish in the same setting as the turkey? Even racing a fast thoroughbred but holding him or her back against lesser horses who are being trained to experience winning can break the spirit and cause discernible depression, as in the case of the much beloved Seabiscuit, the small, ugly underdog winner who bested War Admiral during the 1930s Depression, after a long comeback from injury during which he was used to train others.

9. This is a reversal of what we find today in the world of witchcraft: it is the witch smellers, exorcists, and religious leaders who are making their fortune off accusation and "treatment" of witchcraft, not witches who are paid to curse others. One wonders, beyond syncretism and its insult to the Lord, what the poor soothsayers have done to earn the attention of our laws: Could it be that there is some concern in Leviticus for the animal so pointlessly eviscerated when casting lots supposedly would have done the trick?

10. This is a Christian storyteller's translation of Jesus' statement, "Whoever has ears to hear, let them hear," and in the opinion of this writer captures it perfectly for the modern congregation.

11. Especially not me.

12. As always, this research could not have been completed without the diligent and patient editing of Jennifer Shaw, the support of Craig Fontaine, and the forbearance and encouragement of my friends and colleagues in HR. Thank you all.

PART II

Issues in Numbers

7

Bitter Waters (Numbers 5), Flood Waters (Genesis 6–9), and Some Theologies of Exile and Land

Diana Lipton

In this essay I offer an intertextual reading of the Soṭah ritual of the bitter waters (Num. 5:1-31) and the flood narrative (Gen. 6:1—9:28). I argue that these two texts function as structural, ritual, literary, and theological equivalents of, respectively, divorce as described in Deut. 24:1-4 and exile as interpreted in many prophetic texts, especially in Jeremiah (e.g., Jer. 29:1-14) and Ezekiel (e.g., Ezekiel 36), as a punishment and solution for wrongdoing. The paper was written in the first instance for "Embroidered Garments," a 2008 conference on gender and biblical studies at King's College London, where I was at the time a lecturer in Hebrew Bible and Jewish Studies. The ideas it contains, especially concerning differences between priestly (with a lowercase *p*) and deuteronomic approaches to the three-way relationship between God, the people of Israel, and the land of Israel, had been percolating for many years. I had previously explored possible connections between the flood narrative and the expulsion—or better, divorce—of Ezra's foreign wives (Lipton 2008: 214–64). I had speculated in relation to Ezekiel and the story of Sodom and Gomorrah (Genesis 19) about how the land might be cleansed of sins committed by non-Israelites (Lipton 2008: 108–40). All these themes surface again below.

By the time I returned to the paper, published in the meantime in conference proceedings (Rooke 2009), my life had changed . . . a lot. When I began working on the first version of the paper, my own twenty-three-year marriage had recently ended, not in divorce but because of the death of my husband, Peter Lipton ל״ז. By 2011, I had married again, left my job and my home in London, moved to Jerusalem, and was preparing to teach courses for international students at the Hebrew University and Tel Aviv University. At the time of writing, all being well, I will soon be an Israeli citizen.

I will now proceed with my textual analysis and the theological and literary interpretations it generated for me, and afterward I will reflect a little on how this paper sat in the wider context of my life when I first wrote it in 2008 and how it sits now in 2011.

MARRIAGE AND DIVORCE IN THE HEBREW BIBLE

While this is not the place for a detailed discussion of divorce and marriage in the Hebrew Bible, some preliminary observations are nonetheless required.[2] First, as is well known, the very terminology of marriage and divorce is anachronistic in the context of the Hebrew Bible. Legal, contractual, and other relationships between ancient Israelite men and women were (even) more varied, complex, and fluid than those of our own time. My decision to speak of marriage and divorce, then, is strictly utilitarian; there is no elegant or straightforward alternative. Second, the Hebrew Bible is not homogeneous concerning "marriage" and "divorce." To simplify for the sake of clarity, two basic paradigms are evident—the broadly deuteronomic and the essentially priestly.[3] Neither school has an explicit mission statement on marriage and divorce, but both pay more attention to divorce than to marriage. Nevertheless, it is possible to sketch their perspectives as follows. Deuteronomic marriage is a legal construct based on specific actions and events. It is highly conditional and has an identifiable beginning and possible end (divorce). Just as marriage is not discussed explicitly in its own right, neither is divorce. Divorce is raised in the context of remarriage: should a divorced woman "marry," or perhaps even have sex with, another man following the delivery into her hands of a letter of separation written by or on behalf of her husband, she will render her first husband forever off-limits to herself (Deut. 24:1-4).[4] The lives of deuteronomic children may reflect the behavior and actions of their parents, but they have scope to affect their own destinies by acting or behaving differently. The basic priestly marriage paradigm, by contrast, is articulated most clearly in Genesis 1–3. This account, especially when read in the light of early Jewish interpretations that posit an original androgynous being subsequently divided into two sides,[5] implies that couples are created when a man discovers his original "other half." Not surprisingly, there is no room for divorce in this paradigm; the closest approximation in priestly texts to the divorce provisions in Deut. 24:1-4 is Num. 5:11–31 ("Bitter Waters"), but "Bitter Waters" is not so much a legal response to a dysfunctional marriage as a ritual and psychological response, and, crucially, it makes no provisions for the marriage's termination.[6]

A priestly marriage can cease to function, but it cannot end. The status of priestly offspring is determined by their parentage, so that descendants of an incestuous union, for example, are permanently, or semipermanently, tainted.[7] In the priestly worldview, nature, not nurture, is the order of the day.

MARRIAGE AS METAPHOR

The Hebrew Bible's view of marriage and divorce has broader significance in two related areas. First, it overlaps with, and indeed shapes, biblical conceptions of national and/or ethnic identity;[8] and second, it is the source of one model of God's relationship with Israel. Both are relevant to this essay, but I begin with the second. It is uncontroversial to claim that the marriage metaphor for God's relationship with Israel permeates the Hebrew Bible, and that this metaphorical marriage is related, especially in prophetic texts, to texts that describe marriages, or more often, marital problems, between men and women.[9] I make the more controversial claim, however, that the texts describing relations between men and women, even (respectively) legal and ritual texts such as Deut. 24:1-4 and Num. 5:11-31, show awareness of this metaphorical application, and may be responding to it. In other words, the intertextual engagement occurs in two directions. Readers who assume that the pentateuchal texts in question reflect the sociological *realia* of ancient Israel may find this notion hard to accept. As I read them, however, legal/ritual texts on the one hand, and prophetic texts on the other, share the common endeavor of ordering the world as well as describing and explaining it. On this view, the Bible is at least as likely to respond legally and ritually to the metaphorical marriage between God and Israel as to actual marriages between men and women.

MARRIAGE, LAND, AND IDENTITY

Both deuteronomic and priestly conceptions of marriage and divorce correspond to their adherents' perceptions of the formation of national and ethnic identity and its relationship to the land. According to the deuteronomic worldview, Israel is a national entity with a legal (Sinai) and a historical (exodus from Egypt) basis. Israel's relationship to the land is at once necessary and conditional. Just as the people entered the land at an identifiable, fixed point, so also they can be expelled; but expulsion would threaten their very existence. Israelite identity is dependent, at least in part, upon being resident in the land or aspiring to return, but it is also dependent on historical events, usually subject to change consequent on other historical events. The exception that proves the rule is Amalek, whose deuteronomic identity is fixed by a historical event—what

Amalek did in the wilderness (Deut. 25:17-19)—but that can never change; Amalek is Israel's permanent enemy. Future generations of deuteronomic peoples are certainly affected in this way and others by their ancestors, but it is the *behavior* of their predecessors that is determinative, not the circumstances of their national origins. So just as deuteronomic marriage is event-driven, legal, conditional, and potentially finite, so also Israel's relationship with the land, and the particular identity that this instills, is historical, legal, conditional, and potentially finite. The priestly perception of Israel's relationship to the land, and the identity derived from it, likewise corresponds to the priestly conception of marriage. Israel's claim on the land is eternal and unconditional (Lev. 25:42); exile is but a temporary dislocation. Yet identity is not entirely dependent on being in, or wanting to be in, the land—not, at least, for those "universalist" priestly writers for whom the whole earth is God's. Just as priestly marriage has a biological basis (one divided being reunited), rather than a historical one (no obvious ceremonial beginning), with no legal component, and no possible end (just potential dysfunction), so also the priestly notion of Israel's claim on the land is not based on a historical event that occurred at a particular moment, has no legal basis, is not conditional, and has no possible end.

Divorce and Exile from the Land

The conceptual parallel between divorce and exile fits perfectly in a deuteronomic worldview. Just as human anger could have disastrous consequences in the context of marriage as deuteronomically defined, so was divine anger potentially fatal in the context of the covenant between God and Israel. A single act—the delivery of the divorce document—executed by a husband in the heat of the moment could end a marriage. If this was followed by a wife's "infidelity" (not quite the right term since she was by now divorced), there was no way back; she had rendered herself permanently off-limits to her former husband. When the Babylonian Exile is conceptualized as a divorce, Israel's worship of Babylonian gods (equivalent to sex with other men) was disastrous, forever precluding the renewal of God's contractual relationship.[10] However, the divorce/exile equation fits poorly in a priestly worldview, especially one that espouses anything approaching universalism. A priestly marriage, as we have seen, can cease to function, but it cannot end. Land, meanwhile, is not Israel's possession but God's, which, paradoxically, entails that, having never actually possessed the land, Israel cannot lose it. Moreover, since the whole earth is God's, exile cannot constitute a sending away/divorce, as it does in deuteronomic thought. So I suggest that in place of the deuteronomic concept of divorce, "Bitter Waters" functions within the priestly worldview as a vehicle for reflection on the divine/human, husband/wife metaphor, the key difference being that it does not involve an expulsion or a termination, but focuses on feelings and changes of state. Partly for this reason, and partly because in its most intense form the priestly worldview requires a universalist backdrop, the divine/human scenario that is equivalent to the husband/wife scenario presented in "Bitter Waters" is not played out directly in terms of exile. Instead, it is expressed via the flood, a punishment that pertains to the whole earth (and is thus compatible with universalism), entails no sending away, involves no enemy or human agent of divine anger, and into which restoration—in the form of the survival of a remnant—is built from the outset.

BITTER WATERS, FLOOD WATERS

My suggestion here is that the author/redactor of "Bitter Waters" used the structure, imagery, and theology of Gen. 6:1–9:17 ("Flood") to make the husband/wife paradigm—his most plausible starting point—relevant to the divine/human relationship.[11] Elsewhere, I have tried to show structural and textual links between "Flood" and Ezra's expulsion or (as I think) ritual divorce of foreign women (Ezra 9–10).[12] There I speculated that the redaction was bidirectional, and that just as Ezra owes structure and imagery to Genesis, so Genesis was edited in the light of Ezra. For example, the link with Ezra provides two possible explanations for the two systems of dating for the stages of the flood specified in Genesis 8, one of which includes dates identical to those given for the different stages of Ezra's expulsion of foreign wives.[13] This could indicate either that the author of Ezra recognized in the "Flood" a feature that was extraneous or inconsistent (two systems of dating where one would have sufficed) and used one of them to highlight the connection; or, alternatively, that the Genesis "Flood" redactor incorporated dates from Ezra to highlight the connection from the other end. In the case of a possible intertextual relationship between "Flood" and "Bitter Waters," it seems unlikely that the connections are two-directional. Rather, "Bitter Waters" is more plausibly the later of the two texts, combining elements of known ancient Near Eastern rituals with language and imagery from "Flood," and perhaps also from prophetic sources, to create a priestly alternative to the deuteronomic divorce law. If I am correct, the form of Numbers 5 available to us already incorporates a theological dimension involving God, people, and the land. I shall now work through key elements of "Bitter Waters," showing how they relate to and are illuminated by reference to "Flood."

THE SOURCE OF THE PROBLEM

Often termed "the law of the suspected adulteress," but much better identified (as it labels itself, v. 29) as "the law of the jealous husband," Num. 5:11-31 describes the treatment of a woman whose husband suspects her of a crime that she may or may not have committed. The root problem addressed in "Bitter Waters" is thus not infidelity but jealousy. Whether or not the jealousy is founded is irrelevant, and both scenarios—guilty or innocent wife, "who has . . . or has not defiled herself" (Num. 5:14)—are played out. There is a sense in which this lack of interest in the woman's guilt typifies the priestly worldview in general. Few accounts of priestly mechanisms for dealing with sin entail an investigation of the crime committed and its possible perpetrator. Instead, emphasis is placed on the removal of the consequences of the crime (divine punishment manifested in failed harvests, infertile marriages, and so forth). Thus the failure of "Bitter Waters" to specify at the outset whether or not the woman is guilty may reflect not a different narrative priority (the husband rather than the wife) but the priestly worldview's theological prioritizing of effects over causes.

Turning now to "Flood" in particular, several parallels between "Flood" and "Bitter Waters" help to make sense of "Bitter Waters" over and above the appeal to priestly perspectives in general. First, the Genesis redactor diverts attention from the underlying cause of the flood by offering between two and six explanations for it: inappropriate sex between divine and human beings (Gen. 6:1-4), human wickedness (v. 5a), humanity's evil inclinations (v. 5b), the corruption of the earth (v. 11), human corruption (v. 12), and violence or lawlessness (vv. 11, 13). The abundance of possible causes—any one or any combination of these six could constitute an explanation—creates the sense that there is no explanation.[14] Second, even if it were possible to reconcile these two to six causes, the ultimate cause of the flood is arguably none of the above, but rather God's response to them. Here too, the narrative in its final form generates uncertainty by offering more than one account. To some combination of inappropriate sex, humanity's wickedness, and humanity's evil inclinations, God responds with regret (Gen. 6:6a) and sadness (v. 6b), promising to blot out all living creatures (v. 7). To some combination of corruption (of earth or people) and violence, God reports to Noah his decision to destroy all flesh *and* the earth (v. 13). The highly anthropomorphic tenor of both accounts (see also the reference to God's future intentions in 8:21) further underlines that it is less what humans did that caused the flood than how God felt about what they did. In their different ways, then, both "Bitter Waters" and "Flood" focus on the feelings of the injured party rather than on the precise details of the crime committed.

There remains one important point to make about God's feelings. From our contemporary perspective, the emotions of jealousy and anger are quite different from each other. As Fishbane points out precisely in relation to "Bitter Waters," however, they were not always seen thus. Biblical jealousy, he suggests, corresponds closely to the definition of *A New English Dictionary* (1901), whose "inclusive sense of this term was one of attentive, zealous concern for (personal) prerogative or possessions. . . . By extension this may involve or include fury, anger, and passion" (Fishbane 1999: 493). Anger, then, the predominant emotion that led God to flood the earth, is not so far removed from jealousy, the emotion that led a man to subject his wife to a humiliating public ordeal involving water.

AGENCY AND INTERVENTION

A side effect of the priestly prioritizing of effects over causes is that it allows for third-party intervention. A worldview (such as the deuteronomic one) that emphasizes responsibility, and thus culpability, is unlikely to produce a system in which a priest or a substitute compensates for a crime in place of the guilty party; but this is precisely what happens in Num. 5:11-31. The priest features in "Bitter Waters" when the jealous husband brings his wife, initially to make an offering (v. 15), and subsequently for the bitter waters ritual (vv. 16-22, 26). Both husband and wife are henceforth marginalized in "Bitter Waters"; the priest plays the pivotal ritual roles and effectively manages the couple's relationship. The suspected adulteress remains almost entirely passive (v. 30), neither insisting on her innocence, nor confessing, offering evidence, or promising to change her behavior. While this may be indicative of no more than the authors' attitude toward women, it dovetails both with general priestly cultic practice as described elsewhere (e.g., Lev. 4-6),[15] and, more significantly, with the dynamics of priestly covenants, which are not typically conditional on present or future good behavior (Gen. 9:12-17; 17:15-19).

As noted above, the interplay of people and land begins immediately in "Flood"; people commit crimes, but the punishment is played out on the land. This is reflected in "Bitter Waters" by the focus on the woman's body—emphasized by her passivity, and by the graphically described physical effects—as the arena in which both punishment and cure are executed.[16] In another episode in Numbers, in which a woman commits a crime and is physically afflicted (Miriam in Numbers 12), a physical movement results in a changed status. (Miriam is sent outside the camp to recover from "leprosy"

[12:14], and indeed, Numbers 5 opens with an instruction to remove from the camp anyone with discharge [v. 2].) "Bitter Waters," by contrast, is performed on a single stage. All the action takes place in the tabernacle (5:17), and afterward the woman remains "in the midst of her people" (v. 27), regardless of the outcome of the test.

WATERS, STILL . . .

The equation of bitter waters and flood waters is supported by Frymer-Kensky's suggestion (partly following Lambert) that the verb translated "to swell" (*tz-b-h*) in Num. 5:22 parallels the Akkadian, *sabu/sapu*, "to soak, flood," used in Old Babylonian letters in the sense of saturating the soil (Frymer-Kensky 1999: 468). In their original context, presumably an ancient Near Eastern divinatory ritual, the bitter waters were no doubt intended to determine guilt or innocence. But in the bitter waters ritual of Numbers 5, the divinatory aspect is insignificant. First, as noted above, the formulation of verse 14 ("the woman who has defiled herself," and "although she has not defiled herself") makes the woman's guilt effectively irrelevant. Second, the meal offering—initiated in advance of the bitter waters ritual (v. 15)—presumes guilt, "for it is a meal offering of jealousy, a meal offering that recalls wrong-doing" (vv. 15, 25-26, NJPS), and it is made *before* the woman drinks the water. Why proceed with the divinatory ritual once the priest has dealt through an offering with both the woman's possible guilt and the husband's jealousy? One answer is that waters that began as an ancient Near Eastern test of guilt metamorphosed in priestly hands into a solution to the problem. This represents another parallel with "Flood." The waters of the flood function simultaneously as a punishment and a cure. In this respect, they resemble exile, which is both a punishment and the mechanism that preserves God's damaged relationship with Israel, initiated by God, but executed by an enemy nation. Exile permits purification through separation (a movement from one place to another resulting in changed status), after which a purged remnant is permitted to return. The flood works both similarly to and differently from exile. There is no separation; the waters simply destroy all but a remnant, which survives to provide continuity. This shift to a flood from a punishment involving expulsion not only makes sense but is also logically necessary in the context of full-blown priestly universalism. Once the whole world requires a cure (whence expulsion?), and once universalism renders problematic the use of nations as agents of divine punishment against each other (God is the god of all peoples), exile no longer fits the bill. Natural disaster is an obvious replacement. I see the flood replacing exile as a priestly-universalist cure for the damaged relationship between God and Israel, and

"Bitter Waters" replacing divorce as exile's metaphorical/legal/theological equivalent. The bitter waters ritual might thus have been adopted as the basis of the priestly equivalent to deuteronomic divorce because of its parallel use in ancient Near Eastern marital relations, and because of its structural equivalence to the purging/healing waters of the flood.[17]

A third factor might also be brought to bear. Fishbane sees allusions to "Bitter Waters" in several prophetic texts, some dealing with Israel's infidelity, and some addressing the nations in a dramatic reversal (the nations will now drink from the cup of wrath that God once gave to Israel) (Fishbane 1999: 496–97). Central to Fishbane's analysis here is the figure of a cup (Ezek. 23:28-31, 32-34; Jer. 25:15, 49:12, 50:22), which, it must be said, does not feature in "Bitter Waters," where an "earthenware vessel" is specified (Num. 5:17), nor in the cuneiform parallels Fishbane mentions (Fishbane 1999: 494–95). Nevertheless, the connections are intriguing (especially since the prophetic cup is associated with judgment), and one might ask whether the cup motif in prophetic theology had another source, and its prominence played a role in the formulation of "Bitter Waters" rather than the other way around.

MEMORY

That the offering made by the "Bitter Waters" priest is designated as a memorial of wrongdoing (Num. 5:15, 18) is difficult to explain in the context of cultic offerings. Not only does it have no obvious precedent or parallel, but, as noted above, it also prejudges the outcome of the test.[18] If no wrong has been done, why make an offering that recalls a wrongdoing? Viewed in theological-literary terms, however, the allusion to memory allows the author/redactor of "Bitter Waters" to incorporate an important motif of "Flood" in particular and priestly covenant accounts in general. Descriptions of actual or predicted disruptions in God's relationship with Israel often conclude with a reference to memory. The threatened exile at the end of the Holiness Code concludes with a reminder of the patriarchs (Lev. 26:42), while "Flood" ends with the sign of the rainbow as the reminder/memorial that will prevent God from destroying the earth in the future. Memory functions in these and other cases to heal the rift, variously emphasizing that the relationship has a solid foundation (a promise to the patriarchs) that enables it to withstand temporary dysfunction; that the erring partner has been punished once for the same crime, and since nothing has changed in the meantime, repeated punishment is futile (God's promise never again to destroy the earth after the flood, Gen. 8:21); that since the erring partner was tried once and found innocent, future punishments for the same suspected crime would be inappropriate ("Bitter Waters"); and that the wronged covenantal partner punished disproportionately his opposite number and cannot repeat it. I shall return to this last suggestion shortly, but in the meantime I suggest that the author of "Bitter Waters" identified the meal offering as a *memorial* of wrongdoing in part to evoke this component of priestly covenants in general and "Flood" in particular.

Renewed Fertility

Commentators have long noted the confusing claim that concludes "Bitter Waters": an accused woman vindicated will "bear seed" (Num. 5:28).[19] Since "Bitter Waters" is a ritual response to jealousy and suspected adultery, not an infertility treatment or a pregnancy test, why is this notion introduced?[20] In an ingenious use of the Bible, the Babylonian Talmud (*Ber.* 31b) has the biblical Hannah (1 Samuel 1) parody this claim. Frustrated that God has not given her a child, she creates a mock "Bitter Waters" situation by locking herself into a room with a man and a witness and, once proven innocent of adultery, demands that God allow her to become pregnant in accordance with his promise regarding the "Bitter Waters." Again, however, a seemingly incongruous element of "Bitter Waters" makes sense in the light of priestly covenants in general and "Flood" in particular. Just as a reference to memory offers reassurance that there will be no (immediate) repetition, so the reference to fertility (especially since "seed" is the term used here to designate offspring) underscores the links between the "Bitter Waters" and priestly covenants. The reference to the woman's fertility also serves to demonstrate that the postwater seed is untainted by sin or suspicion. This fits well with the explanation for the flood that emerges from its juxtaposition with the account of illicit unions between divine and human beings in Gen. 6:1-4. "Flood" ends with the assurance that life will go on, triply confirmed, including by a reference to agricultural fertility (Gen. 8:22; the other confirmations are sacrifice [8:20-21] and the reminder/memorial [9:14, 16]). Finally, the swelling of highly anthropomorphized waters (7:18, 24, where the root g-b-r evokes masculine strength and virility) on the earth, immediately following the reference to the male and female animals that will continue life after the flood (v. 16), hints at the land's future fecundity, even as the waters are at present dominating the land (v. 19). This may be reflected in "Bitter Waters" in the water and dust from the tabernacle floor (Num. 5:17), especially given the sense in which the tabernacle already functions as a microcosm of the universe,[21] and the fact that a mixture of moisture and dust is a precondition of the creation of humans in the second creation account (Gen. 2:6-7).

GUILT REMOVAL

Returning now to where I began—the justice or otherwise of God's punishment of Israel by means of the Babylonian Exile—can the intertextual reading I have offered here be construed as a commentary on God's behavior? In twenty-first-century eyes, "Bitter Waters" is unjust and inhumane, but this is not a case of mismatch between ancient and modern sensibilities. Even the earliest rabbinic commentaries are at pains to point out that the ritual was never carried out. The bitter waters ritual humiliates a woman regardless of her guilt or innocence, changes nothing in reality, and serves simply to relieve a jealous man of destructive negative feelings toward his wife. Once "Bitter Waters" is linked to Genesis 6–9, it raises all the same questions about the flood. To be sure, the parallel is not perfect; while the woman in "Bitter Waters" may have been entirely innocent, some members of the generation of the flood were guilty of violence and or lawlessness. Yet was God's seemingly indiscriminate destruction of all life beyond the tiny remnant required for its continuation any more than a mechanism for relieving his hostile feelings toward his own creation? Was his promise that he would not repeat the exercise, with the implication that it was futile from the outset, an admission that the flood was misconceived? Here an intertextual reading between "Bitter Waters" and "Flood" seems to me to put on a chain that prevents the door from opening too far. The chain is constituted by the closing verse of "Bitter Waters": "The man shall be clear of guilt, but that woman shall suffer for her guilt" (Num. 5:31). Various interpretations of this verse suggest themselves, but among them is the idea that the man will not be held responsible for publicly humiliating his wife without cause. Can the same principle be applied to God? Even if the flood were deserved by some, and even if it preserved a remnant, the punishment was arguably disproportionate. Yet God, we might infer from the closing words of "Bitter Waters," cannot be blamed. I am well aware that this sounds speculative, to say the least, but I will draw this to a close with a third innerbiblical intertext that suggests the two I have explored here should be taken seriously, along with the implications, exegetical and historical, that they raise.

A PROPHETIC "BITTER WATERS"/"FLOOD WATERS" INTERTEXT?

A rare biblical reference to the floodwaters outside Genesis occurs in Isa. 54:1-10. The context is God's reconciliation with Israel following the exile, presented as the reunion of an estranged husband and wife:

> Shout, O barren one, you who bore no child! Shout aloud for joy,
> you who did not travail! For the children of the wife forlorn shall

outnumber those of the espoused—said the Lord. Enlarge the site of your tent, extend the size of your dwelling, do not stint! Lengthen the ropes, and drive the pegs firm. For you shall spread out to the right and the left; your offspring shall dispossess nations and shall people the desolate towns. Fear not, you shall not be shamed; do not cringe, you shall not be disgraced. For you shall forget the reproach of your youth, and remember no more the shame of your widowhood. For He who made you will espouse you—His name is "Lord of Hosts." The Holy One of Israel will redeem you—He is called "God of all the Earth." The Lord has called you back as a wife forlorn and forsaken. Can one cast off the wife of his youth?—said your God. For a little while I forsook you, but with vast love I will bring you back. In slight anger, for a moment, I hid My face from you; but with kindness everlasting I will take you back in love—said the Lord your Redeemer. For this to Me is like the waters of Noah: as I swore that the waters of Noah nevermore would flood the earth, so I swear that I will not be angry with you or rebuke you.For the mountains may move and the hills be shaken, but My loyalty shall never move from you, nor My covenant of friendship be shaken—said the Lord, who takes you back in love. (NJPS 1999)

The appeal to the waters of Noah in the context of a marriage is important. The author of Isaiah 54 shares with the "Flood" narrators a universalist perspective, everywhere in Genesis 6–9 and explicit in Isa. 54:5 ("God of all the earth"), and this is reflected in his description of the broken and repaired marriage between God and Israel. In sharp contrast to similar texts in Jeremiah, there is no physical sending away and return, and significantly, neither divorce, nor anything approximating it, is mentioned. Instead, there is abandonment, equated not with movement but with a changed status on the part of the woman (barrenness and widowhood versus fecundity and the promise of future security) and, on God's part, with a turning away of the face (a change of direction, but no change of position). By associating the flood with marriage, the author of Isaiah 54 intensifies the presence of the priestly perception of marriage that has been my concern here. At the same time, he emphasizes the extent to which the flood was caused by a divine emotion, not by human sin. Indeed, Israel's crimes are not even mentioned, and her status as an innocent victim of God's hot temper is underlined. It is impossible to know whether or not this prophetic author knew "Bitter Waters" (Fishbane [1999: 496] thinks that perhaps he did, and I would like him to be correct), but his bringing together of notions of exile, punishment, marriage, divine feelings (as opposed to human actions), and the waters of the flood are at the very least a response in the same spirit.

(Closing) Reflections on the Waters

Underlying this paper is an exploration of two worldviews that I see reflected throughout the Hebrew Bible. They seem to be fundamentally incompatible, and yet both are necessary—in different political contexts, for different people, and even at different times in the life of an individual person. Here are some examples, as gleaned from the passages read in this essay.

Marriage

These two worldviews are clearly manifested, I suggested, in two different attitudes toward marriage. According to the deuteronomic worldview, marriage begins at a precise moment with a legal contract and can end at a precise moment with another legal contract. According to the priestly worldview, marriage constitutes the reunion of two halves of a single being. It is hard to define the precise moment at which a priestly marriage begins. Is it at the point when the two halves are reunited? Or did the marriage begin when the being was originally divided? Can we understand that period between the division of the being and the reunion of its two halves as a kind of temporary exile? And if so, should any period of dysfunction that might occur be understood as another kind of exile, with the two halves awaiting, as long as necessary (even until death), their second reunion? I mentioned earlier that when I began to work on this paper my own marriage had recently ended with the death of my first husband. In truth, I do not know, since I never asked myself the question, which of these two models I would have favored *before* my marriage ended. My strong intuition is that it would have been the deuteronomic model. Although I was very happily married, and at no point considered divorce or separation, the idea in principle of being locked into a marriage does not appeal to me, for myself or for others. When I married for a second time, however, it seemed that only the deuteronomic model could work for me. Since I had already been married, happily and successfully, surely I had found my other half the first time around? On the priestly model, there could be no second chance; no one can have two other halves. Whereas I never once contemplated in detail or at length the end, by whatever means that might occur, of my first marriage, I often think about it now. The main reason for this difference is obvious: I have experienced the end of a marriage; the experience marked me indelibly, and I fear a reprise. And yet it is almost impossible for me to contemplate divorce, not only because I am very happily married, as I was before, but also because I feel that I could not survive separation. Whatever thoughts I have of the end of my marriage involve my own death, and in that respect, my worldview seems more priestly than deuteronomic. I think all this means that I have lived out in my own life my academic *conviction* that these two worldviews are necessary and, however irreconcilable they seem, can function consecutively, and even perhaps simultaneously, within the lifespan of one individual.

THE LAND

In the present essay, I posit two biblical approaches to the land: the priestly (eternal, unconditional, populated by tenants, not owners) and the deuteronomic (capable of ending, conditional, owned by its population). When I wrote the first version of this paper, I had—again—a strong sense that both worldviews are required, the deuteronomic for a time, such as now, when a national connection is possible, and the priestly for a time, such as the period from the Babylonian Exile until 1948, when it was not. The very way in which I have phrased the preceding sentence makes my own view clear. For me, the priestly model is a fallback position, a state of limbo when the people of Israel cannot have autonomous control of their own land. The deuteronomic model must be my ideal. In other words, it seems to be more important to me that a small piece of land in the Middle East is a homeland for Jews, and for me that necessitates autonomous control, since I do not believe that it would remain a homeland for Jews in any other circumstance that can be realistically envisaged today. This second step—the "in other words" paraphrase of my original position—is not a thought that I had ever expressed in these words before I moved to Israel, though perhaps I would have done if pressed (as I never was) to articulate my feelings systematically instead of piecemeal.

Although I was a little surprised to watch the preceding paragraph appearing on the screen as I wrote it, I cannot say that I was totally unprepared. Since I moved to Jerusalem four months ago, I have been studying in a wonderful *'ulpan* (center for modern Hebrew teaching) around the corner from my home in the German Colony. This is my first extended stay in Israel, and it turns out that years of Hebrew Bible and Jewish liturgy did not prepare me to speak on the streets! The classes are one-on-one, but once a week the students gather and give short speeches in Hebrew. Once I had dealt with the questions of where I come from originally, why I want to learn to speak Hebrew, and how many children I have, I decided it was easiest to base my speeches on the *parashat ha-shavu'a*, the weekly reading from the Pentateuch, and its connection to the *ulpan*. On *Shabbat Noah*, the Shabbat when the story of the flood is recited in synagogue, I spoke, naturally, about the tower of Babel, which is recited on the same Shabbat. Before the tower of Babel, I told my teachers and fellow *talmidim* ("students"), there was one tongue and one language. The Bible does not specify, but, as assumed by the ancient Jewish sages, according to rabbinic tradition it must have been Hebrew. Without the builders of the tower of Babel, then, there would be no work for *'ulpan* teachers and *'ulpan* students would have to find other ways to occupy their time: the whole world would already know Hebrew. Not only that. Without the builders of the tower of Babel, there would be no special language of prayer for Diaspora Jews; even in synagogue, Jews would be just like the people who surrounded them. And not only that. The state of Israel would have no linguistic sign of differentiation from the countries around it. In the matter of language, at least, it would be just like Lebanon and Syria. Speaking for myself, I concluded, even though I wish I already knew perfect, fluent modern Hebrew, I find for the first time in my life that I have reason to thank the builders of the tower of Babel!

It is not hard to see the connection between my *'ulpan* speech and my view of Israel's national identity. I am not attracted to the idea of '*Ivrit* (Hebrew) as Esperanto, or to a universalist world in which everyone is Jewish. What attracts me to the priestly worldview as far as the land is concerned is only that it posits an eternal bond, which Deuteronomy lacks. Otherwise, with one other exception, my own worldview since I moved to Israel has become increasingly deuteronomic. The other exception concerns the atonement of other people's sin. I have explored elsewhere the subject of what happens to the sins of non-Israelites living in the land. In the present essay, it arose only implicitly: the floodwater affects everyone, guilty and innocent, as I discuss, and also (had they existed at the time) Israelite and non-Israelite. The priestly worldview, with its universal impulses, cannot concern itself only with the Israelite, and cannot begin with the premise, as Deuteronomy does, that, in an ideal world, all other peoples will have been eliminated. Although my vision of Israel as a homeland for Jews is inevitably nationalist, and despite my fears about its security, I do not want to it to be the home of Jews alone. I must therefore (and do!) care about the fate of non-Jews in the land (and not just in the matter of guilt and the removal of sin, of course), and in this respect my worldview seems to have a priestly component after all. It is hard to see how concern for the well being of non-Jews can be reconciled with the strongly and apparently purely nationalist tendencies of the deuteronomic worldview.

Third-Party Intercession

Finally, I want to say something about third-party intercession. In the deuteronomic worldview, there is no real role, I think, for mediation. It is for the parties involved, whether individuals in a relationship, or peoples involved in religious, legal or territorial disputes, to find a solution and act on it. To be sure, a judge may be involved, but usually in the role of a dispenser of justice, not as a mediator proper. As in the cases I discussed above, I am convinced that there is a role for both models, a priestly worldview based on third-party intercession and a deuteronomic one based on direct action. In my own life, however, I have moved in at least one respect from a bias toward deuteronomic directness to a bias toward priestly intercession.

I mentioned at the beginning of this essay that my first husband, Peter Lipton ז״ל, died unexpectedly not long before I began to work on it. We, together with our two sons, belonged to a Reform synagogue in Cambridge, England. There was no rabbi or *chazzan* ("cantor"), and members of the community undertook many synagogue roles. (Ordination is not required in Jewish contexts.) For many years, I led many Shabbat services and most major festival services, including all the High Holyday services. Although, all things being equal, I would have chosen a different kind of community, this synagogue made sense for us as a family. I was comfortable in the role I had, not because I wanted to be a community leader, but because I felt an obligation to give help where help was needed, because I wanted to help build a community for the sake of my own family, and because it made little or no difference to my own experience of prayer whether I was standing at the *bima* (leader's platform) and singing or reading in a loud voice, on the one hand, or, on the other, sitting at the back of the synagogue and singing or reading quietly.

After my husband's death, I felt that I no longer had the internal resources required to lead synagogue services. I could not depend on my own capacity to sustain a personal divine–human relationship, and wanted to be in a synagogue where the service itself—the liturgy, the music, the rituals, and the rabbi—would function where I could not. More than that, I wanted to be part of a congregation steeped in a commitment to intercession against cosmic disorder, which is more or less how I experienced my husband's death. For this and many other reasons, I moved to London and rented an apartment a few minutes' walk from Lauderdale Road, a Spanish and Portuguese Orthodox synagogue that seemed to meet all my religious needs. My friends cautioned me that it would be hard to make new friends there (but that was not important for me at the time, and in fact it was not hard) and, more to the point, that I would be miserable sitting quietly in the women's gallery after many years of highly visible and audible participation on the *bima*. But I did not feel at all miserable. When I entered the beautiful sanctuary early on Shabbat mornings and saw Rabbi Levy next to the *heikhal*, the ark where the Torah scrolls are kept, and Rabbi Elia on the *bima*, heard the small choir singing beautiful, traditional Sephardi tunes, watched as members of the congregation stood in memory of departed family members, and recited with the congregation the words—every single word, distinctly and audibly, of the liturgy—I was sure that I was in the best possible place in the world. I did not care what individual members did or did not believe about intercession. What cried out to me was that Lauderdale Road embodied, among other things, an utter commitment to positively affecting God in the hope that he might positively affect us, its congregation.

In Jerusalem, my spiritual equivalent of Lauderdale Road Synagogue turned out to be a tiny Moroccan synagogue in the Bak'a neighborhood. This was not completely surprising.

My preferred mode of preparation for leading the High Holyday services in Cambridge had been a week in Jerusalem just before Rosh Hashanah, the Jewish New Year, when I got up every day at four in the morning to attend *selichot* ("penitential") services in the tiny Sephardi synagogues of *Machane Yehudah*, the neighborhood just across from the main Jerusalem *shuk*, the covered market. Now I can attend services similar (in style) to these every Shabbat, though fortunately at the slightly more civilized hour of seven thirty. At *Beit K'nesset Tikvatenu*, "Synagogue of our Hope," the women sit in a separate room, with small (crucially for me—I like to see), curtainless, windows onto the main sanctuary. It is not a beautiful synagogue like Lauderdale Road, and the rabbi and *chazzan* sit among the congregation, not prominently apart from it. But every word of the liturgy is clearly articulated; the singing, though less formal, is as arousing; and the commitment to affecting God is as tangible. It is especially evident at the point in Shabbat and festival services when the rabbi stands before the open *heikhal* and seeks blessings for members of the congregation and their families. People call out their requests with a sense of urgency, and with the same urgency, and utter conviction that they will be heard, the rabbi rephrases the requests and directs them to the *heikhal*. Are all those praying for *refu'ah shelemah*, a full recovery from illness, for themselves and their families convinced that it will come? I do not know, but I am certain that they hope for it fervently. Does the older woman with difficulty walking and barely concealed back pain, who invariably announces at the end of this period of blessings, "God blesses everyone," feel blessed? I am convinced that she does, and also that she hopes every day for renewed manifestations of her blessings.

Do I feel protected from the cosmic disorders I fear? Yes and no, but I feel that I can do no better than this. At least with respect to this important (for me) area of my religious life, I see myself espousing an intensely priestly worldview.

With these closing reflections, I have tried to contextualize in my own life my essay on the bitter waters of the Soṭah ritual and the waters of the Genesis flood narrative. Although the connections I made here, and their implications, seemed self-evident as soon as I sat down to write, I doubt that I would have thought them through without an invitation to contribute to this volume, and I thank the editors for that. At the same time, I want to assure you, the reader, that if what has been unexpectedly therapeutic for me has seemed to you like a misplaced episode of *In Treatment*, the fault is all mine.

Notes

1. *Z"l.*, Hebrew acronym for "let him [the deceased] rest in peace (*Zichrono Li-bhrachah*)."
2. For a detailed historical/sociological treatment of this subject, see Instone-Brewer 2002.
3. I discuss this contrast in greater detail in Lipton 2008: 239–44.
4. On this law, see Tigay 1996: 220–22.
5. I find this the most plausible reading of the biblical text. Levinas (2004: 161–77) analyzes the rabbinic texts that read the Genesis creation accounts thus.
6. See Milgrom 1990: 37–43.
7. The Moabites and Ammonites, for example, following their incestuous origins in Gen. 19:26-38.
8. For a treatment of this in a modern context, see Carter's 2008 monograph charting the development of marriage as a social institution in nineteenth-century western Canada, and the implementation by Christians of lifelong, heterosexual, monogamous marriage as an instrument to impose British-Canadian values on the aboriginal community (Carter 2008).
9. Michael Fishbane has provided an excellent overview of the metaphorical marriage between God and Israel, its sources (Israelite and non-Israelite), its theological applications, and its use of the language and imagery of pentateuchal legal material, especially that drawn from Num. 5:11-31 (Fishbane 1999: 487–502).
10. I offered this reading in a brief Torah commentary, Lipton 2007b: 1185.
11. See Milgrom 1999: 475–82 for a discussion of the composition history of this text. Milgrom follows M. Fishbane and H. C. Brichto, against most other modern critics, in seeing "Bitter Waters" as a unified work, although he argues for two additions, vv. 21 and 31, which he regards as keys that "unlock the redaction and meaning of the text" (475). My reading here is based on the text in its final form, though I see that to read it source-critically to some extent would nuance, and might even strengthen, my exegesis.
12. Lipton 2008: 214–44.
13. For a chart setting out the different stages, see Skinner 1910: 167–68.
14. Greenstein (1982: 114–25) makes this point about how Joseph came to Egypt.
15. Lev. 5:5 does include a term often translated as "confession," but it is by no means clear that this is an appropriate translation, or that "confession" carried then the freight it bears now.
16. This emphasis finds support in recent monographs on the interplay of the female body, warfare, violence, and nationalism in the ancient Near East; see, e.g., Chapman 2004 and Bahrani

2008. For an article on rabbinic bodies and gender containing many valuable insights that can be applied more widely, see Fonrobert 2007.

17. This corresponds interestingly with a point made by Sasson (1999: 483–86), who finds ancient parallels for waters that were at once a source of blessing and a curse.

18. Milgrom (1990: 38–39) relates the "meal offering of remembrance" to 1 Kgs. 17:18, where the widow of Zarephath claims that Elijah has come to "expose" (thus Milgrom) her sin. He could also have mentioned the Pharaoh's cupbearer in Gen. 40:9. Neither, however, indicates that exposure of sin, rather than memorial, is intended in Num. 5:15, where we find both a term that might mean "mention" or "expose," and the term that clearly evokes memory.

19. NJPS renders this "able to retain seed," following from its implication that the ritual does not cause lasting damage to the woman.

20. Frymer-Kensky (1999: 467) offers various explanations, from the naturalistic (this was a term for conception, not delivery) to the supernatural (the woman conceived from the mixture of bitter waters and dust from the tabernacle floor).

21. Sarna (1991: 156) outlines in brief the connections between the Exodus tabernacle narrative and the Genesis creation narrative. See also Hurowitz (1992: 242). Hurowitz does not see an explicit connection between these texts, but sees a reflection here of widespread ancient Near Eastern traditions of describing the cosmos as if built like a temple.

8

From the Well in Midian to the Baʻal of Peor

Attitudes to the Marriage of Israelite Men and Midianite Women

Yonina Dor

A PERSONAL CONTEXTUAL NOTE

My interest in the subject of this essay is first and foremost scholarly and academic, but also political and ideological. Let me explain.

I am an Israeli, born in Tel Aviv. My grandfather was an ordained rabbi; after returning from the synagogue on Shabbat morning, he would give me lessons in the *Teaching of the Fathers* (*Pirkei Avot*). This was one of the sources for my love of ancient Jewish writings and my decision to work on Bible research. As a follow-up to the Zionist-Socialist education in the Youth Movement, I later chose to be a Kibbutz member. I am, until this day, a member of Kibbutz Yagur, near Haifa.

Over the years, however, my deep interest in the biblical text became tinged with moral and ethical criticism of sociopolitical positions found in it, especially in the light of the struggle for peace and equal rights and against a policy of occupation and suppression.

My Ph.D. dissertation, supervised by Professor Sara Japhet at the Hebrew University in Jerusalem, dealt with the separation and exclusion during the Restoration period, and was later modified into a book called *Have the Foreign Women Really Been Expelled?* (Hebrew; 2006). This research fits well with my constant study of the Hebrew Bible, especially the interest in passages that, beyond the text itself, contain aspects of social justice. This is the case in my work on the status of the sojourner (גר, *ger*), the destruction of the native people of the land, and the issue of foreign women.

Part of my work was training teachers for teaching the Bible at schools. In that, too, I was interested in issues of ethics and social justice. In my publications within this area, I present Bible teaching in Israeli state (secular) schools as an opportunity to educate students on biblical values, but concurrently as a chance to criticize outdated values and to reject them. My aim in exposing this complexity that I discern in the biblical text is to reinforce humanist-democratic education in Israel, where Bible study—in this or the other form—is obligatory in all schools, including secular ones.

Beyond studying the biblical text and its background, looking for live, relevant links between the ancient texts and our reality in the Israel of the here and now, as well as introducing critical, academic, and ethical discussions on issues in the texts, is a need of the utmost importance for me. This need was increased by my encounters with students learning to be Bible teachers at schools and with pupils of the same schools—many of whom still accept biblical texts absolutely literally, including nationalistic, racist, antidemocratic messages that I consider obsolete. Such ideas should be openly discussed in every learning framework in the hope that they will promote humanistic education. I believe that, ultimately, the Bible's status in Israeli culture will become stronger when the encounter with its ancient materials creates a discourse on issues of justice and morality.

From this place, I can now move to the article itself, and I hope that various moves I undertake in it are thus made clearer.

***

There is a vivid contrast between the story of the marriage of Moses and Zipporah the Midianite woman (Exod. 2:16-22) and the story of Ba'al Peor (Numbers 25 and 31) in both atmosphere and content. I shall begin my discussion with (1) a description of Moses' conflicting attitudes toward marriage to Midianite women in these two key stories, and follow it with (2) a discussion of various attempts to explain the contrast between them. I shall (3) remark on the characterization of Midianite women, and finally (4) present my own conclusions on the attitude to marriage with Midianite women in the Hebrew Bible.

Moses' Conflicting Attitudes to Marriage
with Midianite Women

As we shall see, Moses' attitudes toward marriage of Israelites with Midianite women are hardly consistent, from his own marriage onwards. In the following we shall trace his conflicting attitudes and attempt to explain them.

Moses and Zipporah

The episode described in Exod. 2:16-22 is based on a type-scene of a meeting between a foreign man and a local woman by a well, a meeting which leads to marriage.[1] Since Moses has helped the daughters of the priest of Midian to water their flocks, their father, Reuel, invites Moses to eat with him. The common meal is a ceremony indicating trust and is the prelude to a contract. Here, therefore, Reuel betroths Zipporah to Moses, a foreigner. We may go further and see in Moses' hastening to the defense of the women an act of deliberate courtship, similar to other episodes in which a man's benevolent action on behalf of a weak woman leads to marriage. The common background to these episodes is the benevolent man's foreignness in the environment of the helpless woman, or her foreignness in his environment. The characterization of Moses as an "other" in Midian is emphasized three times at the end of the story: Moses is described as a stranger; Midian is identified as a foreign country; and Moses names his son *Ger-sham* ("stranger there"):

ותלד בן ויקרא את שמו גרשם כי אמר גר הייתי בארץ נכריה

She bore a son whom he named Gershom, for he said, "I have been a stranger in a foreign land." (Exod. 2:22 JPS)

This emphasis makes it clear that the union of Moses the Hebrew and Zipporah the Midianite was from the first a mixed marriage of which both Moses and Reuel approved. Later, the priest of Midian is called "Moses' father-in-law," and this too expresses approval of the marriage (e.g., 18:1, 2, 5). Reuel and Jethro are read as different names for Moses' father-in-law.[2] Despite the emphasis on Moses' original foreignness, he is faithful to his father-in-law and in their later relationship considers him a reliable source of authority: Moses accepts Reuel's blessing of his decision to return to Egypt (4:18), asks him for guidance in his journey through the desert (Num. 10:31), and puts into practice Reuel's advice to delegate authority in the government of the community (Exod. 18:13-26).

THE INCIDENT AT BAʿAL OF PEOR

In the incident at Baʿal of Peor (Numbers 25) and its terrible consequences (ch. 31), a very different picture of Moses' attitude to involvement with Midianite women is painted. It is not clear why the story is divided between chapters 25 and 31, but the two chapters together constitute a single narrative.[3] Numbers 25 is itself composed of three or four units (vv. 1-5; 6-9; 10-15—or the latter two as one section; and 16-18), and the sequence is not continuous. The details and terminology are not consistent, the account of the actions is not coherent, and it seems that the attempts of commentators to fill the lacunae impair the spirit of the narrative. I shall discuss this noncohesive chapter as it is recorded, and treat the irregular sequence as an authentic expression of the story.

Numbers 25 opens with a short account of the "whoredom" of the people of Israel with the Moabite women, resulting with the Israelites being invited to sacrifice and bow down to the Moabite god—Baʿal of Peor. Here, too, the relationship begins with the Israelites' agreement to a joint meal, but in this case it is a ritual component of a religious ceremony. This relationship is considered a terrible sin, which generates two reactions, one from God and one from Moses: first, God demands to "hang up the leaders against the sun," an unusual punishment, apparently derived from an independent source;[4] and second, Moses commands that each of the judges of Israel should slay every one of his men who worshiped Baʿal of Peor. We have no information about the execution of these two commands, but a new situation immediately arises: an Israelite man takes hold of a Midianite woman in the presence of his brothers and all the people of Israel, and takes her into the tabernacle alone. This sacrilegious act causes the spectators to weep.[5] The Midrash and the commentators explain that the couple go into the tabernacle either to perform a pagan ceremony or to commit whoredom, but there is no indication in the text of an idolatrous ritual. The use of the two verbs בוא (b-w-ʾ Qal) and קרב (q-r-b Hif. and also Qal), each bearing the connotations of sexual relationship, makes it clear that this passage is about intimate relationships.[6] The presence of the crowd of witnesses—the family of the Israelite man and the whole community—suggests that a socially acceptable marriage ceremony was about to take place (Num. 25:6-9; Gray 1956: 384; Noth 1968: 198; Milgrom 1990: 214). Phinehas son of Eleazar, the son of Aaron the priest, reacts by bursting out of the crowd and stabbing to death both partners of the mixed marriage: Zimri son of Salu and Cozbi daughter of Zur. This is the dramatic climax of the story. Their death puts a stop to the plague in which twenty-four thousand people have died, and this is a sign of divine punishment, with the magnitude of the punishment commensurate with the magnitude of the sin. The addition of punishments and their gradually increasing severity in the course of the chapter heighten the terrible impression made by the act. And, indeed, the Baʻal of Peor story left more traces in biblical tradition, such as in Deut. 4:3 (and see also Josh. 12:17; Ps. 106:28-31; Hos. 9:10). Although the cessation of the plague shows that the sin has been atoned for and God appeased, Moses receives another command: to harass the Midianites because of their licentious behavior in Peor and the episode of Cozbi (Num. 25:17-18). Thus all the Midianites, not only the women involved, become a collective target for revenge. Moses orders vengeance, and the people respond by killing all the Midianite men (31:1-7). After the fighting, Moses rebukes the people for killing only the men, and demands that women and children also be killed. In 25:1-15, it is the people of Israel who are the prime offenders, and it is they who are punished or said to be punished. In Numbers 31, Midian is the culpable party, and its punishment is total destruction.

THE CONTRADICTIONS BETWEEN THE TWO EPISODES AND ATTEMPTS TO EXPLAIN THEM

As a private individual, Moses married a Midianite and raised a family with her. He both esteemed and cooperated with his Midianite father-in-law. However, as the public leader of the Israelites, Moses ordered and carried out the complete destruction of Midian. How can the contradiction between Moses' different attitudes be explained? To find out the answer, one has to examine details in the two stories as well as elsewhere in the Pentateuch and in the Prophets, in exegetical interpretations and in research findings.

THE SOURCES OF THE STORIES AND THEIR DATES

It is usually thought that the source of the ideal picture of relations with Midian, as painted in Exodus 6–18, was early literary material from JE.[7] Sources that mention tension and enmity between Israel and Midian, particularly the stories of Balak (Numbers 22–24), of Baʻal of Peor and its consequences (Numbers 25 and 31), and of Gideon (Judges 6–8) are considered late. The most extreme in its enmity to Midian is the story of Baʻal of Peor. It is true that the opening (Num. 25:1-5) is considered a collection of passages from J and E, but the remainder, in its various parts (25:6-9, 10-15, 16-18) is thought to be a combination of different sources from the postexilic period, some of them attributed to P because of their linguistic character and subject matter.[8] The Priestly source is evident in the etiology of the appointment of Phinehas and his descendants as high priests forever. The extreme opposition to mixed marriages probably also dates from this period, following the book of Ezra-Nehemiah and other biblical and nonbiblical texts (Mal. 2:11; Ezra 9:1—10:44; Neh. 9:3; 13:3, 23-30; *Jubilees* 30). But the terminology of the different passages is not consistent, and there is no agreed dating. Baruch Levine maintains that the source of the non-Priestly account was in northern Israel in the eighth century bce and sees in it criticism of the sins of Israel, in the spirit of Hosea (Hos. 9:10). Jacob Milgrom, however, points to indications that this chapter is early (1990: XXXIII). Numbers 31, which describes the destruction of the Midianites, also seems at first sight to be derived from P, in view of the patently Priestly terminology (such as מעל [*ma'al*, "commit wrong"], מטה [*maṭṭeh*, "tribe"], נשיאים [*nesi'im*, "chieftains, leaders"]); the references to purification after the war (vv. 19-24); and the apportioning of spoil to the priests, the Levites, and the tabernacle (vv. 25-54). But scholars consider this account to be a late Priestly midrash because it has no authentic details of the war, and much of it is based on Numbers 25.[9] Even though biblical and non-biblical discourse of the postexilic period reflects opposition to mixed marriages, thence it was assumed that it was the background and date for the story, this in itself is not adequate proof, because there are polyvalent opinions expressed in Priestly writings and others in the postexilic period.[10] Thus we cannot attribute to P complete unequivocal opposition to marriage with Midianites. Moreover, we cannot definitely attribute sympathy toward Midian to JE, if only because the short passage that refers directly to Ba'al of Peor (25:1-5) is assigned to this source. As has been said, although it refers to Moab and not to Midian, it is an integral part of the series of references to the Midianite women that follows on directly from mentions of the Moabite women. Nor is the simple explanation, that the positive attitude to Midian is early while the negative attitude is late, acceptable. This assumption is plausible to an extent; but the chapters are fragmentary, contain insertions, and no doubt have been subjected to deletions.[11] Milgrom gives two instances: If Numbers 31 is a late composition, how can the fact that camels are not included in the list of spoils taken from the Midianites be explained?[12] Similarly, in Num. 31:18, it is permitted to marry female Midianite prisoners of war. This is legitimate in early writings (as in the law of the beautiful prisoner, Deut. 21:10-14), but, in Milgrom's view, it is inappropriate in a late Priestly text. Some Priestly and other writings from the postexilic period are pluralistic and favor the assimilation of foreigners (Lev. 19:33-34; Ruth 4:1-21; Isa. 2:2-3, 56:6-7[13]). There is even compromise in the book of Ezra-Nehemiah, since the demand for ethnic exclusivity was not actually put into practice (Dor 2011: 177–86). Hence, the Persian period cannot be defined as completely separatist.

THE CHARACTERISTICS OF MARRIAGE

The relationship between Moses and Zipporah became a socially accepted marriage through the initiative of her father and under his patronage, as is fitting in an honorable traditional society. Moses the refugee found shelter and a home with his wife's family (Exod. 2:16-22), and built a trusting relationship with his father-in-law. On the other hand, the relationships with the Moabite women are described as whoredom, and the bond of intimacy between Zimri the Israelite and Cozbi the Midianite woman was considered a sin (Num. 25:1, 6, 18). The weeping of the congregation shows how deep a shock the incident caused; the couple's public display of intimacy in the tabernacle infringed the convention that intimate relationships between a man and a woman should take place in private, and the text presents it as provocative immorality, even though this intercourse behind curtains could be interpreted as a marriage ceremony. The fact that it took place in the presence of the family (Zimri's brothers) and the public is an expression of ceremonial formality (Num. 25:6). The hostile description of this ceremony by the author represents it as a sin because it is a mixed marriage. In Num. 25:6-15, it is the mixed marriage, not idolatry, that is the sin, for idolatry is not mentioned at all. The killing of Zimri and Cozbi and the great plague are the consequences of mixed marriages, and not of idolatry. In my view, this passage was inserted after the description of the worship of Baʿal of Peor in order to denounce marriage with Midianite women on the grounds that they lead to idolatry, as is explicitly said at the beginning and end of this chapter (v. 1: "whoredom"; v. 18: "wiles"). The same link between mixed marriages and idolatry is found throughout the Bible, as is the characterization of foreign women as debauched (e.g., Gen. 39:6-19; Ezek. 16:3-45; cf. Dor 2006: 225–27 [Heb.]). In this case, the different attitudes are not explained.

ORIGINS

Midian's friendship and cooperation with Israel is expressed in the common origin of Midian and Abraham (Gen. 25:1-4), and in the inclusion of Midian's descendants among the tribes of Judah (1 Chron. 2:46; 4:17) and Reuben (Gen. 46:9; Num. 26:5; Knoppers 2001:18–28, especially pages 24 and 26). It may be inferred from the positive relationships between the Kenites and the Israelites that this, too, was the result of blood relationship. The family bonds between Moses and his father-in-law Hobab, and between Moses' father-in-law and Heber the Kenite (Judg. 4:11), explain the mutual help between the Kenites and the Israelites. Yael, Heber's wife, killed Sisera (Judg. 4:17-23), and the Kenites helped the Israelites during the exodus and therefore Saul evacuated the Kenites from the land of the Amalekites before going to battle with Amalek (1 Sam. 15:6).

But because the Kenites are the offspring of Cain, the attitude to them is complex. Cain, their eponym, was a criminal, the first biblical murderer, but at the same time a positive figure: the first man who brought an offering to Yahweh, the father of humankind, the originator of human culture (Gen. 4:8, 20-22, 26). Paula M. McNutt explains the ambivalent attitude to the Kenites from the anthropological aspect: the descendants of Tubal Cain were professionally esteemed as smiths and iron workers (2 Kgs. 24:14), but accused of fashioning idols (Isa. 44:17; McNutt 1994: 112–18). The identification of the Kenites with the Midianites through the identification of Jethro with Hobab, in addition to the similarity of the religion of Israel to that of the descendants of Cain (see the section below), enhances the close relationship between Midian and Israel. All throughout the Scriptures, the congruence and exchange of identity between the Midianites and other tribal ethnic groups of the ancient Middle East—such as the Amalekites, the Ishmaelites, the people of the east, the plunderers (שׁוֹסִים, shosim)—is conspicuous. They are nomads, ride camels, steal from the land cultivating Israelites, are traders, and know the ways of the desert. Their origins, their typology, and the nature and strength of the contacts among them are unclear (Abramsky 1984: 128–34 [Heb.]). Although they are usually considered enemies of Israel, some of them share a common origin with Israel (Ishmael: Gen. 16:15; Amalek: Gen. 36:12). Moab is sometimes referred to as an ally of Midian or even part of it, sometimes as one of Israel's traditional enemies, but Moab's eponymous founder is also a blood relation of Abraham (Gen. 19:36-7).[14] This complex depiction of the traditions of the origins of Midian and similar peoples does not by itself explain the different attitudes to them.

RELIGION: THE NAME OF GOD, THE HOLY PLACE, BELIEF, AND RITUAL

While Moses is grazing his father-in-law Jethro's flock in the vicinity of the Mountain of God in Midian, God appears to him for the first time in his own name and speaks with him (Exod. 3:1-2, 13-14). The tradition that God's presence is in the region of Midian is further developed upon the return of Moses from Egypt, when he meets Jethro on the Mountain of God. At this meeting, Jethro's belief in God is revealed: Jethro pronounces a blessing in God's name, acknowledges his superiority to other gods, sacrifices to him, and invites Aaron and the elders to eat bread before him (Exod. 18:5-12). It may be surmised that here, too, the function of the common meal is to cement an alliance. It is not clear whether this is an alliance with God, an alliance between Moses and Jethro under the auspices of God, or some other alliance (Nicholson 1986: 126–27). Jethro's initiative and his authoritative status on this occasion support several scholars' conjecture that it was he who converted Moses to monotheism.[15] The characterization of Jethro as a worshiper of God is consistent with his identification as a Kenite. After Cain is punished by eternal wandering, the sign Yahweh affixes to him symbolizes the protection he and his descendants were afforded. This is an expression of Yahweh's ambivalent attitude to Cain. Joseph Blenkinsopp understands this story as the prehistory of the worship of God, and as evidence of the deep religious connection between Israel and the Kenites (Blenkinsopp 2008: 140–42). These religious features support the theory that the Keno-Midianites were the source of the religion and cult of Yahweh. In addition to the placing of the Mountain of God in the geographical region of Midian, this theory is supported by location of theophanic areas in early poetry: Seir, Edom, Paran, Cushan, and Teman, which are identified as being located on the plains of Midian (e.g., Deut. 33:2, 9; Judg. 5:4–5; Ps. 68:8).[16] Another indication of cult practice common to Midian and Israel is the prohibition of idols (Patrich 1990: 174–75; Na'aman 1999: 391–415). The findings concerning the Shasu, identified with the שסים (shosim, "plunderers"), bitter enemies of Israel (Judg. 2:14), provide further proof of the identity of Midianite religion, with roots from the religion of Israel. Some features of the Shasu's fanatical religion are similar to those of Israelite religion, and the earliest archaeological evidence of the worship of Yahweh—the inscription *Eretz Hashasu Yeho* ("the land of the Shasu Yeho")—was found in their territory. Donald Redford maintains that Israelite Yahwism was derived from the Shasu tribes, and identifies them with the Midian of the book of Exodus. It is not clear exactly to what extent Midian and the ethnic units within it influenced Israel. Although many of the conjectures quoted above are not based on solid evidence, it is impossible to ignore the similarity between the two religions.[17]

Nevertheless, in Numbers 25, Midianite culture is described as blatantly idolatrous; this follows on directly from the description of the encounter with the Moabite women who urge the Israelites to worship Ba'al of Peor. As has been remarked, since the Moabite women are identified with the Midianite women, the Midianite women are unequivocally accused of the transgression of Peor (Num. 25:18; 31:16). Thus, from the viewpoint of faith and worship, one may distinguish between Midian as a religious partner of Israel, against the backdrop of the religion of Jethro and the Kenites, worshipers of Yahweh, and Midian that is linked to Moab and worships Ba'al of Peor.

TIME AND GEOGRAPHIC SPACE

As has been remarked above, the good relationship between Moses and Jethro is believed to have originated in a very early tradition, before the period of the Israelite settlement, in the geographic area of northern Arabia.[18]

However, other sources indicate that Midian was in eastern Transjordan: in the story of Balak, Midian is mentioned as an ally of Moab (Num. 22:4, 7), and the Ba'al of Peor episode takes place on the plains of Moab. In the period of the Judges, Gideon fights against the Midianites, who have come from eastern Transjordan to invade the cultivated area of the land of Israel (Judg. 6:1-5). Gideon is credited with the classic victory engraved in the memory of the nation: "the Day of Midian" (Isa. 9:3).[19]

Eusebius's *Onomasticon* states that the attribution of these two different locations to Midian was ancient. The nomadic Midianites inhabited an unidentified area in northern Arabia, and also the land of Moab, on the shore of the Arnon wadi.[20] Despite doubts as to the veracity of the tradition that Midian was in the region of Moab, recent archaeological evidence has tended to confirm it.[21] Another view is that the Midianites lived not only in eastern Transjordan but also in Canaan itself—in the Negev, in Judea, in Jezreel, in the regions of Issachar and Manasseh, and in the mountains of southern Galilee. Elizabeth Payne bases this claim mainly on the books of Joshua and Judges (e.g., Josh. 15:61; Judg. 4:11; 8:24-27).[22] Her most extreme claim concerning the preoccupation of this essay is that Gideon himself was of Midianite origin, and that his wars were internal battles within Midian itself (Payne 1983: 166). The attribution of Exod. 2:15-22 to an early period and of Numbers 31 and part of Numbers 25 to the Persian period can therefore scarcely be denied. Moreover, the friendly relationship with Midian is typical primarily of southern Midian, in Arabia, whereas hostile relationship is typical of the Midian of eastern Transjordan.

Do the criteria advanced by these scholars explain the difference between the conflicting attitudes to Midian in the Bible? Yes and no. It is probable that the definition "Midianite" included various groups at various times and in various places, each of which maintained a relationship with Israel or parts of it (and Israel too was also not a monolithic, homogeneous entity).[23] In general, it may be said that the good relationship is typical of the traditions of the Kenites, as well as the early southern traditions of the affinity between Moses and Jethro, for which the sources are mainly J and E. Conversely, it may be said that the attitudes to the Midianite groups of eastern Transjordan, such as those that related to the Amalekites, the Shasu, or Moab, were late, and are in line with the spirit of the Priestly source and the worldview evinced at the

Baʻal of Peor episode and its consequent incidents. Such generalizations cannot serve to define the attitude of the Scriptures to Midian in unambiguous terms. What Israel and Midian had in common was deep and ancient. It was based on a combination of hereditary, regional, cultural, and religious factors. It seems that Israel's antagonism toward the Midianites stemmed from the depth of their common features, as well as from the urge to stay aloof from those features. One can understand the struggle between these conflicting forces as a reflection of Israel's tremendous and continuous effort to preserve its detachment from its sources: the autochthonous peoples and nomad tribes of northern Arabia.[24]

Midianite Women: Their Attributes

Despite the extreme diversity of Moses' attitudes to marriage with Midianite women, and despite the differences between Zipporah and Cozbi, some attributes common to both can be discerned. Both were daughters of courageous leaders, and both were brave enough to carry out unusual actions connected with sexuality and matrimony. Zipporah's courageous act is described in the obscure passage about the bridegroom of blood (Exod. 4:23-25). In this act, the relations between Moses and Zipporah are reversed: when they meet by the well, Moses saves the helpless Zipporah and her sisters; here it is Zipporah who saves him from Yahweh's attack. The attacker releases him when she cuts off her son's foreskin, presents it as a valuable sacrifice, and pronounces solemnly: "Truly you are a bridegroom of blood to me. . . . A bridegroom of blood by circumcision" (Exod. 4:25-26). This great sacrifice, part of the male sexual organ that symbolizes the continuity of the family's seed, is accepted as a substitute for Moses' life. The blood of the symbolic substitute wound becomes a symbol of a covenant, and the "bridegroom of blood," at first an enemy, becomes an ally. Although the development of the plot implies that it is the aggressive God who becomes Zipporah's ally, some commentators have maintained that Moses himself is her bridegroom of blood, and that only after he is circumcised, or his son's foreskin touches his sexual organ (לרגליו, le-raglaw, "at his feet" is a euphemism here) is their marriage solemnized. In other words, although the act of circumcision is presented as a spontaneous and sophisticated act of defense by means of a valuable sacrifice, it is performed here in the course of a marriage ceremony (Houtman 1993: 439-49). This is not the recognized, socially accepted circumcision found in later biblical sources: the phrase berit milah ("covenant of circumcision") is not used, and it is the woman rather than the man who is responsible for the circumcision.

It is hard to explain why a mother injures her son in order to save her husband. Is this an instance of an incident, of a type only occasionally mentioned in the Bible, when the son is injured in place of the father?[25] Noth conjectures that the inclusion of the son is secondary. The subject of the beginning and end of the story is Moses, and the strange solemnization of the circumcision ceremony, with the concluding oath, proves that this is an allusion to an ancient marriage custom whose main feature is the circumcision of the bridegroom (Noth 1968: 49–50). When Zipporah injures her son's body, she is not acting as a mother, with compassion, but endangering herself and heroically standing up against God in order to save Moses' life. This is a courageous feminine rebellion, which has no parallel in the Bible. In this respect, Zipporah is a unique personality, standing above the image of usual women, who cherish their sons' lives more than their own (Gen. 27:13; Judg. 17:3) and accept their husband's authority. Zipporah is presented almost as a divine figure. Ilana Pardes maintains that when Zipporah resists God's plan in order to protect her husband, she embodies, to some extent, the personality of a goddess (Pardes 1995: 93–94 [Heb.]). She adduces a source very similar to the story of the bridegroom of blood: the Egyptian myth of the goddess Isis, who defends her husband/brother, Osiris, and saves him from death. Both female figures dare to struggle against a threatening male divinity, both succeed in saving their husbands by an act affecting the penis, and both have birdlike features. Zipporah thus owns characteristics of a feminine figure in pagan culture.

In the story of Ba'al of Peor, the women of Moab-Midian also dare to perform acts of contrivance, although their artifice is not unique. They use their sexuality as temptation to idolatry, thereby causing the Israelites to sin (Num. 25:1-2). Their deeds are therefore described as "wiles" (Num. 25:18, 31:16).[26] The Kenite woman Yael—who offers food and hospitality to Sisera, shares her bed with him, and then kills him—plays a similar trick in order to ensure that the Israelites' victory over Canaan would be complete (Judg. 4:17-21).

Just as the ceremony of Zipporah's bridegroom-of-blood covenant can be understood as a wedding ceremony, so too, as has been remarked above, can the union of the couple in the tabernacle. The elevated social status of Zimri in Israel and Cozbi in Midian is intended to emphasize the importance of the occasion and the power of its sociopolitical message. What the onlookers see is not simply a marriage ceremony but a demonstration of support for marriages of Israelites and Midianite women and a declaration that these are permitted and honorable, not an individual, random, one-time aberration. The intercourse of a couple behind a tent-cloth "in the eyes of all Israel," in order to pass on a message to the community, is reminiscent of the story of Absalom. In order to signify David's deposition as king official and to confirm his own rule, among other acts Absalom has intercourse with David's wives "in the eyes of all Israel," in a tent on the roof of the royal palace (2 Sam. 16:22).

In response to the union of the distinguished couple in the tabernacle, Phinehas son of Eleazar the priest attacks them and stabs them to death. Not only does he enter the tabernacle with a spear in his hand; but he also strikes the Midianite woman in her "stomach" (euphemism for the vagina, according to the traditional commentators) and kills both her and her Israelite partner.[27] This action purifies the people of Israel from the desecration, and the deadly plague comes to an end. Explanations of Phinehas's act, such as that it is a spontaneous expression of rage, or that he is doing his duty as a priest by protecting the sanctity of the tabernacle,[28] are unsatisfactory. This extreme and flamboyant reaction is first and foremost a powerful ritual expression of the call for the complete prohibition of mixed marriages. In the same way, the Levites attack the people who sin by worshiping the golden calf, and kill three thousand men (Exod. 32:1-29). In both instances, the act is a reaction to a terrible sin committed in public, and the slaughter purifies the congregation. As a sign of esteem, the Levites who did the killing are blessed and rewarded for their zeal (Milgrom 1990: 211). The two stories evoking mass punishment are analogous: we can suppose that many Israelites are killed because many Israelites have married Midianite women, just as that numerous worshipers of a golden calf bring punishment upon many. It is difficult to believe that all the Midianite people were liquidated because of one woman's sin, or that "twenty-four thousand" Israelites were killed because of one man's sin.

The two accounts of the collective punishment—of Israelites in Numbers 25, and of Midianites in Numbers 31—must be understood as a midrash, a myth warning about the bitter results of mixed marriages. This is the essence of the whole story. Commentators have discussed at length the question of what happened inside the tabernacle—idolatry, sexual licentiousness, or pagan ritual prostitution.[29] These interpretations are tendentious; their purpose is to vilify contact with Midianite women and to justify the terrible punishment it incurs. Even without these interpretations, the message is clear: those who are involved in mixed marriages can expect death and catastrophe, and the temptresses are most to blame.

The Ambivalence of the Attitude to Mixed Marriages

Attitudes to mixed marriages in the Hebrew Bible are mixed: at times they are positive or at least indifferent, at others negative, at others ambivalent. Here I analyze examples of several instances: the story of Dinah and Shechem, the story of Ruth, the book of Chronicles, and the book of Ezra-Nehemiah.

The Ambiguous Attitude to Mixed Marriages in the Bible

In the story of Dinah and Shechem (Genesis 34), two voices can be heard: the voice of Jacob and the voice of his sons. Jacob does not oppose the marriage of his daughter Dinah to Shechem son of Hamor the Hivite. But his sons, Simeon and Levi, do not accept this marriage; they attack the inhabitants of Shechem deceitfully, kill all the males, and take whatever remains as booty. Jacob soundly castigates his sons for their dangerous deeds, but the blunt rhetorical question with which they reply, ויאמרו הכזונה יעשׂה את אחותנו, "But they answered, 'Should our sister be treated like a whore?'" is intended to justify their violent reaction (Gen. 34:31). It is similar to the definition of the actions of the Moabite women as whoredom in the episode of Ba'al of Peor. The brothers' demand that the men of Shechem be circumcised is also parallel to Phinehas's stabbing Cozbi's pudenda. Despite the separatist conclusion of the story, it is significant that the moderate pluralistic voice is attributed to Jacob—the most honored personage—and his prestige adds weight to the attitude that he represents. This parallels the role of Moses, the revered leader, who takes a Midianite wife.

In the book of Ruth, Ruth's positive personal qualities are emphasized even though she is a Moabite: her faithfulness, her modesty, and her agreement to the purchase of the family plot prove that she is worthy of joining the Israelite community. The birth of Obed, who becomes the grandfather of David, is the high point of the legitimation of marriage with this Moabite woman. But, aside from the pluralism evident throughout the book of Ruth, there is also some criticism of her: the erotic story of nocturnal temptation on the threshing floor (Ruth 3) is reminiscent of the sin of Ham, who uncovers the nakedness of his father, Noah (Gen. 9:21), and the rape of Lot by his daughters (Gen. 19:31-35). The worst blow to Ruth's standing is struck by her neighbors when they give a name to her newborn child: ילד בן לנעמי, "A son is born to Naomi!" (Ruth 4:17), and Naomi takes steps to adopt him (Ruth 4:16)[30] in order to Judaize King David's ancestry, and thereby to neutralize his relationship with his biologically Moabite ancestress. This is a separatist attitude that undermines the pluralist message otherwise dominant throughout the book of Ruth.

In Chronicles, Israel is conceived of as a community of all its citizens, and it discloses mixed marriages that are kept hidden in First Temple literature (e.g., 2 Chron. 24:26 as against 2 Kgs. 12:22).[31] But Chronicles ignores and even hides the tradition of Solomon's marriage with foreign women in its account of the

House of David. Thus this pluralistic account reaches a compromise with the separatist approach.

Ezra and Nehemiah demand that all the foreign women and all their children be expelled, and the assembly assents, decides, and even swears to its agreement. But this concept is not put into practice. The impressive ceremonies in which it is decided to expel the foreign women, and which perhaps includes a symbolic performance of expulsion, is no more than a formal purification of the community. This enabled the men to continue living with their foreign wives without breaking up families. The ceremonial nature of the treatment of foreign women proves that it is no more than a ritual performance that exhibited what is desirable and required, and hides the fact that the foreign women were actually *not* expelled (Dor 2011).

AMBIVALENCE IN MOSES' ATTITUDE TOWARD MARRIAGE WITH MIDIANITE WOMEN

Despite the positive assessment of Zipporah, there are remarks and hints that undermine this positive attitude. The first one is echoed in the statement that Moses has sent her away (Exod. 18:2). The reason for the divorce is her foreignness, as can be deduced from Miriam and Aaron's criticism of Moses because of the "Cushite woman whom he had married" (Num. 12:1). The definition of Moses' wife as "black," without mentioning her name, is intended to show that she is an "other."[32] Even though the text does not state categorically that the black woman is Zipporah, the idea that she is indeed the one referred to is based, first of all, on the synonymous parallelism of Cushan and Midian, as in אהלי כושן . . . יריעות ארץ מדין ("The tents of Cushan// the pavilions of the land of Midian," Hab. 3:7). Furthermore, referring to the identification of the black woman as Zipporah, and also as the Kenite wife of Moses (as seen in Judg. 4:11), Gerhards maintains that the fact of these several versions of the foreignness of Moses' wife is a definite proof of the reliability and authenticity of the Moses tradition (Gerhards 2005: 162–75). Gerhards follows ancient commentators, who believed that Cush was one of the tribes of Midian, and sees "Midianite woman" and "woman of Cush" as variations of the same identity. He considers the claim that Moses' wife was a Kenite derived from concerns that arose after the Israelite settlement, when Midian was thought to be an enemy to Israel and an ally of Amalek. In order to improve the status of Moses, the tradition that his wife was a Midianite was replaced by a tradition that she was a Kenite, which was considered more positive.[33] After the divorce, Zipporah returns and joins Moses during Israel's wanderings in the desert (Exod. 18:5-6). Miriam and Aaron speak against her because she is black—foreign and other—but God defends Moses against his family's criticism, thereby legitimating the black wife and confirming Moses' leadership (Num. 12:6-10).

A minor reminiscence of the criticism of Zipporah may be discerned in the disparagement of her grandson, which besmirches her good name, in that "children's ill deeds reflect on their parents." The superscript *nun* in the genealogy of the Levite who sinned by building a temple in Dan—so that we read מנשה (*menashe*) instead of משה (*moshe* = Moses)—reveals the existence of a tradition that Moses and Zipporah's grandson was the Levite who instituted the worship of the statue in Dan (Judg. 18:30). The difficulty involved in attributing the misdeeds of Jonathan to Moses led to the concealment of Moses' name by its corruption to Manasseh.[34] However, the fact that the *nun* of Manasseh is written above its natural place in the line preserves the criticism besmirching Moses' reputation in the scriptural text of the *Massorah*, and challenges the perfection of Moses' family, the mother of whose sons was a Midianite. Although the criticism is faint and subdued, the traditional version of the Scriptures makes it impossible to ignore.

A double message can also be seen in the story of Ba'al of Peor. At the end of the incident, the people are ordered to attack Midian (Num. 25:17-18). The Midianites as a whole, and not only the women involved, have become the target of collective punishment. The reason for the accusation that all the Midianites practice deception is not stated, and it is apparently only a consequence of the Moabite women's behavior (25:1-2) and the result of Balaam's suggestion that the Israelites be tempted to sin (31:16). Moses' command to kill all the women who are not virgins and every male child emphasizes that the goal is to prevent any possibility of revenge and to ensure complete destruction of the progeny of the defeated (31:17; Snaith 1967: 195). Later, Moses expressly orders that the virgins be kept alive for the conquerors (31:18):

וכל הטף בנשים אשר לא ידעו משכב זכר החיו לכם

But spare every young woman who has not had carnal relations with a man (NJPS).[35]

Hence, these women have no evil in them, and the fact that they have not lain with Midianite men cleanses them completely of their Midianite nature. As has been noted, both the Bible and other accounts of ancient genocide in different cultures describe the obliteration of the original identity of virgins in order to allow them to be taken by the men who have destroyed their people.[36] This ancient attitude contradicts the hegemonic message of the story, that intimate relationships with the Midianite women are a terrible sin and a source of disaster. Through this crack in the uncompromising account can be heard the silenced voice of reality, in which marriages with the daughters of Midian actually did take place.

Summary

The extreme contrast between the Bible's positive attitude to the marriage of Moses and Zipporah the Midianite, and the negative attitude to marriage with Midianite women conveyed in the Baʿal of Peor incident, is modified by the voices that express reservations about each of these two extreme views. The attempts to explain the contradictions between these two attitudes by categories such as the written sources and their dates, the origins of the ethnic groups, and religion and ritual do not provide a completely satisfactory answer. Israel was involved with Midian from a very early period, and the boundaries between the two groups are sometimes unclear—as are the differences between Midian and Moab, or Midian and Amalek. The complex picture portrayed by the present discussion shows that the attitude to relations between Israel and Midian, which reached their peak in mixed marriages, changed from time to time and from case to case. Together with the dominant view expressed in the Bible, which is opposed to marriage with Midianite women, one can hear voices that speak sympathetically, or at least as normal, of the relationships with these women.

So how should we relate to this ambivalence? Does it arise from the long process of Israel's detachment from the peoples from whom it originated, in which case it can be understood as one of the features of any cultural revolution? Does the dialogue described here express a complex human attitude to others—a combination of strong attraction and longings for common roots—alongside a fanatical aspiration to separateness and uniqueness? Or does the difference lie in the contrast between reality and the aspirations of didactic literature? In the latter case, it may be that mixed marriages were actually widespread, and that ideological separatist literature painted such unions in demonic colors in order to educate the community. Furthermore, throughout the Bible there is an ongoing dialogue about the question of marriage with the other, in his or her many guises. In that sense, the Baʿal of Peor incident, together with its bitter ending, seems to be an extreme ideological response to the narrative of Moses and Zipporah's marriage.

Epilogue

Studying the dilemma of marriage with Midianite women, as set forth in this discussion, can contribute to contemporaneous understanding of points such as the following.

1. The Bible is constructed of various sources. Hence, it is no surprise that it contains disparate views on mixed marriages. The stories about Moses, in which he takes a Midianite wife but also commands Midian's total annihilation, can be explained along this line.

2. Ancient Israel was established, inter alia, out of a mixture with various ethnic elements of the land's inhabitants. This undermines the idea of the "holy seed" and ancient Israel's ethnic uniqueness.

3. The message concerning the annihilation of the "other," the land's ancient inhabitants, is unethical, even a crime.

4. Regarding Midianite women and girls as vessels for identity-less childbearing is unethical, a crime.

5. It is dubious whether the information about Midian's annihilation is historically sound.

Such critical ideas contradict traditional and religious norms that justify humiliating and oppressive treatment to non-Jews, especially to Arab Israelis, even in times of bitter conflicts with some of those "others." The issue of Midianite women is just an example of the non-democratic traditions modern Israel has to confront. The Bible is both source and religious legitimation for such traditions; it cannot be ignored. The only way to live with it is to reinterpret it anew in each and every generation. Doing precisely this within the school education system, as part of the regular Bible classes, is an important humanistic aim with political implications.

In 2011, an experiment was carried out in five eleventh- and twelfth-grade classes (the last two grades before matriculation), 120 pupils in all from various schools in Israel, concerning the teaching of our topic in the spirit of this essay. The aims of this experiment were to find out the pupils' attitudes toward Moses' marriage with a Midianite when he himself is responsible for both the destruction of Midian and mixed marriages. Other questions were: What was the pupils' sensitivity to women's status in the Bible, as reflected in the relevant text; and how critical were they about the Bible's historicity? In sum, we wanted to know how they assessed the road taken here, in spite of its disagreement with contemporary Israeli norms. Did they find this topic concretely relevant?

Here are our results of this quantitative survey. Differences between girls and boys, and between various schools, are not meaningful. 41 percent of the pupils see Moses' marriage with Zipporah as a mistake; nevertheless, 60 percent think that the story about Midian's destruction aims at showing that mixed marriages result in catastrophe and should be avoided, although such marriages were acceptable against the positive relationship between Israel and Midian. Surprisingly, the discrepancy between Midian's destruction according to Moses' command and his marriage to the Midianite Zipporah seems to have caused no difficulty. Most pupils—67 percent—explained it as emanating from the different Israelite concepts of mixed marriages.

Finally, pupils were asked for their opinion concerning the open approach to this topic, an approach that exposed the Torah's violent attitude to other nations and to women as procreation vessels only. Most pupils—65 percent—wrote that this approach of teaching the topic did not destabilize their respect for Moses in particular or the Bible in general. On the contrary: many—52 percent—wrote that this study unit challenged them toward further reflection and explanations, and that such an approach is beneficiary for high school Bible classes (62 percent). Half the pupils thought the topic was relevant and actual. One-third argued that mixed marriages are topical. One-third supported fresh thinking. Nevertheless, 10 percent wrote that the topic was neither relevant nor actual. Most of those contended: "The Bible is no longer relevant," "The Bible is only a school subject," "The Bible has no influence on my life," "We are secular."

The teachers who took part in this experiment said that the topic should be included in the curriculum, and that an experiment such as this one is worthless if not linked to the regular curriculum. This is indeed the point: the Bible curriculum in Israeli secular education, as dictated by the Ministry of Education, does not included chapters that are difficult to digest, such as the alleged destruction of Midian or Joshua's conquests.

This experiment illustrates my point. Difficult issues, not only exempla, should be taught and studied. If we wish to make Bible classes spaces for live social exchange, "difficult" cases and passages are essential for the debate. And without such a debate, without studying conflicting and uneasy passages, no critical discourse about values and justice can be undertaken.

Notes

1. E.g., Gen. 24:1-67; 29:1-30; See Alter 1981: 54–57.

2. For a discussion of the relation between these names, and of the name Heber (Judg. 4:11), which is also considered a name of Jethro, see Moor 1949: 33.

3. For a critical review of the reasons for this division, see Licht 1995: 113 (Heb.).

4. See also 2 Sam. 21:1-11; Levine 2000: 300–301. Joseph Ginat writes about *tashmish*—a desert punishment: Ginat 1987: 90–112.

5. Num. 25:6. This chapter, which begins with the whoredom of the Moabite women, continues with intimate relationships with one Midianite woman, and thereafter all the Midianite women are accused of the same sin. The medieval commentators explain the transition from Moab to Midian by an interchange of Midianites-Kinites, Moab, Amalek, and Edom: so Rashi, Maimonides, and Hizkuni for Num. 24:20-22. Modern criticism relates the change from Moab to Midian to the different sources integrated here: Num. 25:1-5 is attributed to JE, and the continuation to a priestly source. See Noth 1968: 194–99; Levine 2000: 279–85; Klingbeil 2007: 43–49.

6. בוא as in Gen. 16:2; קרב as in Gen. 20:4. And see BDB בוא e, 98; קרב a, 897.

7. Noth 1968: 33–35. Noth points out the early date of the stories of Moses and Jethro and relates them primarily to J, with additions from E. On the early date of the story, see also Stager 1998: 143.

8. According to Gray's analysis, the Priestly material is derived from at least two sources (1956: 380–87). Noth conjectures that Num. 25:1-5 is derived partly from J. In his view, the continuation of the chapter (vv. 6-18) is late and partly, though not entirely, appropriate to P; it contains different sources and late additions (1968: 195–99). See also Levine 2000: 283–300.

9. Noth 1968: 228–30; Sturdy 1976: 214–16; Levine 2000: 466. Levine considers that the source is definitely Priestly only from v. 13.

10. Japhet 1977: 286–99 (Heb.); Knoppers 2001: 28–30; Douglas 2002 (1966): 2–3, 14–19.

11. For instance, the deletion of the execution of the first two punishments (Num. 25:4-5), or the deletion of information about the events that followed the plague. See the *Massoratic Piska be-emtza pasuk* (Num. 25:19).

12. Milgrom (1990: XXXIV) compares the mention of camels, which were characteristic of Midian, in connection with spoils in Judg. 8:21.

13. According to Van Houten 1991: 154–65.

14. E.g., Num. 22:4, 7. In *Targum Jonathan* to Num. 22:4, Balak son of Tsipor is a Midianite king in Moab. See Ben David 2008: 78–88. (Heb.) about the connection between Midian and Moab from an archaeological point of view.

15. Stager 1998: 147–48; Alberts 1992: 50–52; McNutt 1994: 126; Knohl 2008: 78–90 (Heb.).

16. Noth 1968: 30–33; Stager 1998: 142–48; Blenkinsopp 2008: 131–40.

17. Redford 1992: 275–80; On *Eretz Hashasu Yehu*, see Hacohen 2006: 1–22. (Heb.).

18. Stager 1998: 143; Abramsky 1984: 128–34; Stager (1998: 145) claims that the ancient town of Qurayyah, in the northwest of Arabia, was their principal site in the heart of the land of Midian.

19. The mention of the enemies—Oreb, Zeeb, Zebah, and Zalmunna—in this connection (Ps. 83:11) proves that the reference is to the wars of Gideon.

20. Eusebius of Caesarea 2003: 143.

21. Soggin 1987: 105–7; see Ben David 2008: 78–88 on six Midianite sites east of the Dead Sea.

22. Some of her arguments are as follows: Midian was situated in the territory of the tribes of Manasseh and Issachar; Ophrah was the town of Gideon, and is similar to Epher son of Midian (Gen. 25:2); Epher was one of the families of the tribe of Manasseh (1 Chron. 5:24); Jether, like the name Jethro, was the firstborn son of Gideon (Judg. 8:20)—Payne 1983: 163–72.

23. Num. 24:20-21 marks the different attitudes to various Midianite tribes: they are mentioned in sequence—Amalek is doomed to extinction, while the attitude to the Kenites is favorable. According to 1 Kgs. 11:18, Midian helped Adad the Edomite, and this demonstrates hostility to the kingdom of David. See Liver 1974: 4:687 (Heb.); Aharoni 1974: 6:289–92 (Heb.); Soggin 1987: 105–8.

24. Na'aman 2005: 1–24; Finkelstein 2007: 73–84; Knohl 2008: 50–76.

25. Canaan was punished for the shameful deed done by his father, Ham (Gen. 9:22-27); Amon and Moab were cursed because of their mothers' incest (Gen. 19:30-35).

26. Even though it is hinted that Balaam was responsible for this plot, the women are held responsible.

27. Rashi: "Aimed at the male parts of Zimri and her female parts"; Hizkuni: "To her stomach (*kevata*) = to her pudenda (*nakvuta*)." See Milgrom 1990: 215.

28. Phinehas is mentioned in 1 Chron. 9:19-20 as commander of the temple guard. See Milgrom 1990: XXXIII.

29. Licht (1995: 43–46) discusses these interpretations in the light of the context. Since Phinehas was commended for his zealousness for God, and since zealousness for God was required as a reaction to idolatry, prostitution, and intercourse with foreign women, he draws conclusions about what went on in the tabernacle. Levine 1990: 296–97, summing up these interpretations and others, mentions the connection that some surmised with Mesopotamian ritual prostitution (ἱερὸς γαμός), and rejects them all, on the grounds that the principal issue in the story of Ba'al of Peor is the religious rebellion against Yahweh.

30. On her action's accordance with the ceremonial norm of adoption, see Malul 1988: 480n109 (Heb.).

31. The book of Chronicles specifically mentions marriage with sons and daughters of foreign parents, but considers them to be Israelites. Japhet 1977: 286–99.

32. Abraham Melamed maintains that one of the characteristics of the black person in the Bible is his or her otherness. See his discussion of the black woman in Melamed 2002: 68, 202–8 (Heb.).

33. See above, under the heading "Origins."

34. Rashi on Judg. 18:30; and see Burney 1970: 435.

35. This is similar to the purification of the four hundred virgins of Jabesh Gilead, who were given to Benjamin as wives and were not slaughtered like their fellow townspeople (Judg. 21:12-14), and to Pharaoh's command to cast into the Nile all the sons who were born to the Israelites, but to let the daughters live (Exod. 1:22).

36. Deut. 21:10-13. And see Smith 1994: 316–19. Smith cites Numbers 31 as a foundation story for accounts of genocide.

9

Numbers 25 and Beyond

Phinehas and Other Detestable Practice(r)s

Anthony Rees

THIS MUSIC: BEGINNING WITH EZRA

In Ezra 9, having returned to Jerusalem from captivity in Babylon and finding that the "holy seed ha[d] mixed itself with the peoples of the lands" (Ezra 9:1), Ezra is appalled (9:4). His response takes the form of a lamenting prayer (vv. 6–15), which is really a sermon, addressing what he perceived as faithlessness on the part of the returned exiles and those who had not been deported. Ezra 9 three times uses the word *to'ebhah*, "abomination," or as the NIV renders it, "detestable practices." Ezra makes clear his view on the state of Judahite society and institutes a series of social reforms to purify the nation once more. The story we read in Numbers 25, which tells of an Israelite man and a Midianite woman speared through on the occasion of their marital embrace, is in effect an illustration of Ezra's reform. It is clear through the way the story is told who we are to believe the detestable practice(r)s are.

While Ezra's words, as translated by the NIV Translation Committee, are the inspiration for the title of this paper, it should be clear that I am interested in reading against the colonial ideology brought to bear. The paper itself is guided by a story told by an Australian aboriginal elder. Indeed, it is a story told to him by his mother. The story is brutal, bringing together three images of abuse and violence committed against Australian aboriginal people in the first half of the nineteenth century. These three images will be put in dialogue with three biblical texts with which there are clear resonances.

This methodological practice is not without precedent, or problems. In some respects, it is contrapuntal, a musical term borrowed by Edward Said (Said 1994: 59) to describe the practice of reading two texts together, from both sides of the colonial collision. This practice is consistently championed in biblical studies by R. S. Sugirtharajah (Sugirtharajah 2012: 143). Of course, using the Bible in such a way presents its own unique problems, it being in some way the great legitimating tool of colonialism while itself being a witness to the experience of colonization. The Ezra text already cited gives expression to this dilemma: Jerusalem has been razed by one empire, and another empire appoints Ezra to rebuild. The citizens of Jerusalem continue to have foreign rule imposed on them, Babylonian rule having given way to Persian, whose own practices are said to be detestable. This imposition of foreign rule is, in some sense, the very definition of colonialism.

In contrapuntal music, different musical lines are woven together, with themes developed side by side. Melodies appear time and time again, perhaps disguised by different timbres or registers, perhaps played by a different instrument; but as the music progresses, the melodies converge: after all, contrapuntal music—in the manner of its great master, J. S. Bach—is consonantal, the tension of dissonance always and only temporary, a part of the building of drama that will be resolved in the end. Perhaps, then, *contrapuntal* may be an inappropriate term for reading colonial texts. Are we necessarily reading for consonance? For resolution? Of course, these questions assume the consonance that ultimately characterizes contrapuntal music, but such an assumption need not be made. Indeed, the word itself lends itself to the expression of dissonance, in that one "point" (*puntus*) is pitted "against" (*contra*) another.

A Cross-Textual Approach and the Reading "I"

Perhaps it may be better to describe this approach as "cross-textual," a term favored by Archie Lee, who articulates the goal of such an exercise as "each text . . . illuminat[ing] the other" (Lee 1999a: 199). That is, each text brings new ways of understanding the underlying complexity that gives rise to each; reading two texts together allows each to (in)form how we read the other. Rather than working in counterpoint, we look at one text from the vantage of another, before leaping (crossing) the divide and peering back to where we jumped from. So in this model, the texts continue to exist independently from each other, even as they come together in the creation of a new (con)text.

Lee's project is to read Asia (a social "text") with/against the Bible (Lee 1999: 161). The present essay reads a variety of biblical texts with/against the experiences of Australian aboriginal people in the colonial period. Are these two texts related in any way? Certainly there is much that separates them, geography and time by no means the least significant differences between them. One set of texts has been, and indeed continues to be, used as religious literature; the other is the recollection of an individual. However, there is a mutuality of experience that crosses both and so enables the two texts to be crossed through the mediation of reading.

In reading this way, it is important for me to be clear about who I am: a white, middle-class Australian man with a touch of English ancestry. The two primary texts under consideration bear on me in different ways. As a white Australian, I believe the mistreatment of aboriginal people, both historically and its aftermath, which continues down to the present day, is a reality that demands our attention. As a Christian, indeed, as a church minister, I have been shaped by the Bible as a formative text. Its difficult passages continue to trouble me as I seek to make sense of this book that comes from a different time and place, yet which continues to inhabit our world. Given my interest in postcolonial studies, my whiteness is of course an issue. With Daniel Smith-Christopher, I ask "What is a white, [Christian] liberal to do?" And with him, too, I respond, "to listen to, engage and support our colleagues from more or less dissimilar backgrounds or social locations" (Smith-Christopher 2008: 132). To be silent on these issues is to be complicit; so with a measure of humility, I offer my thoughts, hoping that they may in some way contribute to a conversation that leads to understanding, to reconciliation, to a better world.

ABUSE OF ABORIGINAL WOMEN IN AUSTRALIA

They spent most of the day raping the women, most of them were then tortured to death by sticking sharp things like spears up their vaginas until they died. (Roberts 1981: 19)

The sexual abuse of indigenous women is highly documented in the history of colonial Australia. Roberts notes that similar events to the ones found in the story cited (from northeastern Victoria) occurred throughout the interior of New South Wales, where communities were spread out and isolated. With no equitable recourse to the law, such crimes were largely ignored, the victims left to suffer both the savagery of the detestable crime and the injustice of the legal system, which likened their evidence to the chattering of the orangutan (Roberts 1981: 20).

This view of aboriginal people as chimps was widespread. A letter to *The Australian* newspaper in 1838 says this very thing: "I look on the blacks as a set of monkeys" (Elder 1988: 83). Of course, this blatant lack of respect for the aboriginal people both forms and informs white attitude toward them in a cruel circularity: We don't respect them, and so we treat them disrespectfully. Or, using our terms: We think they are detestable, and so we treat them detestably. The letter goes on, "The earlier they are exterminated from the face of the earth the better. I would never consent to hang a white man for a black one" (Elder 1988: 83). In November 1838, men were tried in the Supreme Court in Sydney for the murder of twenty-eight aboriginal people. The evidence was overwhelming; the chief justice acknowledged that a heinous crime had been committed, referring to the aboriginal people as "fellow creatures" and reiterating that the life of a black person was as precious and valuable under the law as that of a white person. In just fifteen minutes, the jury found the perpetrators not guilty. Thankfully, some of the men were retried and with the same evidence were later found guilty and sent to be hanged. They confessed their crimes, their moral defense resting on their ignorance of the fact that killing aboriginals was illegal. On the street, it seemed that the citizens of New South Wales agreed with them (Elder 1988: 92–94).

But we return to the matter of the rape and cold-blooded execution of aboriginal women. Most commonly, "rape" is used in discussion of forced intercourse; it describes an act of overpowering and domination. The effects on the victim are of course catastrophic on all levels. The act is a violation of human dignity, an act of dehumanization, so perhaps we should be unsurprised to find such acts in the history of colonization, itself a project built on assumed power and superiority.

On a broader scale, rape is a weapon of war and conquest. It destabilizes, even destroys the community that suffers from it. The children born of the illicit unions are routinely ostracized from their communities and families, and create significant problems for family systems, particularly those based on patriarchal figures. Discussing the rape of Dinah in Genesis 34, Helena Zlotnick Sivan notes that a woman's great power is the ability to generate patriarchs, and so to perpetuate or disrupt patterns of succession (Sivan 2001: 74). Aboriginal society is based around clearly defined, intrafamilial behavior, requiring certain categories of kin to avoid each other (Howie-Willis 1994a: 356). For example, brothers and sisters must avoid social contact, or should behave in formal, patterned ways. So too the relationship with the mother-in-law is a well-established taboo through much of Australia (Duncan 1994: 978–80). Marriages were generally contractually organized, partners brought together who met certain kinship rules (Howie-Willis 1994b: 664). Acts of rape therefore cut a swathe through these family systems, doing untold damage to women and their communities, and decimating important cultural values and norms.

The violent and degrading sexual exploitation of aboriginal women fits neatly within the postcolonial concept of ambivalence. The idea that an aboriginal woman could be married to a white man was almost implausible, given that the prevailing wisdom was that it would be "degrading to the man, even in the instance where the man was of a very low type" (Roberts 1981: 26). Such views were common in contemporary scientific journals. One such journal, *Science of Man*, declared in 1907 that "hybrid and mongrel mixtures of mankind are as unsatisfactory as those of the lower animals and they usually degenerate and become extinct" (Roberts 1981: 26). A mother to such children bore no rights to them, and her children were almost universally taken from her. It was thought that the white blood in their veins gave the children some cause for hope, but only away from the degrading influence of their mother (Roberts 1981: 27). Despite this, the absence of white women in the early days of settlement seemed to ensure the enslavement of aboriginal women, who were often locked up for the use of their owners and their owners' staff, traded between cattle stations, forced into labor, and isolated from their communities. In every way, they were put to shame.

Raping women from outside your group is not a practice confined to the classical colonial period. It is an ancient practice that "speaks to one of the most basic dilemmas in human social relations—namely, how to steer the proper course between endogamy and exogamy" (Niditch 1993: 107). Here is the "them-us" dualism that is so destabilized by the theory of ambivalence. The difference that is meant to keep us apart is in some way alluring. Desire and derision are never too far apart, and when issues of power are involved—that is, when there is not an embrace of the other—the consequences, for the colonized, are tragic. "Just as proper marital relations are constructive for peacemaking, relations formed by rape . . . are destructive" (Niditch 1993: 107).

Our story of aboriginal experience doesn't merely end with the rape of women though. The story quite graphically describes acts of murder; the women are literally raped to death, reminding us of the story of the Levite's concubine in Judges 19. The murder is accomplished by the spearing of women's vaginas, and here we come close to the story of Cozbi, Zimri, and Phinehas.

Cozbi: Murder and Rape in Numbers 25

Now, a man from the sons of Israel came, and he brought a Midianite woman into his brothers in view of Moses, and in view of the entire congregation of the sons of Israel. They were weeping at the entrance of the tent of meeting. And Phinehas, son of Eleazer, son of Aaron the Priest saw, and he stood up from the midst of the congregation and he took a spear in his hand. He went after the man of Israel, into the tent and he pierced through the two of them, the man of Israel and the woman, in(to) her stomach. (Num. 25:6-8)[1]

On the surface, the relationship between Zimri and Cozbi appears to be that of the newlywed couple coming to their new home for the consummation of their new marriage. What we appear to have is a proper marital arrangement between two families. Such relationships were not unknown in Israel. Moses, Israel's leader, was married to Zipporah, the daughter of a Midianite priest. There is nothing in our tale to suggest that anything has happened out of order. So the rape of Cozbi is not effected by her new husband, but rather by the zealous priest Phinehas, who rapes Cozbi to death. The spear, a great phallic symbol if there ever was one, penetrates Cozbi and causes her death.

The physical point of Cozbi's penetration is an interesting conundrum. Different versions have translated the difficult Hebrew *el-qobhatah* in a variety of ways. Most commonly, this is rendered "through the/her belly" (for instance JPS, NRSV) or "through the body" (WEB). However, other translations see a more aggressively sexual act taking place. For example, the 1899 Douay-Rheims translation suggests "through the genitals." Such a choice is not without precedent. Stefan Reif's article "What Enraged Phinehas" alerts us (Reif 1971: 202) to an ancient tradition stretching back to the Babylonian Talmud and other rabbinic sources that read this as a penetration of Cozbi's genitals. Other sources—the LXX, Peshitta, and Vulgate choose to render the word as "womb," which too has a sexual connotation. It is far different to penetrate a womb than a belly. *Targum Onqelos* uses מעא, *me'a'*, a form that most often refers to the belly, bowels, or intestines, but that may also be rendered "womb" (Jastrow 1903: 812). For instance, *Targum Jonathan* of Isa. 49:1 uses this same form, translating "when I was in my mother's *womb* he named me."

Phinehas's action, as we read, must be seen as more than an act of blind rage or, as the text puts it, zeal. Rather, the death of Cozbi in this manner is highly symbolic. Her textualized death, in such an act, is sexually related again: violence serves as an official, or perhaps better, ideological delegitimation of her relationship with an Israelite. The text tells its readers that it is acceptable to treat foreign women in this way.

Controlling the sexuality of foreign women is an obvious ploy of the colonizing power. If you control what, if any, children the women produce, you control the sort of society you wish to build. This of course brings Ezra's prayer-cum-sermon of Ezra 9 into focus, where foreign wives and their children are to be put away for the sake of the purity of the holy seed. Is this too far removed from the experience of Australian aboriginal women and their children? Sivan suggests that underlying the story of Cozbi, Zimri, and Phinehas is a process of redefining family and society (Sivan 2001: 78). It perfectly illustrates the unspoken terror of Ezra's sermon. The same must surely be said of our elder's story. The tragedy is, of course, that the "putting away" of foreign women has continued to be far more difficult in practice than in rhetoric. It is exactly Cozbi's foreignness that is so appealing and that, sadly, is a matter of tragedy for her. The irony of Cozbi's story is that even though she suffers such a tragic, violent death, her virgin Midianite sisters are spared in the ensuing war against Midian. Derision and desire are never too far apart.

BACK TO AUSTRALIA: RAPE THE WOMEN, KILL THE BABIES

> I lived because I was young and pretty and one of the men kept me for himself, but I was always tied up until I escaped to another land to the west. (Roberts 1981: 20)
>
> My mother would sit and cry and tell me this: they buried our babies in the ground with only their heads above the ground. All in a row they were. Then they had a test to see who could kick the babies' heads off the furtherst [sic]. One man clubbed a baby's head off from horseback. (Roberts 1981: 19)

It seems implausible that there could be a more detestable act than the one described above. The actions of the settlers are despicably cruel and appallingly calculated. If anything could be worse than what is recalled above, it must surely be the trauma of having to remember it. This story is told because there was someone, an unnamed mother, who was a witness to it, and whose life was lived haunted by the things she had seen.

Atrocities against children in the theater(s) of war are a common practice these days. Genocide, ethnic cleansing, and other such detestable acts have been widespread in the latter part of the twentieth century: from the killing fields of Rwanda through to the Serbian carnage wreaked on Bosnia,[2] the child soldiers of the Tamil Tigers and the still-untold stories of Afghanistan, Iraq, and so on. Children, those who have no part in any battle or conflict, seem to be more vulnerable than ever before. Even those who escape death do not escape the effects of war: orphaned, made homeless, destitute, disowned, they become a shame to their communities (Boniface-Malle 2008: 77).

KILL THE BABIES: BACK TO THE HEBREW BIBLE

But we are wrong to assume such actions are new in our world. There is a strong biblical tradition of violence against children, both real and imagined. 1 Sam. 15:3 records the king, Saul, ordering the ruthless slaying of the Amalekites, saying they are to be "utterly destroyed," including the *yoneq*, the suckling ones. The verb "utterly destroy" here (Hebrew *h-r-m* Hif.) is also the root of *herem* ("ban"), which lends the extermination a sacred element. Those things that come under the ban are devoted to YHWH (Niditch 1993: 28–55). Verse 15:8 records that all the people were put to the sword, though some of the more valuable sheep, cattle, and fatlings were spared. As the narrative is told, it was in sparing the life of these animals that Saul's kingship began to unravel.

In 2 Kgs. 8:12, Elisha predicts that young men, little ones, and even pregnant women will be put to the sword by a rampant Hazael. This instance is slightly different from the example in 1 Samuel, in that the Samuel example comes to us as a direct order from the king, and an unspoken assumption that his orders are followed. In Kings, Elisha is speaking of something that may come to be, rather than issuing an order. Nonetheless, Hazael goes onto to become a king, as Elisha predicts, and is responsible for the oppression of Israel. Again, we are left to assume that Elisha's predictions come to pass.

Moving to the writing prophets, the nature of the delivery changes once again. Hosea 14:1, in an oracle against Israel, declares that their "little ones will be dashed in pieces and their pregnant women ripped open." This is the second instance of this image in Hosea, the first coming at 10:10,[3] though in this instance there is no ripping open of pregnant women, just dashing in pieces of little ones. So, too, in Nah. 3:10, a remembrance is made of infants dashed in pieces as a result of the exile of Thebes. Surely, Nahum seems to suggest, Nineveh should expect the same.

Clustered together in this fashion, it is clear that the image of children being killed in such cold-blooded fashion was simply a part of the practice of ancient warfare or, perhaps, a part of the rhetoric that surrounded warfare (Goldingay 2008: 609). Either way, the idea is detestable. This tradition takes a cruel twist in Psalm 137.

> O Daughter Babylon, you devastator!
> Happy shall be they be who pay you back
> what you have done to us!
> Happy shall they be who take your little ones
> and dash them against the rock! (Ps. 137:8-9)

The style of discourse here is telling. The psalm is an act of remembrance, of recollection, and looks forward to recompense. But as a psalm, its language is metaphorical, poetic. The previous examples talk of the killing of children in similarly poetic forms. While this psalm takes up the oracular imagery of the prophets, the examples that form part of the narrative account of Israel's history contain no such concrete descriptions of the murder of the children (Goldingay 2008: 609). Othmar Keel points out that Middle Eastern writing much prefers such concrete imagery, but that such images often signify something far greater than reality. The suggestion is that "the little ones" or "children" actually represent the ruling class that perpetuates the dynasty, and so the verse may be rendered "Happy is he who puts an end to your self-renewing domination," which is far less troubling than the actual image offered (Keel 1978: 9). Yet it is the image offered that concerns us. Why this image? Why this sick fantasy of violence against children?

Allen suggests that the "spiritual framework of the psalmist" provides a key to understanding this image (Allen 2002: 309). Such images are inextricably linked with the theological concepts of the chosen nation, of the territory possessed by divine right, of the holy city and its corollary, holy war. Such passionate nationalism is considered a virtue in the Old Testament record. The desolation of Jerusalem, the ignominy of the exilic experience, is an affront to YHWH, and so the psalmist's lament is related not only to those things the community has experienced but also to the sin committed against YHWH, the killing of the children coming in some way to represent "satisfaction of divine justice" (Allen 2002: 310). The act of speaking the psalm, of performing the remembrance, is an act of clinging to historical identity in the face of humiliation and distress. It is in the expression of such violent fantasy that the lust for revenge is sated and that such hopes are committed to the god of (presumed) universal justice, so that even those who mouth such things submit themselves to this justice. Actually, as Goldingay suggests, this is even more than hopefulness: in the end, this is an expression of confidence in YHWH's willingness to fulfill the promises made by the prophets (Goldingay 2008: 610).

Such arguments can only be made by those who have such atrocities in their sacred texts, and these arguments are presumably of shallow comfort to those who exist within the communities that are the supposed victims of such imagined violence. As we have established, this psalm does not devise in itself the most detestable image it can fathom. Instead, it borrows from prophetic tradition[4] (Goldingay 2008: 610), which in turn develops an older, less graphic narrative tradition in which children become the target of imperial aggression.

It is surely no surprise that such brutal, now canonized images continue to cause tension and violence as they are held up as sacred and authoritative.

To this point, we have been consumed by the image of the murdered children. As awful as this is, it is at least matched by the description of the perpetrators. *'Ashre* is an important word in the Psalter. Indeed, it is the first word of the psalter, an instance where it is traditionally translated as "happy" or "blessed": so, for instance, in the NRSV, "Happy are those . . ." Sigmund Mowinckel saw no difference between *'ashre* and the more common term for blessing, *barukh*, though Hans Kraus discerns a more secular tone in the former. Happiness never refers to God, whereas blessing demands certain behaviors (Cited in Cazelles 1974: 445–58).

Athalya Brenner, who reads this psalm with Jan T. Gross's book *Neighbours*, a story of the total destruction of a Jewish community in Poland in 1941, argues persuasively for a translation of *'ashre* as "praised" (Brenner 2003: 90–91). Indeed, she argues that the choice of the translation/understanding of "happy" or "blessed" as the first word of the Psalter is ideological, despite a long-honored tradition. However, either of the traditional choices presents a significant ethical dilemma for readers of Psalm 137. Are we content that those who murder children can be either happy or blessed? Even as an act of revenge, surely there is nothing uplifting in the destruction of innocents. Brenner's choice of "praised" softens the extremity of this outburst, noting that a verbal assault on the most defenseless of the enemy constitutes affirmation, in the sense of "righteousness" perhaps (see Psalm 1), and/or is praiseworthy for the avenger, but does not in any way solve the moral problem. Nonetheless, it is altogether different to suggest that the perpetrator of violence may actually be "happy" about the cruel actions, or in some divine way "blessed" on account of them (Brenner 2003: 91).

What we are speaking of is a verbal or textualized fantasy of violence. It is one thing to talk about, or to write about, committing such horrors, but it is another thing altogether to carry it out. The concluding verses of Psalm 137 call for revenge, but there appears to be little if any evidence that such atrocities were committed against Jewish children[5] (Brenner 2003: 84–85). The textualized image of the crushed children, then, serves as a symbol to remember the catastrophe of the exilic experience and the desire for revenge, without the actual intention of fulfilling the detestable wish that the symbol represents.

The great tragedy of this image is that in our story of aboriginal recollection, the brutality moves from the fantasy of one's[6] mind, from the pages of a book, to cruel, calculated execution of a barbaric crime.[7] The grim reality of this story is that the various understandings of the psalmist's *'ashre* appear to resonate within the performance of the psalm in colonial Australia. This story inverts the relationship of the psalm. The Psalm speaks from the position of the subject, desiring revenge against the imperial aggressor. The Australian story, however, is about the unbridled expression of colonial aggression, a clear statement of presumed superiority. The depravity of the action is in the game that it becomes. Not content with the destruction of innocent lives, not content with committing this atrocity in the faces of the children's family, the killing becomes a contest. One can imagine the banter and laughter that accompanies sporting contests—the urging on, the sledging, the laughter. In a sick, detestable way, these murderers enjoy their work, they are *'ashre*, happy. Sadly, as we will see in the following section, community attitudes toward aboriginal death was at best ambivalent. Many statements were made about the uselessness of the aboriginal people. Many wished for their extermination. So again, these men may well have been *'ashre*, praised. And as Mark Brett has shown, colonial attitude toward aboriginal people, even among the missionary movement, reflected a belief in the colonizers' divine right to their land and to the widespread belief that aboriginal people were degraded, "on the level of the beasts" (cited in Brett 2009: 12). Perhaps, in a sick way, these men had a sense of being *'ashre*, blessed.

Castrate and Kill the Men: Australia

They tied the men's hands behind their backs, then cut off their penis and testes and watched them run around screaming until they died. (Roberts 1981: 19–20)

In recent times, it has become common, or perhaps less uncommon, to hear about women who have cut off the penises of men who have cheated on them. The dismembering of the offending man has become the ultimate act of female retribution. It is an enormously powerful statement about sexual control: the ones who were unable to control themselves have the tool of their indiscipline forcibly removed. The result is that manhood—that is to say, the thing that makes one so obviously a man—is lost, or more specifically, taken.

But the penis is more than the marker of manhood. It also plays a reproductive function. In an incisively symbolic way, slicing off a penis is a way of saying that this is a person who does not deserve the right to have children; or put differently, no child deserves this man as a father. Even more coarsely, we don't want the progeny of this man to be a part of our society. Unborn, even unconceived children are in some way condemned by this action.

Colonial attitude toward Australian aboriginals, as we have already seen, was contemptuous and violent. Already we have heard the story of the women, so dreadfully raped and murdered in such brutal, detestable, sexually violent ways. But here too we have a story of sexual violence committed against the men of aboriginal Australia. What we have is a story of rape against men as well.

What differentiates this story from the example of the wronged woman exacting her revenge is that the aboriginal men were not perpetrators of violence against their assailants. Instead, the invaders of the colonial project mutilate the men in a way that sends the same symbolic message: their sexuality is controlled, and furthermore, their women's children will not be theirs. This is, quite simply, a method of racial extermination. Once again: if you control sexual activity, you are able to go a long way toward shaping the society that you want to produce or, more pointedly, eliminating the parts of society that you find undesirable.

UNMANNED MEN: THE HEBREW BIBLE

No one whose testicles are crushed or whose penis is cut off shall be admitted to the assembly of the Lord. Those born of an illicit union shall not be admitted to the assembly of the Lord. Even to the tenth generation, none of their descendants shall be admitted to the assembly of the Lord. (Deut. 23:1-2)

These verses introduce a series of prohibitions against people who may enter *qehal yhwh*, the "assembly of the Lord" (vv. 1-8). The *qahal* is the group of people able to join together for worship, for reading and hearing the law, for the celebration of religious feasts, and so on. In this sense, it is a smaller, more exclusive group than the entirety of the people of Israel, which necessarily includes people that fall outside the parameters set by this legal code. Indeed, the latter half of Deuteronomy 23 deals with concerns around the *machaneh*, the "camp," in which the entirety of the population lives together. Verses 3-8 go on to exclude other groups on purely national grounds, with varying degrees of severity.[8] Clearly what is being promoted is a "holy seed" people, much like the society envisioned by Ezra. The standards once required only for the priesthood (Lev. 21:20) are now expanded and required across all of the assembly.

Why this prohibition? Why must YHWH's men[9] be fully equipped? Most commentators see this as a regulation against those who have been mutilated in the context of the worship of other gods (McConville 2002: 348), and so Peter Craigie suggests that those who have suffered these injuries as a result of illness or accident are most likely not in violation of this law (Craigie 1976: 296). Consequently, their view tends toward interpreting this text using the holy seed ideology of Ezra: these men are disqualified because of prior allegiances to other deities. But of course, without functioning testicles or a penis, reproduction is impossible in any event, and so these men provide no danger to the holy seed of Israel. Perhaps, then, these prohibitions are more about purity and order, and are consequently closer to the Holiness Code provisions from Leviticus. Such men are to be excluded because of some injury that places them outside the realm of the "whole"; they are blemished, permanently, and so they are excluded, permanently.

Jione Havea suggests another, simpler reason. These people are not real men.[10] They are unable to penetrate or be productive (Havea 2010: 11). Having had their tools of productivity taken away, having been "dismembered," these men are relegated to the sidelines of the Israelite community, never to penetrate the boundary of the *qahal* again, never to be fully functioning members. It seems unlikely that one with a sliced-off penis would live very long anyway; certainly the aboriginal story suggests that this was an act of murder, although one who had suffered from crushed testicles almost certainly would not die immediately. Either way, these men were to be excluded from the worshiping community, unwelcome at the religious feasts, never to hear the very law that made them outcasts.[11]

Deuteronomy 23:2 deals with those born of an "illicit union" (NRSV). Such people, too, are barred from entering *qehal yhwh*. The word used is *mamzer*, a form that is used in only one other place in the Tanakh, Zech. 9:6, where the NRSV translates it as "mongrel," suggesting some form of colloquial expression for a mixed race. Older translations render it here as "bastard." Commentators are agreed that the expression involves children born to a relationship that breaks the "prohibited degrees of relationship" (Wright 1996: 245), and so goes beyond the notion of the bastard as the child born out of wedlock. This includes, as McConville recognizes (McConville 2002: 348), marriage with foreigners, citing Deut. 7:3. Craigie sees a cultic element: that is, according to him the term might denote children born of cultic prostitutes, thereby conceived in an environment directly related to foreign religion (Craigie 1976: 297). For ten generations, the descendants of these "bastards" are to be excluded. The form, *mamzer*, seems to lean on the element *zur*, meaning "foreign," "strange," even "forbidden." This word is commonly used of the foreign woman, the *zarah* (Prov. 2:16 and elsewhere), and so also suggests a feminization of sorts and a relation to the *mamzer*.

What is evident is a concern to promote purity and wholeness and a lack of willingness to include those, nor the direct descendants of those, who fail to fit within established guidelines. Indeed, as Deut. 7:4 suggests, any tolerance of intermarriage will lead to swift punishment and quick destruction.

All of this serves to bring us back to our aboriginal story. The aboriginal men have their penises forcibly removed. In the context of these verses from Deuteronomy, those who are inside take matters into their own hands, and, cutting off the men's penises, they make sure of their exclusion. What is at stake here is not membership in *qehal yhwh,* but there certainly is a sense in which membership or participation in the community is at stake. The dismembered men, robbed of their (re)productivity, are no longer "real" men and are condemned to a life on the outside of the privileged community. The blemish, inflicted on them by insiders, serves to keep them perpetually outside.

What is more, the children born of the aboriginal women will now inevitably be seen as a *mamzer,* born to illegitimate relationships and condemned to life as outsiders. They will be born of "mixed" relations, as children of rape, as mongrels, as half-castes, as misbegotten children. Sadly, these children will be thought of as detestable, though it will be the actions of their fathers where the true crime lies. In a tragic way, like the foreign wives and children of Ezra 10, aboriginal children were "put away," by which I mean taken away from their mothers to be cared for by the very people who looked down on them for their aboriginal blood. They too become excluded, their lives lived outside the privileged community, always looking forward to a time when—perhaps—they may be allowed to enter.

Back to Ezra, by Way of a Conclusion

We began with the words of Ezra 9 ringing in our ears: remove yourselves from the (results of your) detestable practices! Perhaps we have not come that far, seeing as how we end with Ezra 10, and the putting away of foreign wives and their half-caste children. I hope, though, that the notion of both who and what is detestable has been subverted.

Cheryl Kirk-Duggan, in the introduction to *Pregnant Passion,* writes:

> Violence is that which violates, destroys, manipulates, corrupts, defiles and robs us of dignity and true personhood. Violence is the use of thought and deed within a continuum of the physical, the philosophical and the psychological that oppresses and robs an individual or community of their gift of freedom and the sacredness

of their person. Violence is a practice of idolatry: that which defames God's created order. (Kirk-Duggan 2003: 3)

We have considered a number of texts that have, at their core, the very type of thing Kirk-Duggan describes: acts of violence intended to damage individuals and communities physically, philosophically, and psychologically. We have read of innocent victims, robbed of their dignity and their personhood, who have had their sacredness demeaned. We have witnessed the defamation of the sacral nature of the created order.

It is this violence that is the truly detestable thing. It is this violence that we must condemn. It is the victims of this violence that we must stand with, lest we too, like Phinehas and the rest, become detestable practice(r)s.

Notes

1. Author's translation. All biblical material that follows is taken from the NRSV.

2. As I write, former Serbian general Radko Mladic is on trial at the Hague for war crimes. At a football match between Australia and Serbia just in the last few weeks, a banner was unfurled that cried for his release, a sure sign that violence lingers not far from the surface.

3. See also Isa. 13:16.

4. Goldingay notes that this prophetic tradition also images Judah's children as the victims of Babylonian violence. See Jer. 13:14 and 51:20-23.

5. This, as Brenner points out, stands in stark contrast to commentators' assertions that child killing was part of the mechanics of ancient warfare.

6. Albeit a "collective" one.

7. This too is the case in Brenner's article (following Gross's account), where the fantasy of the violence is played out against the Polish Jews of Jedwabne.

8. Of special interest to us is the harsh treatment leveled against the Moabites (See Num. 25:1-5). Their welfare or prosperity are not to be promoted "as long as you live" (v. 6).

9. Clearly, this prohibition is relevant only to those who have or have had a penis and testicles.

10. This echoes the idea of purity and wholeness mentioned previously. These men are "blemished," they are not "whole."

11. As Havea (2010: 11) playfully notes, perhaps such individuals would not, under the circumstances, have any desire to join such an assembly!

10

Indicting YHWH

Interpreting Numbers 25 in Oceania

Nāsili Vaka'uta

The Bible, of all books, is the most dangerous one, the one that has been endowed with the power to kill. (Bal 1989:8)

The Bible does not demystify or demythologize itself. But neither does it claim that the stories it tells are paradigms for human action in all times and places. . . . Perhaps the most constructive thing a biblical critic can do toward lessening the contribution of the Bible to violence in the world, is to show that certitude is an illusion. (Collins 2003: 20, 21)

What I intend to do here is simple and straightforward.[1] First, I will begin with a brief overview of popular European depictions of Oceania, which will serve as a contextual platform for my reading of Numbers 25. Second, I will discuss Anne McClintock's concept of "porno-tropics," some aspects of which will also inform my reading. Third, I will reread Numbers 25 as an Oceanic islander, and from the perspective of island women.[2]

OCEANIA DEPICTED

Speaking of island women, I want you to ponder the following images of Polynesian women painted and/or taken by Europeans. (Viewer discretion is advised.)

Illustration 1

Illustration 2

Illustrations 1–2. Old depictions of Tongan women from the Godeffroy album.[3]

Illustration 3

Illustration 3. "The Seed of Areoi," by Paul Gauguin.[4]

Such sexualized representations of Polynesian women continue today in tourist literature distributed worldwide. I would like to make three points based on these images.

First, the visual and literary depictions of Oceania—by those who crossed our boundaries—are preoccupied with island women, as if there were no men in the islands. This is the colonial *feminization* of Oceania.

Second, island women are portrayed as promiscuous figures who offer themselves to be penetrated by imperial white male travelers/intruders. This is the colonial *sexualization* of island women. This imperial (mis)representation can be found in works like Margaret Mead's *Coming of Age in Samoa* (1928), which talks about the so-called sexual freedom of Samoan women, and Paul Gauguin's visual depiction of Tahitian women (*The Writings of a Savage* [1978], *Noa Noa* [2009], and *Gauguin Tahiti* [2011]) in nude and seminude states. The visual portrayals of women represent a common perception that Polynesia is a white man's paradise, a place of sexual freedom with women readily available to be viewed, and perhaps more.

Third, the *feminization* of Oceania has in some ways turned the region into what McClintock in her classic work *Imperial Leather* calls the "porno-tropics" of the European or imperial imagination.

The "Porno-tropic" Tradition

McClintock defines "porno-tropics" as the European tendency to sexualize foreign (non-European) women as "a fantastic magic lantern of the mind onto which Europe projected its forbidden sexual desires and fears" (McClintock 1995: 22). She also speaks of a "porno-tropic" tradition that goes as far back as European explorers such as Christopher Columbus.

In 1492, Columbus feminized the earth as a cosmic breast to which the epic male hero is a tiny, lost infant, yearning for the Edenic nipple. That image, according to McClintock, is invested with an uneasy sense of male anxiety, infantilization, and longing for the female body. At the same time, the female body is figured as *marking the boundary* of the cosmos and limits of the known world.

In the European porno-tropic tradition, unknown continents are depicted as "libidinously eroticized"; women are figured as the epitome of sexual aberration and excess. The hallmarks of the porno-tropic tradition are its obsession with the *feminization* of foreign lands and the *sexualization* of foreign women.

In the following, I summarize McClintock's description of the process of feminization.

First, feminized foreign lands are spatially spread for male exploration, then reassembled and deployed in the interests of imperial power.

Second, in feminized lands, women served as boundary markers, and female figures are planted like fetishes at the ambiguous points of contact. At the contact zone, women serve as mediating figures, by means of which men orient themselves in space as agents of power and knowledge.

Third, unknown lands are considered "virgin" territories, awaiting exploration, discovery, and naming. Feminizing terra incognita is a strategy of violent containment.

Fourth, feminizing foreign lands appears to be no more than a familiar symptom of male megalomania, and thus betrays acute paranoia and a profound, if not pathological, sense of male anxiety and boundary loss.

Fifth, in the feminization process, the erotics of imperial male conquest become also an *erotics of engulfment*. Feminizing foreign lands serves as a compensatory gesture, disavowing male loss of boundary by reinscribing a ritual excess of boundary accompanied by an excess of violence.

Sixth, the feminization of foreign lands represents a ritualistic moment in imperial discourse, as male intruders ward off fears of narcissistic disorder by reinscribing an excess of gender hierarchy.

Seventh, when travelers sailed beyond their charted seas, they entered a liminal condition: men in these states become marginal figures on the border between the known and unknown; they become creatures of transition and threshold—there they are in danger and emanate danger to others. Men at the margins usually resort to violence. At the margins, foreign lands are feminized and destined to be inseminated with the male seeds of civilization. At the margins, feminized land is renamed—naming is an extension of the male intruders and stakes their claim to the female body. At the margins, however, male anxiety and male crisis of identity are exposed.

Eighth, and finally, fear of engulfment by the unknown is projected onto colonized peoples, thus leading to imperial violence to ward off being engulfed.

These aspects of the feminization of foreign lands (and the whoring of foreign women) feature in biblical border-crossing narratives, and Numbers 25 is a vivid example.

Turning to Numbers 25

Numbers 25 opens with Israel encamping at Peor en route to Canaan. There the people (העם, *ha-'am*, presumably men, though women are not ruled out) pollute (חלל, *ḥ-l-l*) themselves by "whoring" (the JPS rendition of זנה, *z-n-h* Qal) with Moabite women (בנות מואב, *benot mo'ab*, "daughters [of] Moab"). Jacob Milgrom notes that this is the only occasion in the Hebrew Bible where the verb *z-n-h* takes a masculine subject (Milgrom 1990: 212). In this case, the *benot mo'ab* are not responsible for the situation. The narrator, however, points his finger to the latter. Pollution happens because the *benot mo'ab* invite the Israelites (*ha-'am*) to join them as they offer sacrifices to their gods. Those who accept the invitation "eat" (אכל, *'a-kh-l* Qal) with them, "bow down" (וישתחוו, *vayishtahawu*) to their gods, and "attach" (צמד, *ts-m-d* Nif.) themselves ("transferring allegiance"; Milgrom) to Ba'al. (The other gods remain nameless.) In the narrator's opinion, the "daughters of Moab" are as guilty as their Israelite male counterparts.

For this reason, YHWH's[5] anger is fired up (ויחר אף, *wayichar-'ap*), and Moses is ordered to "take all the heads of the people" (v. 4b, קח את כל ראשי העם; JPS reads: "take all the ringleaders") and "expose[6] them to YHWH before the sun" (v. 4c, והוקע אותם ליהוה נגד השמש; JPS reads: "have them publicly impaled before the Lord"). The wording of this verse is unclear, thus inviting other possible readings. First, it is possible that the command is holding the Israelite tribal leaders (ראשים, *rashim*) responsible for what their people (העם, *ha-'am*) had done (Grossman 2007: 57). Second, it is also likely that the reference here is to those who actually attached themselves to Baal; they are to be publicly executed. Such display of punishment would perhaps serve as deterrent. Third, it is likely still that the divine order demands the beheading of the people (העם). After all, they were the ones who whored with the *benot mo'ab* (25:1) and bonded with Baal (v. 3). This reading cannot be ruled out, given the intensity of YHWH's wrath,[7] which can only be averted by the shedding of the guilty blood.

Moses, instead of conveying YHWH's command directly to the people, consults the judges of Israel and gives them a license to kill those who were involved in the Peor affair. In addition, he offers a modified version of the divine order (v. 5b), by limiting the punishment to those responsible, but not all the people, as YHWH demands. Again, Moses alters the language of the punishment. The שפטים (*shophetim*, "judges") are told to kill (הרג, *h-r-g* Qal) those involved in the Peor affair, rather than to impale (יקע, *y-q-'* Hif.) them before the sun as YHWH commanded.

What appears to be a Moabite gesture of hospitality is ideologically (mis)construed as apostasy, and thus provokes YHWH to react violently. *Why is YHWH so angry? Who is YHWH really angry at?*

Verses 6-18 introduce a new event and new characters into the story: Zimri, Cozbi, and Phinehas. The target of attack is no longer the Moabites, but Midianites. There is also a notable gap between the preceding unit and this one. In 25:1-5, there is no indication of a plague as punishment for the Peor affair. Here, in 25:6-18, a certain plague is being referred to (vv. 8-9), though its nature is unclear. The two units are nonetheless connected by a common denominator: hostility toward all that is foreign (non-Israelite).

As the people have entered the religious space of the Moabites, so this Midianite woman enters into the camp of Israel as she accompanies her Israelite male companion. Neither entry poses a threat. The first (25:2) introduces the Israelites to the Moabite's way of worship and their typical ritual. The second (25:6) is possibly an attempt by the Israelite man to introduce his Midianite companion to his family and the Israelite way of worship, since they are at the entrance to the Tent of Meeting (פתח אהל מועד, *petach 'ohel mo'ed*).

Perhaps the two have just got married, and if that is the case, it raises the question of endogamy (Sivan 2001: 71). But if they are lovers, then they are adulterating within the boundary of the Israelite camp; the very act that causes YHWH's anger to burn in the preceding unit, and brings death upon the people. In either case, both are doomed to die. From this point forward, events move swiftly, and take a brutal turn.

The narrator tells us that the couple does not sneak into the camp. They enter in the sight of Moses and the weeping congregation. Nobody sees any cause for alarm, except Phinehas ben Eleazar ben Aaron. His reaction is described in a succession of five verbs: he saw, he rose, he took, he came, he pierced. These verbs epitomize an *act of terror*: he saw the couple; he rose up and took a spear in his hand; he followed them into their קבה (*qubbah*, "tent"); and he pierced them both through קבתה (*qobhatah*, "[her] belly").

By killing an innocent couple, according to the narrator, Phinehas has averted YHWH's burning anger (in the form of a plague; 8b). Given the cultic setting of the story, Phinehas's act may be seen as an atoning act for the sake of the community; the couple becomes the offering. From a Midianite standpoint, however, this barbarous act is no atonement at all.

This unit ends with the report of the number of deaths from the plague. About twenty-four thousands of the Israelites are killed for appreciating the ways of the Moabites. *Is this what the narrator calls aversion of YHWH's anger?* Such a mass killing of people because of their social and religious preferences is unbelievable to the modern reader. But that is how YHWH, at least from the narrator's vantage point, deals with adultery and apostasy. The deity who took Israel out of Egypt (without their asking) in the name of liberation has now decimated them for exercising their freedom. *If this is the manner of YHWH's liberation, I would rather stay in Egypt.*

Verses 10-13 open with the narrator's introduction to YHWH's speech to Moses. Terrified by Phinehas's act in the preceding unit, one may still have hope for divine intervention. But when YHWH speaks, instead of denouncing and punishing Phinehas's brutality, YHWH (like the narrator) redefines killing as *a zealous act of atonement*—a senseless murder is stamped with divine approval.

In addition to this divine approval, there is the granting of a dual pact: a pact of peace (v. 12, את בריתי שלום) and a pact of eternal priesthood (v. 13, ברית כהנת עולם). Both pacts are unique to Phinehas. Both may have shocked Moses, as YHWH had not granted him a personal pact of that magnitude. Here again, the political orientation of the text resurfaces, as YHWH's favor drifts away from Moses to Aaron's grandson. Such a grand affirmation of violence, from the victim's standpoint, offers only *words of terror. What is wrong with YHWH?*

The murdered Israelite and his Midianite companion, unnamed in life, are identified in death by the narrator as Zimri ben Salu (son of a Simeonite tribal leader) and Cozbi bat Zur (daughter of a Midianite chief [31:8]). Both are from important families, and have positions of honor in their respective communities.

What have they done to deserve such a terrible death? What is wrong with marrying a Midianite woman?

As if the death of Cozbi were not enough, YHWH now orders the destruction of her people: the Midianites. The fulfillment of this divine command is the concern of Numbers 31. The rationale behind this terrifying command is herein given (v. 18), thus providing closure to the text: because of the Peor affair, and Cozbi's affair with Zimri. *Is YHWH having a memory problem? Does YHWH not remember that the affair at Peor involved Moabites, not Midianites? Why should a whole nation be decimated because of an offense committed by one person? What is Cozbi's offense anyway?*

What's in Numbers 25 for Oceanic Women?

Let me retrace the orientation of the story.

First, the land is *feminized*—there is no reference to any Moabite male, only women. In contrast, the Israelite camp is *masculinized*. No female is mentioned (how boring!).

Second, the female figures mentioned (Moabite and Cozbi) are *sexualized*—they are portrayed as seductresses/prostitutes who are responsible not only for seducing and polluting Israelite males but also for the divine punishment that befalls the Israelite camp.

Third, male figures in Numbers 25 exhibit not only megalomania but also confusion and fear of engulfment. Because they are men at the margins, they exert, on the one hand, power and control as if they are stable people with lands. On the other hand, there are internal tensions among themselves (in the camp) simply because of foreign women.

Fourth, the deity, YHWH, is depicted as powerful, jealous, but violent—YHWH punishes the people violently, justifies the violent killing of Zimri and Cozbi with a pact of peace, and commands that the Midianites be harassed.

Fifth, violence against other peoples is justifiable as long as it is done in the name of YHWH. Ethnic cleansing is necessary for maintaining religious purity. In other words, to be with YHWH requires no free choice; *one has to be a faithful servant.*

As an Oceanic reader, I opt to drift away from YHWH's camp. I cannot sacrifice my freedom for a deity who offers legitimacy to violence. I cannot worship with a congregation that ignores the suffering of oppressed subjects like Zimri and Cozbi. I indeed cannot be so zealous for a god that finds joy in shedding innocent blood. I would rather dwell in Peor if entering the Promised

Land requires me to abandon my sanity and to annihilate those who rightly belong to that land. As an Oceanic islander, I yearn for freedom, but I would not pursue it to the detriment of others.

From the border of Peor to the shores of Oceania, Numbers 25 is a *pornotropic text* where foreign lands beg for *defeminization*, and foreign women—like those in Oceania—plead to be *desexualized*. With island women, YHWH deserves an *indictment* for tolerating and justifying violence.

A text like Numbers 25 poses a challenge to the reading task. One must not be lured by the ideology of the text. To do so would make the reader as guilty as those in the text itself. As John Collins aptly puts it, "There is much in the Bible that is not worthy of humanity, certainly much that is not worthy to serve as a model for imitation" (Collins 2003: 20).

Notes

1. A revised version of a paper delivered at the SBL Unit on Contextual Biblical Interpretation, SBL/AAR Annual Meeting, San Francisco, November, 19–22, 2011.

2. There is no claim here whatsoever that I am representing the views of the women of Oceania; neither am I "speaking *for* them." The view presented hereinafter is solely mine as a Tongan native, an Oceanic islander.

3. Courtesy of the Godeffroy Museum.

4. Courtesy of Wikimedia Commons.

5. YHWH is referred to strictly in this work as a character in the narrative rather than the revered God of Judaism. Likewise, ethnic groups like Israelites and Moabites are treated as social groupings within a story.

6. Here I am following the variant reading from the Greek (LXX) and Syriac (SyrVer).

7. For another opinion on the wording of v. 5, see Havea 2004: 46.

A Queer Womanist Midrashic Reading of Numbers 25:1-18

Wil Gafney

What makes an interpretation feminist?[1] A feminist interpretation is one in which gender forms a, if not the, critical lens through which the object—text, artifact, performance, culture, and so on—is interpreted. The gender lens is a multifocal tool, so gender as an interpretive medium includes gendering disclosed in and constructed by the text, artifact, performance, or culture being interpreted and the gender configurations and implications of those configurations of the interpreter.

Does "feminist interpretation" refer to the method or the hermeneutical lens one uses, or does it refer to both? A feminist interpretation is not a single method or hermeneutical lens. Feminist interpretation employs and deploys a variety of methodologies and lenses in addition to the gender lens. None of the literary, social, cultural, or religious texts, artifacts, or performances that we interpret is one-dimensional; neither are their interpreters one-dimensional.

Given the diversity of feminist scholarship in biblical studies, is it possible or desirable to speak of a single feminist method? It is possible to speak of a feminist method, but I believe it is the height of arrogance to speak of a singular feminist method.

These questions framed our discussion at the *Journal of Feminist Studies in Religion* section at the annual conference of the Society of Biblical Literature in 2011, and the initial, simple answers we gave trouble me, because they do not get at what I mean and understand by feminist or womanist interpretation. I have wrestled with these and similar questions in conversation with wonderful students, teachers, colleagues, congregants, and editors. Finally, it dawned on me: the difficulty I was having articulating what I mean by feminist and womanist interpretation was similar to the difficulty my aunt had when I asked her for one of my grandmother's recipes. She couldn't tell me how to make the dish, but she could show me. But I wasn't there. She had to make the dish herself and then reverse-engineer it because neither she nor my grandmother wrote their recipes down. They just cooked. Perhaps the hermeneutical equivalent of reverse engineering a recipe is *praxis*. Praxis is most simply the practice of an art or skill; in divinity school, I learned that praxis is best supplemented with reflection that leads to more praxis in an action-reflection cycle.

So to respond more deeply to the framing questions, I would like to borrow from the methodology of Katie Geneva Canon and offer a vignette modeling of a womanist and feminist methodology in my praxis repertoire. (Dr. Canon regularly frames her public lectures and academic presentations with vignettes as a womanist discursive practice.) I call it *womanist midrash*, combining the deployment of the African American sanctified imagination as a womanist and feminist interpretive lens with the broader tradition of rabbinic and postrabbinic tradition of midrash.

> While Israel was dwelling in Shittim, the people began to have unsanctioned-intimate-relationships [*liznot*] with the women of Moab. And the (Moabite) women invited the (Israelite) people to the sacrifices of the God of the (Moabite) women, and the people ate and bowed down to the God of the (Moabite) women. (Num. 25:1-2)[2]

Numbers 25 extends the previous Torah portrayals of foreign women as dangerously seductive to a new realm. The people, *ha'am*—an inclusive term that includes women and men—began to "whore" with Moabite women (see the Fox [1995] and GSJPS translations of *liznot*). The use of "people" suggests a large group between "some" and "all." (Num. 25:9 offers a possible tally of at least twenty-four thousand.) Adults, categorized by the ability to be sexually active, are indicated here. The Israelites are regularly accused of prostituting themselves with other gods or their intermediaries in the scriptures, for example, in Lev. 17:7; 20:6; Deut. 31:6; and Ezekiel 16 and 23. Worship of other deities is regularly characterized as adultery and prostitution, for example, in Jer. 5:7; Hos. 4:14; 1 Chron. 5:25. The charge of prostitution, from *z-n-h* Qal, can mean sex for money or worship of other deities or intermarriage with non-Israelite peoples. This last is accompanied by the presumption that intermarriage will lead the Israelite spouse to non-Israelite worship; interestingly, the canon does not presume authorized Israelite worship will draw outsiders into its fold. Yet all intermarriages are characterized as whoring; Yosef (Joseph),[3] Moshe (Moses), and David are among the prominent Israelites who escape being labeled whoremongers for their unions with non-Israelite women, as is Hosea (ch. 1), even though he marries a woman the text actually calls a whore. The notion is further complicated by the passages that call, after armed conflict, for Israelite men to abduct women and girls of non-Israelite peoples as breeding stock (see Num. 31:18; Deut. 20:14, 21:10-17; Judg. 21:10-12) in the name of God, without critique for the men in these unions; neither men nor the prepubescent girls whom they preferentially abduct or even abducted sexually experienced women are accused of *zenut*, "whoredom."

The Numbers 25 passage is unique in its assertion that the *people* of Israel are perversely intimate with the *women* of Moab, leaving open the possibility that both Israelite *women and men* are intimately involved with Moabite women (but not Moabite men) through its grammar: "While Israel was dwelling in Shittim, the people began to have unsanctioned-intimate-relationships with the (daughters) women of Moab."

There is no other comparable text even suggesting women's same-gender erotic activity in the Hebrew Scriptures. Other passages accuse the people as a whole of sexual (or sexualized religious) perfidy by describing Israel collectively as God's female spouse; and the foreigners in plural terms that indicate collective maleness (that is, the male Egyptian and Assyrian "lovers" and "warriors" in Ezekiel 23) or by specifying heterosexual unions, for example, in Exod. 34:16: "And you will take women from among their daughters for your sons, and their daughters who prostitute themselves to their gods will make your sons also prostitute themselves to their gods."

Conversely, Num. 25:1 can be understood as excluding women from the category "people" if the text is read as heteronormative, therefore referring only to male Israelites in relationship with Moabite women. However, this would read against the use of the term *ha'am* in Numbers and the remainder of the biblical corpus, where it is clearly an inclusive term. In any interpretive framework, this is a queer—in every sense of the word—text. The passage continues with the Moabite women inviting the people to participate in their religious rituals—again "people" is *ha'am* and gender inclusive. At these sacrificial feasts, the Israelite women and men willingly yield themselves to the Moabite God in the worship of Ba'al of Peor. Peor was the mountain from which Bil'am (Balaam) repeatedly blessed the people of Israel in the preceding chapters (22–24). He paid for those blessings with his life. I'll return to the relationship between Ba'al Peor and the God of Israel later.

The compression of time in this text makes it difficult to know how these events and relationships developed over time in the scenario envisioned by the text. The scant reference gives rise to many questions: Did the Israelites settle in or just near a Moabite community? Did the two peoples share grazing land, water sources, and markets? Was there regular daily contact between the two peoples? Did the Moabites welcome the Israelites to their community? Were there other peoples resident in the area? Did the Moabite women extend invitations to their sacred meals, as an expression of their culture, to welcome their new neighbors? Why did the Israelites find Moabite worship so compelling? Did any Moabites find Israelite worship compelling? What was the nature of the relationships between the Moabite women and Israelite women and men—were they sexual, marital and/or religiously but not physically intimate? For the authors and editors of the Numbers 25 text, the relationships between the peoples are deeply problematic, as signaled by the verb z-n-h used here, meaning sex for money in a literal sense and infidelity to the Israelite God in the broader sense. However, there is no suggestion that commercialized sex work is performed in the passage.

God through Moshe pronounces judgment on the Israelite people for these queer relationships. God calls for the "heads" of the people to be executed. The heads, or leaders of the people, are never defined in the text; they are presented as a group. There is no clear articulation of how many persons occupied this leadership role in the wilderness. (Ezra and Nehemiah will provide lists of these persons in their time—without attestations of gender—in their respective writings.) While they are traditionally read as an all-male group, there is no grammatical reason to do so. The text does not say if the heads were themselves involved with Moabite women and also participated in the sacrificial meals. It does not seem likely that all of the heads of the people did so. Yet Num. 25:4 says that all the heads are to be executed; this suggests that they are being executed for failing to keep the people from yielding to the temptation of the Moabite women and their religion. If that is indeed the case, then it is surprising that neither Israelite women nor men, nor the Moabite women with whom they were intimately involved, were sanctioned by the Israelites.

This is a surprising conclusion to the text, particularly since the maligned foreign women are not ill treated by the Israelites, who instead intend to execute their own people. Instead of complying with the divine command in verse 5, Moshe commands the judges, perhaps synonymous with the heads of the people, to kill the Israelite women and men who have joined the Moabite community. In so doing, he abrogates the divine command without consultation or consequence. However, the judges never execute their fellow Israelites in the narrative. Moshe's command has fared no better than God's. In the next unit, a Midianite woman and her Israelite husband are executed, impaled, but not by a judge. They are leaders among their own peoples, but certainly the two of them are not "all the heads of the people" as called for in 25:4—"people" here would seem to be restricted to Israelites. In Numbers 31, the Midianites will be savaged by the Israelites (possibly as surrogates for the Moabites), but the Moabites and their tempting women and inviting God and religious festivals largely pass out from the narrative as it is written.

One of the hermeneutical keys to this text is the identity of the Moabite God. In v. 2, 'eloheyhen appears twice. It can either mean "their [the women's] god" or "their [the women's] gods." The traditional translation choice has been the plural "gods," which offers the greatest contrast with the singular Israelite God—traditionally affirmed by use of the capital letter in translation, although Hebrew lacks capital letters. However, verse 2 only mentions one deity, Ba'al Peor, and 'elohim is also used for an individual non-Israelite deity (see 1 Kgs. 19:37). The translation choice ought not necessarily be based on how many deities one can identify in ancient Moab, that is, the full Canaanite pantheon, but rather on what is going on in the passage. Choosing the singular to reflect the specificity of Ba'al of Peor, I also chose to capitalize "God" to reflect the view of the Moabite women who are the subject of this text and not the judgment of those who produced the text. I also suggest that the Israelite and Moabite gods were not viewed as polemically opposed by their worshipers as they were by the framers and many interpreters of this text.

Many contemporary religious readers and hearers of this text will see and hear in the name Ba'al of Peor something irreconcilable with the God of the Scriptures with whom they identify. It may help to remember that the title Ba'al means "lord" and/or "master," and that the God of Israel was also called by that title, leading to no small amount of confusion with the Canaanite god of the same name (such as in Hos. 2:16). The Canaanite deity Ba'al Haddu, or Lord Haddu, was so often called just Ba'al that the title came to be synonymous with his name. Ba'al Peor, then, is simply Lord/Master of Peor.

In addition, ba'al occurs frequently in the text as a noun, without reference to any deity, and did not necessarily evoke heterodox religion. Examples include the Gen. 37:19-20 quote engraved on the tomb of the Rev. Dr. Martin Luther King Jr.: "Here comes ba'al ha-chalomot, this master dreamer. Come now, let us kill him. . . . And we shall see what will become of his dreams" (originally said by Joseph's brothers). Most translators regularly omit ba'al here. Other designations include "husband," as in Exod. 21:3 and elsewhere; "horse-master," as in 2 Sam. 1:6 and elsewhere; and in many place names, for example Ba'al Gad (Josh. 11:17; 12:7; 13:5); Har Ba'al Hermon (Judg. 3:3; 1 Chron. 5:23); and Ba'al Shalisha (2 Kgs. 4:42). Along with Ba'al, the God of Israel shared the names El and Elohim with Canaanite gods along with some psalms, hymns, imagery, and sacred stories, so there was a good deal of overlap between religious traditions (Cross 1976). All of this is to say that Ba'al Peor may have not been perceived as significantly different from the Israelite God, whom the people knew by many names and associated with a number of specific places, including Peor, where the Israelite God had so recently demonstrated lordship and mastery by having the prophet Bil'am bless the Israelite people when Balak king of Moab conspired to have them cursed.

Reading from the perspective of those for whom Ba'al of Peor is the God they have chosen to worship—perhaps not differentiating Ba'al Peor from the God of Israel as Ba'al Sinai—provides the contours of this midrash. My sanctified imagination suggests to me that the Moabite women, and the Israelite women and men who are intimately involved with them, represent a type of womanist community. Alice Walker's classic definition of a *womanist* as "a woman who loves other women, sexually and/or non-sexually. Appreciates and prefers women's culture. Committed to survival and wholeness of entire people, male and female" offers a framework for understanding these relationships (Walker 1983: xi-xii).

In this reading, the Moabite women, first, are proto-womanists. They are *other* in the Israelite scriptures as women of African descent and are frequently *other* in Western discourse. The relationships between Israelite and Moabite women suggested by the bombastic text include sexual and non-sexual relationships: The stem *z-n-h* can indicate erotic intimacy or any other relationship, worship, or act that is perceived as disloyal to the Israelite God. I suggest that the Israelite and Moabite peoples rediscovered their common ancestry; perhaps some Israelites thought they had reached the land of promise when they experienced the hospitality of their distant cousins. Perhaps a significant number of Israelite households defected from the caravan and settled in Moab; that would explain why others were punished in their stead. In any event, the women and men of the Israelite people entered into a number of differing relationships with the Moabite women, including intimate unions and more formal interactions, conjugal child-producing unions, and non-sexual relationships. And perhaps the women of Israel and women of Moab loved each other sexually and non-sexually, as intimated or at least allowed for in the words of the text; in other words, the people began to have unsanctioned-intimate-relationships with the women of Moab.

Second, the Moabite women offer sacred hospitality. For this reading, I am suggesting that their hospitality be read as "women's culture," in part because it is restricted to the women of Moab in this text. There is also a suggestion that Moabite culture can be read as women's culture in the book of Ruth: When

Naomi tells the Moabite women Ruth and Orpah to go back home to Moab in Ruth 1:8, she tells them to return to their "mothers' households," *le-bet 'immah,* describing Moabite culture in matriarchal terms. There is something compelling about these invitations; enough Israelites accept them to provoke the censure in the text. The rituals themselves may well have been nearly indistinguishable from the Israelites' own slaughter-sacrifice rituals, or the distinctions may not have been as significant to the people participating in the liturgies as they appeared to the framers of the canon and its articulation of orthodoxy.

Third, womanists are committed to the well being of the whole people of their community and indeed the larger world. So are the Moabite women in this text. This is indicated by the presence of Israelite men, boys, and girls—all included in "people"—forming relationships within their host community. This is, I think, what makes this a queer text, not the possibility of same-gender sexual contact between women, or the specter of an Israelite-Moabite orgy masquerading as worship of a god-who-is-not-God, but the choice of an untold number of the Israelite people to leave their pilgrimage and prophets for a different promise, a new home among a people who welcomed them to their tables, sacred spaces, homes, and communities. And because so many accepted that hospitality, someone had to die. Those to be executed did not join the protowomanist transcultural, transgressive community. They were presumably to be executed for permitting or not preventing the flowering of an alternative expression of Israelite religion and culture.

The manner of execution for the surrogate victims reflects the charge of *z-n-h,* unauthorized intimacy, specifically penetration. The verb *y-q-ʿ* Hiph. means to "impale" or violently penetrate. There may not be penetration or even sexual intimacy in all of the relationships between the Israelite people and Moabite women, but their surrogates will be penetrated on their behalf (Num. 25:4). The heads of the Israelite people will not be the last surrogates penetrated on behalf of the Israelite people who chose to live and worship with Moabite women. Women, girls, boys, and men from Midian will be penetrated sexually and non-sexually, lethally and non-lethally. The subunit ends with the commission of the judges—who may or not be the same as the heads of the people—to kill the Israelites who have joined the Moabite community (v. 5). Moshe commands their deaths. He does not speak to God. God does not speak to him. The silence of God in the story so far is deafening. Before they can carry out their task, the command seems to fall off the page; it is never fulfilled and not mentioned again.

The ongoing narrative is interrupted by a new narrative. The following two stories, those of Cozbi bat Tzur and the women of Midian, are part of one large narrative told in serial episodes. Suddenly, unexpectedly, an Israelite man brings his Midianite—not Moabite—woman, Cozbi the daughter of Tzur, home to his people and their sacred space, the Tent of Meeting. Instead of being offered a place at the welcome table, they are violently penetrated at the hands of Pinchas (Phinehas), Aharon's (Aaron's) grandson.

Let's go back to our framing questions. The communal grounding and perspective of womanism and black feminism create an inclusive interpretive framework that transcends the interests and questions of those who most easily identify with woman-centered approaches to biblical interpretation. In womanist practice, the voice and perspective of the whole community is sought and valued. Womanist interpretation *does not* privilege the embodiment and experiences of black women *at the expense of other members of the interpretive community*. Rather, while affirming the interpretive practices of black women as normative and as holding didactic value for other readers, womanist interpretation makes room at the table of discourse for the perspectives of the least among the community and the honored guest of any background: the child who is invited into "adult" conversation around the table with "Baby, what do you think?" and the extra place at the table for whoever may come by. In addition, as black women who reside in communities (and families) whose constituent members include black men and children and biracial bodies and multicultural families, we have courted the voices of those around the table without regard to race, ethnicity, gender, age, ability, or orientation.

Both womanism and feminism begin with the writer/thinker/interpreter as the starting place for scholarship. Womanism particularly emphasizes the bodiliness, incarnation in Christian terms, of the writing/thinking/interpreting person. I am a woman of African descent in the Americas. As is the case for many in the African diaspora, I identify as black while acknowledging that I also share European and Native American heritage. I am cis- and hetero-sexual. I am Christian, specifically an Episcopalian Anglican. I am also a member of a Jewish Reconstructionist minyan. Each of these aspects of my self affects the ways I hear, understand, translate, and interpret Scriptures.

Womanists and feminists (and those reading from a variety of other perspectives—often in concert: liberation theology, postcolonial studies, queer, ethic perspectival studies, and so on) begin with ourselves, distinguishing ourselves and our scholarship from those scholars who do not disclose their selves as they produce scholarship that they imagine is culturally neutral because they imagine and proclaim that their gender and cultural norms are normative for everyone else.

While feminism has contributed much to biblical studies, countering one-sided (male-stream) scholarship, exegesis, and interpretation, feminism as it exists in the Western academy is frequently severely hobbled by racism and classism. Womanism offers remedies to the myopia of racist and classist feminism. Womanism has evolved to include the radical egalitarianism of feminism, the emancipatory ethic and reverence for black physical and cultural aesthetics of the black liberation movement, and the transformational trajectories of both movements. The primary womanist principle that shapes my work is the *inherent value of each member of a community*. In this work, that principle means that each character in (and often those missing from) the narrative is an exemplar of the values of the scriptural text and its revelatory portrayal of God. And this work is womanist because it is *womanish*. That is, I am talking back to the text, challenging it, questioning it, interrogating it, unafraid of the power and authority of the text—just like a girl-growing-into-a-woman talks back to her elders, questioning the world around her in order to learn how to understand and navigate it. I call this work womanist and feminist, recognizing the intellectual, religious, and moral integrity of womanism and the essence of uncorrupted feminism. Let me add that I see the trajectories of womanism and feminism as parallel, intersecting, and overlapping streams.

Womanists and feminists ask different questions of a text than do other readers. We also ask some of the same questions, and we arrive at similar and dissonant conclusions. Privileging the crossroads between our afro-diasporic identity (embodiment and experience) and our gender (performance and identity), we ask questions about power, authority, voice, agency, hierarchy, inclusion, and exclusion, offering ways of reading biblical texts that go far beyond reading oneself into the dominant roles. The questions we ask enrich our own understanding and the understandings of those with whom we are in conversation. For religious readers, womanist and feminist biblical interpretation can help women and men make sense of an overwhelmingly masculine text while affirming its scriptural status.

What makes an interpretation feminist? Or womanist? You tell me.

Notes

1. This article was initially presented as a paper at the *Journal of Feminist Studies in Religion* section, Society of Biblical Literature annual meeting, 2011, San Francisco, Calif., and is being published with the permission of Westminster John Knox Press, which is also publishing it in the forthcoming collection *Womanist Midrash.*

2. Translations of biblical passages in this essay are the author's, unless otherwise indicated.

3. It is my practice in translation to use the names of biblical characters as they appear in the Hebrew text, preserving their literary and cultural identity, rather than further colonize them with Western spellings and sometimes completely different names, even when they are familiar. The names' Western spelling follows their first occurrence, in brackets.

12

Assessing Female Inheritance of Land in Nigeria with the Daughters of Zelophehad Narrative (Numbers 27:1-11)

Amadi Ahiamadu

INTRODUCTION

The choice of the narratives about Zelophehad's daughters is intended to highlight its relevance to understanding the inheritance rights of women in Nigeria. The side-by-side reading of the two disparate cultures, across time and place, helps us analyze a problem in the Niger Delta areas that demands an attitudinal change with respect to female inheritance of land among the Ogba and Ekpeye.[1] It serves as a textual example from the Bible that can be used to assess the Nigerian understanding of the whole concept of inheritance. In order to effectively harness the theological and ethical implications of the narratives concerning Zelophehad's daughters, certain basic methodological concepts have to be defined.

DEFINITION OF BASIC CONCEPTS

Definition of concepts here used such as "culture," "cultural relativism," and "patriarchy," among others, will be necessary for clarity, and are hereby given below.

Culture refers to a people's way of life as reflected in their values, institutions, symbols, and social structure as an entity distinct from those of other ethnic groups (Deist 1990: 62). Culture can also refer to human work "detached from the nexus of individual experience and action, consciously given shape as a construct, to be appropriated in the understanding, and then passed on to others. It can be reproduced in their experience and deeds and can be transformed by them, but it also forms them. . . . We are creators of culture but also its creatures" (Bromiley 1999: 746).

Cultural relativism. Deist has pointed out in his definition that "cultures differ to such an extent that it is illegitimate to transfer analytical anthropological categories from one to another, or to measure one culture by the standards of another, since each culture establishes its own social categories and norms of conduct" (Deist 1990: 62). Thus a universal human culture is a misnomer.

There are certain aspects of human culture that run across all societies, such as marriage, procreation, inheritance, respect for elders, the quest for religious harmony, and the desire for means of livelihood. In other words, a comparison of certain features of culture can be done on a cross-cultural basis, whereas other aspects of culture can be contrasted—such as language, technology, agricultural procedures, attitude toward gender, education, and religious practices and beliefs.

Patriarchal refers to a system of rule in which men exercise control over women and children in all aspects of life, including political, economic, social, sexual, and religious aspects, and in which male interests override those of their female counterparts (McKim 1996: 204).

Patriarchy, in turn, refers to a male authority system tending toward the oppression and subordination of women through social, political, and economic institutions and practices (McKim 1996: 204).

Patrilinial refers to family descent that is traced through the father and his ancestry. In other words, descent is traced through the paternal, instead of the maternal, line.

Patrilocal refers to the location centered on the residence of the husband's family, instead of the wife's.

A Short Analysis of Existing Research

In this section, we will first briefly look at scholarship on the book of Numbers more broadly, and then at the daughters of Zelophehad narrative more particularly.

The Book of Numbers: Some Relevant Notions

"Numbers" is the title given to the fourth book of the Pentateuch. The translators of the Septuagint (LXX) gave it this name apparently to reflect its two censuses listed in Numbers 1 and 26, which according to Olson (1996) also divide the book into two unequal parts. Each respective part deals with what Olson describes as "the death of an old generation and the birth of a new." The title was passed on through the Latin Vulgate to the European and present-day English versions (Lasor 1996: 100).

Scholars like Ashley (1993: 2–3) prefer a tripartite division of the book that is closely related to geographic locale: Section 1 at Mount Sinai (1:1—10:10); section 2 at and around Kadesh Barnea (10:11—19:22); and section 3 on the plains of Moab (20:1—36:13), where the events of our narrative on the daughters of Zelophehad takes place. Within the narratives, Ashley traces the movement of the children of Israel from Sinai to Kadesh Barnea (10:11—12:13) and from Kadesh Barnea to the plains of Moab (20:1—21:35), spanning a period of more than thirty-eight years (Martens 1997: 985).

The journey from Sinai to Kadesh Barnea, by way of the Gulf of Aqaba, would normally have taken only a few days (Deut. 1:2). Instead, as told, it took more than thirty-eight years due to the nonbelief of the older generation, which Yahweh promptly punished by denying them access to the promised land. Therefore, Numbers is, more or less, a recital of the acts of Yahweh. In it is set the divine providence of Yahweh—his faithfulness, presence, provision, and forbearance—against Israel's unfaithfulness, rebellion, apostasy, and frustration (Lasor 1996: 99). Numbers follows Leviticus and like it contains the cultic regulations given at Sinai. Much of its regulations for both priests and people are similar to Exodus, Leviticus, and Deuteronomy. (Ashley 1993: 2–3). Against this background, we can now read the stories relevant to our case.

NUMBERS 27:1-11

This text section has been identified as of a Priestly provenance by many scholars, such as J. Wellhausen, A. Kuenen, H. Holzinger, B. Baentsch, and G. B. Gray (Budd 1984: 300). And according to Noth (1968: 210), who has been followed in his view by J. Sturdy and J. de Vaux, this Priestly material appears to be of a later redaction. In his commentary on Numbers, Budd is satisfied that a consensus of scholarly opinion ascribes the materials in this section to the Priestly editor.

Closely associated with this pericope are parallel narratives like Num. 36:1-12 and Josh. 17:2-6, which deal with the same inheritance issues of the daughters of Zelophehad. How is the second census in Numbers important for understanding the plight of the daughters of Zelophehad, for which they had to petition Moses? Why did the Priestly editor choose that context for the placement of this narrative?

In response to the second question, the Priestly editor placed this pericope (Num. 27:1-11) against the background of the second census (Num. 26:52-55) to highlight its importance for the subsequent partitioning of the promised land, based on those listed by name. And in response to the first question, Zelophehad's daughters anticipated that they would be left out without a family inheritance, and so they took action to preempt that likelihood (27:1-5; Levine 2000: 341).

The request the daughters of Zelophehad make in 27:1-11 is implemented with modifications: in Numbers by restricting the marriage options of the heiresses (36:1-12); in Joshua by a land-allocation panel headed by Joshua the son of Nun, and by Eleazar son of Aaron the priest (Josh. 17:3-6). Any detailed discussion of the fundamental inheritance issues raised in Numbers is reserved for the subsequent sections below. Meanwhile, some observations can be made with respect to the pericope in Numbers 27.

Our pericope presents a legal issue about women inheriting land through a male line in exceptional cases, when there is no male descendant to possess the inheritance. In these verses, we also read about the initial ruling given on the case at the entrance to the Tent of Meeting before Moses, Eleazar the priest, the leaders, and the entire congregation of Israel. We are also given a family tree for Zelophehad's daughters in verse 1, which is part of the second census list, representing an entirely new generation, and which for that purpose repeats the clan structure of Manasseh outlined in 26:28-35 (Olson 1996: 162–63).

The problem of inheritance that the daughters of Zelophehad are concerned with is not covered in any of the existing law codes in the Torah. Their inheritance problem creates an ambiguous legal situation requiring special revelation for its solution. As Ashley (1993: 542) has observed, a matter of such importance would have formed part of the Torah in order to provide a general legislation for similar cases in the future. What was the problem of the daughters?

The daughters' problem is of a legal nature (27:3-4). Their father Zelophehad had died in the wilderness without any male heir to inherit his property. In view of this, they request the right to inherit it. They claim that their demand is necessitated by the desire to perpetuate the clan name of their father, who died "for his own sin." In other words, Zelophehad did not die because of his part in the rebellion of Korah and his group, whom the Lord swore would not inherit the land—but because of the general sin of unfaithfulness that characterized the entire first generation; and therefore, like the rest of the younger generation, his descendants deserved to be granted an inheritance. Such a request, coming as it was from females, was without any precedent, and Moses had to refer the matter to God (vv. 5-11). God consents to the demand of the daughters and rules in verse 7 that Moses should indeed transfer Zelophehad's inheritance to his daughters (Ashley 1993: 542–43). The book of Numbers ends with the second generation still waiting on the plains of Moab, where Moses has died, in order to enter the land of Canaan; and the leadership then passes on to Joshua the son of Nun.

Space does not permit an elaborate, in-depth description of the land-tenure practices of ancient Israel and the ancient Near East (ANE). We might, however, examine in brief such practices in the wider ANE community, including ancient Israel, before taking up the issues raised by the inheritance traditions elicited by the narrative about Zelophehad's daughters, which can then be applied to the Nigerian experience.

A Brief Analysis of Land Use and Land Tenure in the Ancient Near East and in Israel

Land was used for agricultural and residential purposes in both the Ancient Near East and in Israel. While in the former, conceptions of land were inextricably bound up with the traditional religions, in the latter case, it is similarly centered on the Yahwistic religion. In most ancient societies, sacrifices had to be offered at certain periods of the year as one way of acknowledging that the land belonged to the deity, and that the living held land in custody both for ancestors and for future generations.

In the case of ancient Israel, this was a highly developed concept, whereby all land was seen as belonging to Yahweh and with the people as mere stewards of land and its temporary residents. Land was therefore not to be sold or alienated on a permanent basis, and every arrangement was made to guarantee that. On the other hand, at this point the surrounding culture of the ANE differed slightly because land could be sold and given out without scruples (Boecker 1976: 18).

This discussion is of importance when one considers what constitutes the land use and tenure practices in the ANE, particularly among the Canaanites. This is set out below in order to show how it compares and contrasts with parallel use in ancient Israel.

As part of the ANE, Israelites and the Canaanites had many cultural traits in common, such as kinship structures in which members of a tribe were regarded as descendants of a common ancestor (Curtis 1994: 46). There seem to be some contrasts, however, when it comes to land tenure. Communal land tenure was practiced in the ANE, and the tendency in both Egypt and Mesopotamia was toward a joint ownership of land (Dybdahl 1981: 24).

LAND TENURE IN THE ANE

In Egypt, for instance, the people owed allegiance to the gods for the land on which they dwelled and which they used to make their living. The same was true of the Babylonians, whose religious practices became inextricably woven into their land-tenure system (Boecker 1976: 18). In general, land ownership in the ANE could be communal and private. In Egypt, women were allowed to own land in principle, but in practice, we know of hardly any existing examples of such a practice. The land was used in such a collective manner and for agrarian purposes that it was difficult to distinguish between owners and non-owners (Dybdahl 1981: 25).

Features of joint ownership in the ANE also included a common way of land cultivation, as well as of uniform crop planting. The same was also true of a timetable of operations. "There was . . . a common agricultural calendar followed by all peasants" (Dybdahl 1981: 29). This extended from plowing time to harvest time, and even to fallow periods.

One remarkable feature observable in the ANE is a system whereby landholding was rotated among the people, based on an annual redistribution of land to every land user (Dybdahl 1981: 29–30). Moreover, as has been pointed out earlier, unlike in the Old Testament land law, land renting and land sale were features of land tenure in the ANE, particularly among the Canaanites and to some extent among the Babylonians (Boecker 1976: 88).

Three basic concepts governed land-tenure practices in the ANE, including Egypt and Mesopotamia, namely: (1) Society, or a segment of it, was the basic controlling group in relation to land. Right to land was dependent not on individual merits but on social obligations, such as marriage and maintaining a family. (2) Land so communally held could not be sold or given away by individuals—especially to those outside the kinship unit or group. And (3) nonmonetary periodic redistribution took care of the changes in membership due to births, deaths, or other factors such as adoption or temporary residency (Dybdahl 1981: 36).

This is in a sense similar to what obtained in ancient Israel as well, but as we shall see, the Israelites had a more egalitarian approach to the retention and use of land. The basic landholding unit was the clan (*mishpachah*), and every individual had access to land on the basis of equality and accountability. Let us elaborate further on this egalitarian feature by looking at land tenure in ancient Israel in some more detail.

LAND TENURE IN ANCIENT ISRAEL

Much like its ANE counterparts, ancient Israel practiced land tenure that was both communal and in some sense also private or egalitarian. In this way, everyone's right to land was inalienable, and no one was above the law (Matthews 1988: 134). As a bona fide gift from Yahweh, the land was not to be sold or alienated on a permanent basis. That basic concept of land tenure remained intact until the inauguration of the era of the monarchy, when, as it were, a twofold land-tenure practice became the vogue in ancient Israel—one favoring the more egalitarian land tenure and the other adhering to an elitist land-tenure system (Dybdahl 1981: 35–36). The reasons for this can be seen from the discussion below.

One of the inevitable results of an incomplete conquest was the presence of Canaanites living on the land that Yahweh had originally intended for Israel alone (Hawk 1991: 43). It is instructive, therefore, to note that tribal inheritances received either by conquest or by lot presented an incomplete possession, distorted by the presence of aboriginal strongholds (Hawk 1991: 21). These aboriginal strongholds were of such an intense nature that it was difficult for the Israelites to completely take the land, and from time to time there was war between the parties. For instance, the Jebusites occupied a central area in Judah's allotment, and the Judahites could not dislodge them (Josh. 15:63). Ephraim had the Gezerites to contend with in the area they both occupied (16:10), and Manasseh had a list of cities and the valley areas that they could not completely possess due to the Canaanites' superior military strength (17:11-13, 16).

The effect of this was the practice of a dual land-tenure system, as has already been described. While the Canaanites practiced a tenure that tolerated individual ownership, the Israelites held on to a tenure system that left ownership with the clan, to which several individual household units belonged. This practice stuck with Israel until the monarchy was instituted. During the period of the united monarchy (1200–922 bce), it was clear that both Israelite and Canaanite land-tenure customs were practiced side by side (Westbrook 1991: 23). This meant that Israelite tenure laws governed the rural communities, whereas in the cities the kings preferred to use the Canaanites' more individualistic tenure customs. By this, they were able to appropriate land needed for public projects such as the temple, the *millo'*, and the palaces. However, it meant that the poor were robbed of vital landed assets (Dybdahl 1981: 100–101; Matthews 1988: 142–43). The move therefore from an egalitarian to a centralized system was not without its ideological roots and social consequences.

The original land tenure of ancient Israel was based on three overarching principles, namely: (1) Land belonged to Yahweh; (2) land was given to the twelve tribes of Israel as a lasting inheritance; and (3) land so given was not allowed to be sold or alienated on a permanent basis, so that every individual Israelite's means of livelihood would not be impaired (Wright 1989: 57–58). However, by the time of the First Temple period (922–586 BCE), the kings saw themselves more as Yahweh's vice-regents than as ordinary citizens. In the matter of land ownership, some of them used the land to gratify their political and economic interests, to the detriment of their subjects and contrary to well-known conventions (Matthews 1988: 134–35), thus fulfilling Samuel's prophecy against a monarchical rule (1 Sam. 8:14; 14:52). Therefore, land in ancient Israel occupied a prominent place as an economic resource (Wright 1989: 46). It was given to the twelve tribes by Yahweh, who also prescribed how it had to be shared among them (Nelson 1997: 28, 198; Butler 1983: 171–73). The principles of conquest, lot and donation, governed the distribution of land among the tribes and their respective clans, *mishpachot* (Deuteronomy 32; Joshua 13–19). In ancient Israel of the early period (1200–1000 BCE), the principle of inalienability of land was deeply ingrained in the land-tenure practice, and land was distributed on an egalitarian basis, with permanent land sale considered a forbidden matter.

We can now proceed to examine the views on women against the background of the influence land-tenure practices could have had on such views.

Views on Women in the Ancient Near East and in Israel

Generally speaking, there are various views on women that stressed their property rights in the ANE. In the case of Zelophehad's daughters, we are presented with a paradoxical situation in which a norm "which prohibits the inheritance of property by women and a norm which mandates the preservation of property within the lineage are in conflict and are resolved in these narratives" (Olson 1985: 97). The resolution that a man's daughters could inherit his property in the event of there being no male heir was given the status of a "lasting ordinance" and was aptly observed even in the stressful days of the monarchy in ancient Israel (Brueggemann 1977: 10–11).

The world of the Old Testament (OT), which for all intents and purposes appears to have been a male-dominated society, was nevertheless far from antiwomen (Wright 1989: 198). Meyers (1988: 78) expresses the view that women's roles in the OT were disguised under the male-dominated culture and male-skewed inheritance laws of ancient Israel. Bird (1992: 951) looks closely at the cultural impact of patriarchy on women, and states that, according to records, in ancient Israel women played significant and essential roles. Women, though subordinated to men, are some of the best-known actors in the biblical story. In other words, women were seen as fulfilling very significant roles in the social life of various communities, even though such roles had been assigned to them by their male counterparts.

In the *bet 'ab* ("father's house"), women sometimes became heads when the male head had abdicated that role through long absence or death, although such headship by women was considered an aberration, to be corrected as soon as a male heir could be found (Wright 1989: 219). Outside the *bet 'ab*, women were engaged in productive endeavors as much as their male partners (Meyers 1997: 18–19). They were also involved in nurturing the younger generation toward covenant loyalty.

Inheriting the land and Yahweh's guarantee of a lasting and fruitful inheritance (Brueggemann 1977: 108) depended exclusively on how well informed the younger generation was in the words of Yahweh (Ashley 1993: ix). Besides instructing the children in their homes, women also had their share in the sacrificial meal (Deut. 12:12; 14:26), eaten together with other members of the *bet 'ab* (Evans 2003: 900). Their involvement with the covenant meal was as important as their commitment to the educational development of their children. In both ways, women served as reminders to the younger generation of the tenets of the covenant Yahweh had established with Israel. The responsibility this entailed for women was of enormous magnitude within the faith community (Bird 1992: 951).

With this background in mind, let us now examine the views on land in Nigeria, before highlighting the challenge posed to its overtly patriarchal values by the positive image of women in ancient Israel, as exemplified by the special inheritance granted to Zelophehad's daughters.

Inheritance Rights of Women in Parts of Southeastern Nigeria and the Niger Delta

African inheritance laws, like inheritance laws in most of the ANE, were also not explicit in matters such as the inheritance rights of women. Nevertheless, certain laws that protected the rights of women in the countries of the Bible had parallels in African cultures (Ukpong 2001: 11–28). In fact, there exists such an undeniable parallel between African cultures and lifestyle and the "customs and manners" of ancient Israel (see Matthews 1988: 24–25) that many are tempted to think of culture in an African context as resonating more with ANE cultures than with culture as it is understood today in postmodern Western societies (Bosman 2002: 360).

The similarity between ancient Israel and other cultures with respect to land-tenure systems has also been pointed out (Boecker 1976: 17). In several ways, the similarities are even more pronounced by comparison to local African landholding practices (Moiseraele 2001: 397). For instance, in Africa, the Deity is recognized as the primary owner of all land, and the kinship group as the main custodians of land on behalf of past, present, and future generations (Ayandele 1966: 69; Yakubu 1985: 6–8). Another similarity lies in the observance of land laws intended to preserve the land so as to make it fruitful (Moiseraele 2001: 395).

In ancient Israel, the basic landholding unit within the country was the *mishpachah*; similarly, in most of sub-Saharan Africa the *kindred* are the basic landholding unit (Meek 1957: 186). Although individuals are associated with sharing the land both for domestic and agricultural purposes, such individuals must be married and raising a family to be considered eligible for a share in the land (Dybdahl 1981: 36). Moreover, no individual, not even a unit of kindred, has the right to alienate any land permanently apportioned to them, as such an apportioning is only temporary and depends on membership in a kin group (Ayandele 1969: 69).

The Land Use Decree (1978) and the Rising Status of Women

The land-tenure situation in Nigeria has gradually been changing for the better over the last three decades. In 1978, in order to facilitate economic and social development, the Federal Military Government under General Olusegun Obasanjo (who, incidentally, was the third Republican Civilian Democratic President of Nigeria up until 2007) promulgated a decree tagged "Land Use Decree," which vested the title to all lands in Nigeria's city and urban areas in the hands of state governors, rather than in local chiefs or kinship groups.

The law also defined some hitherto traditional communities and elevated them to "urban" status by law, bringing such areas under the government's radical land laws, and facilitating both individual and corporate land acquisitions in such areas for purposes of social, agricultural, industrial, and economic development.

This decree empowers corporate bodies and individuals to acquire land for developmental purposes in any part of the country, and the authority to make such land grants has been vested in state governors, no longer the traditional kinship groups, which of course still hold such rights in the nonurban areas

(Yakubu 1985: 74–75, 257). The decree has greatly enhanced the economic and social status of women, as they can now own land of their own in any part of Nigeria, provided the guidelines for land acquisition under the land-use decree are followed.

Land Use Tradition in Nigeria and the Rising Status of Women

There are two ways in which the inheritance rights of women are fostered traditionally, namely, through marriage and the levirate, and by direct purchase. We shall consider each of these briefly before drawing our conclusions.

First, land, as we have seen, is treated more as belonging to the lineage or kin group, and in some cases to the extended family unit. Individual rights over land and its use are co-terminus with the membership of the group. No male is considered eligible to a share in the land until he is married to a woman. In this way, both male and female are granted equal rights to the land, with inheritance passing through the male line.

Moreover, marriage is patrilocal, and it is the female who moves to the man's home and stays with him on his inheritance. Since female members marry away from their ancestral home, they are not given land as inheritance, but are given dowries, which compensate for the land they do not receive (Nwabueze 1972: 170-71). Again, to ensure that land remains within the kinship group, a woman is introduced into the levirate marriage in a manner similar to that used in biblical texts: when a woman has lost her husband, one of her late husband's brothers or cousins may remarry her. If she remarries outside of her husband's kin group, she automatically loses any land rights she formerly enjoyed within his group. Meek observes that land inherited by women through levirate marriage can sometimes include land acquired by her parents, and that she simply holds it in pledge, so that on her death it passes on to her children, or to her husband should the children still be minors (Meek 1957: 69).

Meek's observation does not necessarily reflect land-inheritance practice in all parts of Africa. In Nigeria, for example, it is rare for individual nuclear families to own land except, as we have seen, within the context of the kinship group of which they are a part. This was even truer of precolonial Nigeria, which was the focus of Meek's ethnological studies during the late 1950s. She is right, however, in underscoring the general subordination of women on the continent then, especially as it is reflected in the area of land inheritance.

Second, like all other women in Nigeria, women in southeastern Nigeria are theoretically given the right to own land under the general provisions of the Land Use Decree of 1978. The decree has enhanced women's ability to own land, as they can now purchase and retain land in the cities and urban areas of Nigeria. Land so purchased becomes a woman's property and at death is passed on to her sons, or male relatives if she has acquired the land before entering into marriage. As has been observed, this practice is not new (Yakubu 1985: 186). It has, however, received an added impetus as a result of sociopolitical changes in the country. The decree does not also alter the traditional patrilineal inheritance. However, it is not explicit on the inclusion of females from the inheritance line. Females are still defined as daughters of their fathers or as wives of their husbands. This will become clearer as we look at a specific context below.

Inheritance Rights of Women in Southeastern Nigeria and the Niger Delta

Let us start with the Igbo, who occupy predominantly the southeastern section of Nigeria, before looking at the Niger Delta, which is situated geographically as a crossroad between the Igbo in the southeast and the Yoruba in the southwest of Nigeria. There are indications that in traditional Igbo societies, women were never marginalized: they had access to property and enjoyed commensurate rights with their husbands in using ancestral land once they had been brought into the family through marriage (Nwabueze 1972: 170–71; Uchem 2001: 42). However, at present, Igbo society is pervaded by a culture of subordination that has also robbed women of inheritance rights and hedged them in with ritual prohibitions or taboos. By means of this, men's preeminence and women's subordination were and are still enforced and perpetuated. This has invariably resulted from a conflict of paradigms in the cultural contact of the Igbo with Western European and Christian ideas of headship of the home (Uchem 2001: 142).

With respect to women in the Niger Delta, particularly among the Ogba and Ekpeye, they are theoretically given the right to own land, but hardly any instances of this obtain. Even when they do own land, it has to be in partnership with their husbands or male relatives. This custom has been carried over into the general provisions of the Land Use Decree of 1978. Thus only in rare cases are women allowed to own property on their own, a situation that parallels the case of Zelophehad's daughters.

In Nigerian culture, be it Igbo or Niger Delta, patrilocal marriage is the vogue. This means that on getting married, a woman moves into a home provided by her husband, usually in his own home or one provided by his kinsmen. Whatever land or property acquisition she subsequently makes are considered as jointly owned with her husband. If she has acquired property prior to getting married, it is considered as jointly owned with her male relatives. Since land cannot be transferred, land is not included in the dowries that fathers and relatives provide for their daughters when they get married. The end result is that this strongly patrilineal, patrilocal culture exercises subtle control over women's quest for a personal inheritance of their own.

However, since the promulgation of the Land Use Decree in 1978, the situation has been changing for the better, as some women are known to have taken advantage of the decree by buying their own land for the purposes of building a house or for setting up a business. There is still the nagging problem of not being able to do so without a male counterpart as a guarantor. Moreover, patrilineal inheritance rights are restored when a female landowner dies and her sons or brothers lay claim to her estate as primary claimants.

Conclusion

There are three ways in which the narrative of Zelophehad's daughters (Num. 27:1–11) has helped us to assess the Nigerian understanding of female inheritance.

First, in spite of the bias toward patriarchy and patrilineality in ancient Israel, as in contemporary Nigeria, we have in our pericope an example of women who, due to the unavoidable absence of a male child, were brought into the inheritance line to receive the inheritance. The general tendency in the ANE points to land inheritance by males only; and in the exceptional cases, where land was given to women, such women were not allowed to marry outside of their father's kindred. In other words, under exceptional circumstances a man's daughter became heir to his patrimony, provided she married within the kindred. This stands in sharp contrast to Nigeria's overtly exogamous marriages and male-skewed inheritance patterns of the post-1978 era.

Second, the narrative of Zelophehad's daughters, when examined against the background of the land grant narratives in the OT, reveals that there indeed were religious and theological structures that guaranteed the security and integrity of tribal inheritances (Wright 1989: 90–91). Those structures ensured that the inheritance rights of women who did not have the direct economic support of their male relatives, for one reason or another, were guaranteed (Bird 1992: 952). Religious structures, which included the levirate, Sabbatical year and Jubilee laws, enabled the faith community—and especially women—to fit into an essentially male focused land-tenure practice (Dybdahl 1981: 86). When applied to the Nigerian experience, it is fortunate to find that the levirate, for instance, is practiced in both southeastern Nigeria and the Niger Delta as well as among the Igbo, Yoruba, Bini, and Ogba-Ekpeye peoples of Nigeria (Meek 1957: 186; Ayandele 1969: 69). The important place occupied by women in matters of land inheritance can be further appreciated when cultural institutions such as the levirate are evaluated. Whether in the ANE, in ancient Israel, or in contemporary Nigeria, the intention is the same: the protection of family name and patrimony through special inheritance concessions granted to women along with their male counterparts (Ashley 1993: 541; Boecker 1976: 120–21). It is in that sense that the land grant covered in our pericope can be described as supplementary, because women who received such inheritances were later to pass them on to their male descendants or relatives as the case may be, thereby restoring the normal pattern of patrilineal inheritance (Ashley 1993: 541; Nelson 1997: 9).

Third, socially and religiously, no stigma has been attached to any woman inheriting land in Nigeria (Nwaoru 2002: 55–60). Instead, as we have seen, the Land Use Decree of 1978 enables both men and women who aspire to acquire land for residential, industrial, and agricultural purposes to do so (Yakubu 1985: 257). The underlying assumption, however, is that women who inherit or acquire land do so either as partners with their husbands or with the support of their male kin. In Nigerian society, neither men nor women are considered respectable and credit-worthy without the other (Amadi 1982: 48). Therefore, the inheritance rights of women are considered a veritable part of their family life, not for women as single entities but as partners with their husbands or male counterparts.

Notes

1. The Ekpeye and Ogba are kin-groups occupying the upper recesses of the Niger Delta of Nigeria and inhabiting the areas between the Nkissa/Anyana and Orashi river tributaries of the Niger. With a combined population of 900,000 they practice a land tenure system which excludes females and for which this Biblical example is necessary.

13

Reading Iconoclastic Stipulations in Numbers 33:50–56 from the Pluralistic Religious Context of China

Archie C. C. Lee

INTRODUCTION

Christian evangelical missionary work in the religiously plural Asian context is more often than not characterized by iconoclastic polemics for undermining the value and integrity of Asian religious cultures.[1] Missionaries, regardless of their religious persuasion as either liberal or conservative, have the ultimate goal of converting the so-called pagans. Though practically impossible, conversion is said to be complete only when it involves severing oneself from the native culture and its religious beliefs and practices. Most missionaries still see it as their mission to endeavor to convert. Paul Cohen, a well-known scholar in Chinese missionary history, raises the question as to why the missionary, who came not to take but to give and intended to serve the interest of the Chinese, had "inspired the greatest fear and hatred." Cohen points to the answer in the missionary's negative attitude toward Chinese culture and religion and unbending iconoclastic position:

> The vast majority of missionaries, Protestant and Catholic, were intolerant of Chinese culture and unwilling or unable to make meaningful adjustments to it. They devoted themselves tirelessly to religious proselytizing and tended to relegate secular change to a position of secondary importance. Although narrowly conservative in personal and religious outlook, their impact on the Chinese scene was the very opposite of conservative. For these were the missionaries whose demands on the native culture were the most

unyielding—and hence, from a Chinese standpoint, the most overly iconoclastic. (Cohen 1978: 543)

Cohen goes on to suggest that this Western cultural imperialism posts a revolutionary challenge and threat to the traditional Chinese order. He further claims: "It is for this reason, more than any other, that so many Chinese felt so threatened" (p. 544). The bitter experience of the painful conflicts between the Chinese Christian converts and the so-called idolatrous Chinese during the missionary era in the nineteenth and twentieth centuries supplies ardent testimonies to the religious and cultural war brought about by the Christian iconoclastic commitment. In the Thirty-fourth Annual and Public Meeting of the Religious Tracts Society, held in London on May 7, 1833, it was reported that the operation of the society should continue

> till the visions which our faith may regard as about to take place, shall be fully realized; when the idolatry which now darkens and covers the earth shall be no more, when the last triumphs of the cross shall be celebrated in the demolition of the last heathen temple, or in the burning of the last heathen book, the pile of which we may conceived to be set fire to by the hand of the last convert from idolatry, and which shall be accomplished by the shoutings of the triumphant multitude who shall be assembled on that day, and who shall exclaim Hosanna! (Drew 1833: 294)

Such condemnation of idolatry and its vanity has been widespread in missionary writings and addresses. Indigenous communities would have great difficulty identifying themselves with this kind of imperial attitude toward other religions and the triumphal celebration of their destruction. Missionaries, however, have great confidence in the divine order to remove idolatry, based on biblical iconoclastic stipulations embodied in biblical passages such as Num. 33:52, "You must drive out all the inhabitants as you advance, destroy all their carved figures and their images of cast metal, and lay their hill-shrines in ruins."[2] Local inhabitants, however, are dismayed to read this and other similar passages advocating iconoclastic polemical attitudes toward their religion and the people of their native land.

In this essay, I intend to understand the charge of the Israelites to expel the Canaanite inhabitants and destroy their religious practices in Numbers 33 in the context of the religious and political schism between communities in the exilic environment, and the aspiration to strengthen the monotheistic faith of the desperate Israelites. In order to understand the impact of the iconoclastic movement in a particular context, we will proceed by first looking at the missionary Christian understanding about the prohibition of idolatry, which inspired the Taiping Rebellion in China. The insurgence brought about tremendous destruction to Chinese religions and communities of faith. It is perhaps an extreme case of actually implementing the biblical command in a political context. But, in converting believers from pagan and heathen religions, the basic missionary attitude toward other religions created schism and conflicts between the new converts and the local communities. The Christian polemic against local religions has also inspired fear and growth in anti-Christian sentiments among the Chinese in recent history. In the second part of this essay, I will examine the command of Numbers 33 to destroy idolatry and expel the local inhabitants of Canaan sociohistorically, in Israel's exilic context, in order to see how the command was and should be understood and appropriated.

Missionary Christianity and Taiping's Radical Policy on Iconoclasm

The Asian history of colonization witnesses to the fact that the iconoclastic stipulations have inspired the Protestant Christian missionaries and given them license to bring about tremendous destruction to the pluralistic religious context of Asia in general and China in particular. The missionaries' intrinsic iconoclastic outlook created religious and cultural polemics between communities. Since part of the missionaries' preaching was based on biblical iconoclasm, they demanded that new converts turn away completely from the so-called pagan religion and its practices, thereby severing themselves from all sociopolitical connections with their old world. In so doing, the new converts became a new person, absolutely detached from the native cultural environment. In a way, the absolute discontinuity is necessary in the redefinition of identity for these new converts in the Christian culture; however, most Chinese Christians were left hanging in the air as a result of their detachment from the local community, from which their particular ancestry, history, and social networks, along with the meaning of existence they provided, were primarily derived. Many of them thus became desperate and miserable Christians, living in tension, with split personality, alienated from their own family and neighbors.

Besides the problems of individual alienation, the most destructive effect of iconoclasm is obviously the incalculable violence it brings to other religious traditions and institutions. In the case of Shanxi in China, which missionaries refer to negatively as "a temple land" in the sense that it is "a god-saturated, idolatrous place, the seat of Satan" (Austin 2007: 154), Alvyn Austin sees "the decimation of the idol population of Shanxi" as a result of the conversion of the people by the iconoclastic Protestant missionaries who "burn the paraphernalia of idolatry given up by their converts" (p. 160). In terms of large-scale destruction at the sociopolitical level, the iconoclastic Taiping Rebellion (1850–1864) led by Hong Xiu Quan (1814–1864) is by far the most typical. The rebellion was inspired by Christian ideology of destruction of local religions and their idolatry. It created a political entity designated as Taiping (Peace) Kingdom, which covered a wide area of China south of the Yangzi River. Its capital was established in Nanjing in 1853, and was renamed the Heavenly Capital (*Tianjing*), the earthly Jerusalem. During his stay in Guangzhou in 1836 for the civil examination, Hong was given the pamphlet *Good Words to Admonish the Age*, written by Liang Afat, the first Chinese Protestant preacher (McNeur 1934), but only got to study it seven years later, in 1843. The booklet, which contains Bible quotations on condemnation of idolatry, enlightened him and gave him a Christian explanation of his dream of ascension to heaven to meet God and his elder brother Jesus, when he fell ill in 1837 after his repeated failure in examinations. In 1843, Hong converted his two relatives, Hong Rengan and Feng Tunshan, and together they reread Liang Afa's apologetic tracts. They were so convinced of the teaching of iconoclasm that they decided to implement God's order to strike down all idols and icons in the village where Hong had been a teacher at the local school. He and his two friends removed all the tablets dedicated to Confucius and his disciples, including the replica of the "Model Teacher of Myriad Generations," which was written by the Qing emperor Kangxi in 1686. It was legally required to erect that centerpiece in every school hall to pay homage to the Confucian sage. As a result of their act of "purging their schoolrooms of the heathen icons" (Spence 1966: 68), they broke off their basic social relationship with the community. Subsequently, they turned down the offer of one of the village leaders to point out the errors in Liang's Christian teachings. In his verse responding to the village leaders' accusation that he was convinced of slanderous words, Hong declared his dedication to God's commandments and that the division between their two different ways is unbridgeable:

> Not because of slanderous words did we reject your offer,
> But because we follow the True God's commandments.
> Sharp must be the line between the roads to Heaven and Hell—
> How can we muddle through this earthly life mindlessly?[3]

They then set off on their journey in southern China with the mission not only to condemn Confucius but also to banish and destroy all idols and idol worship. In addition to the Ten Commandments, Hong had also read the Bible with the Baptist missionary I. J. Roberts in Guangzhou for a couple of months (Shih 1967: 147–48). Besides adopting biblical concepts and terminology in his construction of Christian ideology, Hong followed Liang Afa's strong anti-idol attitude in condemning Chinese idolatry, which has been explicitly expressed by Liang in his chapter "Perverted Gods Transform Themselves into the Snake Devil."[4] He received the clear vision of the Lord's strong prohibition against idolatry from reading the Decalogue and passages such as Psalm 115.[5] They continued to carry out their movement in smashing images and toppling idols in temples and local shrines in the name of *Shangdi*, the Chinese term for the biblical God '*Elohim*.[6] Hong founded the "Religion of the Worship of *Shangdi*" (*Bai Shangdi Hui*) and gained popular support from numerous peasants of southern China, where famine, social unrest, and unjust oppressions had been on the rise. The new iconoclastic religion angered the local gentry and alienated magistrate officials to the extent that it was renounced as "illegitimate heterodoxy," and its followers were pronounced offenders and criminals.

Hong based his belief on the Ten Commandments of the Hebrew Bible and considered it to be the will of God to bring about destruction to other religions and their idols. In the Taiping writing, *An Exhortation in the Origin of Virtue for the Enlightening of the Age*, Hong condemns the setting up of idols and the worship of images as "in absolute defiance of the Supreme God's expressed will" and being "deceived by the demon" (Michael 1971: 2:41). Hong recapped the Old Testament themes of creation and cited the tradition of Mount Sinai to drive home the points of the prohibition of images and the worship of other gods:

> By referring to the Old Testament we learn that in early ages the Supreme God descended on Mount Sinai and by his own hand he wrote the Ten Commandments on tablets of stone, which he gave to Moses. The Supreme God commanded Moses, saying, "I am the Lord, the Supreme God; you people of the world must on no account set up images resembling anything in heaven above or on earth below, and bow down and worship them." Now you people of the world who set up images and bow dawn and worship them are in absolute defiance of the Supreme God's expressed will. You people of the world on the other hand say these images are meant to assist the Supreme God in protecting mankind. How extremely foolish you

are to let your minds be so deceived by the demon! Do you not know that when the Supreme God in the first six days created heaven and earth, mountains and seas, human beings and things, God did not require the assistance of anyone? (Michael 1971: 2:41)

Here idol worshipers are accused of stupidly bowing down to senseless objects, as they are caricatured in satirical style in Ps. 115:4-8 and Isa. 44:9-20. People are admonished to worship the heavenly Father of all humanity, who promises to answer prayers, as expressed in Matt. 7:7:

> Alas, while it is very evident that there exists a true Spirit, most honorable and most exalted, the universal and Heavenly Father of humankind throughout the world, who ought to be worshipped and adored every morning and evening, you do not worship God, but on the contrary worship only the demon who deceives, entangles, and captures the souls of humans! How stupid is this! It is very evident that there exist a true Spirit who is most responsive and most manifest, the universal and Heavenly Father of all humans throughout the world, who says, "Ask, and it shall be given you; seek, and ye shall find; knock, and it shall be opened unto you." (Michael 1971: 2:42)

The Taiping documents use over forty different Chinese terms to designate the devil and its multitude of idols.[7] Many of these terms are popular names used by Buddhism and folk religious beliefs. Some of them have been adopted in the early translation of the Bible in China.[8] The devil, the archenemy of *Shangdi*, is singled out as the embodiment of evil and perversion. The Old Testament Decalogue constitutes the core of the Taiping Religion to the extent that it was referred to as the "Ten Commandment Religion" (*Shijie Jiao*). Hong modified the Decalogue in *The Book of Heavenly Precepts* (*Tiantiao Shu*). "Thou shalt have no other gods besides me," one commandment in the Decalogue, is divided into two commandments in the *Tiantiao Shu*: (1) Thou shalt honor and worship the Supreme God. (2) Thou shalt not worship false gods (Michael 1971: 2:119–20).

The aniconic tradition of the second commandment in the Decalogue is left out and replaced by a prohibition against the worship of other gods, condemned as false gods.[9] The representations of these gods are to be utterly destroyed and their worshipers eliminated. These two commandments take up a paramount position in shaping the Taiping mission, expressed in the slogan of "exterminating the demons and establishing the righteous," and they "served as the essential standard of Taiping religious practice" (Reilly 2004: 134). The third commandment, not to take God's name in vain, received great attention as well. The Taiping army portrayed the imperial Qing political order as the devilish embodiment of blasphemy of God's name and a usurping of the authority of the supreme God. "The emperor, in referring to himself as Emperor (*Huangdi*), had transgressed the law of Heaven and so was judged to be worthy of execution" (Reilly 2004: 143). Hong saw his role as being charged with Heaven's mandate to destroy iconoclasm and execute the divinely ordained anti-imperialistic movement (Reilly 2004: 170). In *The Trimetrical Classic*, it is stated that the devil, being embodied in all the emperors of China, had deceived the Chinese for seven hundred years. *Shangdi* was angry and sent Hong, as "God's Chinese Son,"[10] to deliver China:

> In the *ting-yu* year [1837]
> He was taken to Heaven
> Where the heavenly matters
> Were first revealed to him
>   The Supreme God
> Instructed him in person,
> Gave him poetry and documents
> Which expounded the *Dao*
>   God bestowed upon him a seal,
> And also gave him a sword
> Conferred upon him authority
> And majesty inviolable.
>   He commanded him and his Elder Brother
> Namely Jesus,
> To drive away the devilish demons
> With the assistance of angels
>   The *Red Eyes,*
> King of the Underworld
> Displayed much malignity
> This devilish Serpent. (Michael 1971: 2:158)
>   Although you smoke and smoke, smoking does not satisfy;
> Why foolishly turn yourself into a living demon?
> Ridding of opium and dying of sickness is better than death by condemnation;
> Casting aside the demons and becoming a real human being is really great. (Michael 1971: 2:598–99)

People are repeatedly instructed and invited "to cast aside the demons to become real human beings."[11] They have to return to the supreme God, their "Real Father" (Michael 1971, II: 150). Reilly is of the opinion that iconoclasm and blasphemy of the Qing Empire constituted the core of the Taiping ideology, and these two aspects of the Taiping legacy are the Taiping contributions to Chinese Christianity (Reilly 2004: 164–71). But from the point of view of Chinese culture and religion, the iconoclastic program of the Taipings brought tremendous destruction to the local religious institutions and practices. Reilly's endorsement of the Taipings' contextualization of Christian teaching is questionable in the setting of a religiously plural China.

READING ICONOCLASTIC STIPULATIONS IN NUMBERS 33:50-56

We now come to the biblical material in Num. 33:50-56 to see how the conception of idolatry and the socioreligious function of prohibition of idols should be understood in the historical context of the people of Israel. First, we have to review the structure of the whole book of Numbers before we can appropriately locate meaning for Numbers 33.

In the book of Numbers, the fourth book of the Pentateuch, Israel is portrayed as coming to the end of the long journey from Egypt through Sinai to the wilderness, witnessing the death of the old generation and anticipating the birth of a new one that is about to enter the promised land. With the structural and literary devices of the two chapters about taking census in Numbers 1 and 26, the book of Numbers is assumed to have been divided into two major parts: chapters 1–25, and chapters 26–36. Scholars are mostly convinced that Numbers intends to portray a rebellious, old wilderness generation, which is to be punished with the denial of the promised land, and a hopeful, new generation about to enter God's land (Olson 1985).

I believe that by reading the poetic recitation of history in Psalm 106 and the narrative account of Israelite historical traditions in Numbers in parallel, we come to understand the underlying ideological function of Numbers. The traditions narrated in the latter part of Numbers are only recited otherwise in Psalm 106. The tragic end of the Exodus-Sinai generation is characterized by the rebellions against God (Num. 11:1—21:35; Ps. 106:6-25) and apostasy in the worship of the foreign god, Baʻal Peor of the Moabites, in Numbers 25 (Olson 1997: 232). Phinehas, the grandson of Aaron, punished the congregation with a terrible plague and was credited with perpetual priesthood (Num. 25:6-13).[12] Psalm 106 refers to the same tradition in its historical recitation, with parallel understanding of the reward to Phinehas of priesthood for generations (vv. 28-31). The epistle may have originated from the context of contestation of the priesthood of Phinehas in the postexilic era (Ezra 8:2; 1 Chron. 9:20). The generation of the wilderness and the exilic disaster are put together in parallel in Psalm 106:

> Then they despised the pleasant land,
> having no faith in his promise.
> They grumbled in the tents,
> and did not obey the voice of the Lord.
> Therefore he raised his hand and swore to them
> that he would make them fall in the wilderness,
> And would disperse their descendants among the nations
> scattering them over the lands. (Ps. 106:24-27)

The latter part of Numbers (chs. 26–36) exhibits a strong sense of life and hope for the new generation. The appeal of Zelophehad's five daughters to inherit their father's land (Num. 26:33-34) so that the land remains in the family's possession results in a compromise in dealing with traditional laws in new social reality (27:1-11; cf. 36:1-12).[13] Negotiation and reinterpretation tend to characterize the new generation (Olson 1997: 236). The text goes further, taking up the theme of leadership. While Moses is not allowed to enter the land (27:12-14), the election of Joshua anticipates the new leadership that is to emerge (vv. 15-23). The text has God proclaim the sin of Moses at the waters of Meribath-kadesh in the Wilderness of Zin: "Because you rebelled against my word in the Wilderness of Zin when the congregation quarreled with me. You did not show my holiness before their eyes at the waters" (v. 14). Again, Psalm 106 indicates the passing away of the old leadership, and even Moses, as the great leader, is not exempted from the blame directed at the old generation:

> They angered the Lord at the waters of Meribah,
> and it went ill with Moses on their account;
> For they made his spirit bitter,
> and he spoke words that were rash. (vv. 32-33)

Psalm 106 goes further than Numbers to lay blame on the older generation for not listening to the command of God to destroy the inhabitants of the land, but for mingling with them instead and serving their idols (Ps. 106:34-36), whereas Numbers 33 presents the same concern as God's command and a warning of it not being executed.

The first part of Numbers 33 (vv. 1-49) represents a record of the itinerary supposedly followed by the Israelites on their march from leaving Egypt to the region of Moab.[14] It has been observed that many of the stations and campsites listed in the wildnerness itinerary are unique to this passage and not found elsewhere in the Bible (so in 33:13, 19-29; see Olson 1996: 184). In Moses' recapitulation of the significant events along the journey, there is, besides the theme of the announcement of Aaron's death (33:38-39), the strange topic of the conquest of the Canaanite kings in the wilderness setting (33:40). At the beginning and the end of the list, the reiteration of God's victories over the gods of the Egyptians (33: 3-4) and the Canaanite king of Arad (33:40), respectively, function to induce faith and hope in the community (Olson 1996: 184–85). After the recapitulation of the long trek in the wilderness for the old Exodus generation (Num. 33:1-49), the chapter turns to the instructions for the Israelites to observe when they approach the land (vv. 50-56), which is a forward-looking warning to the new generation stationed at the edge of the promised land and about to enter it. The five pericopes that follow all begin with two identical phrases: "God commands Moses to transmit instructions to Israel" (33:50; 34:1, 16; 35:1, 9) and "when you cross the Jordan to the land of Canaan" (33:51; 34:2; 35:10) (Milgrom 1990: 282). The whole chapter, therefore, concludes with a warning that if Israel fails to drive out the Canaanites, the latter will remain a temptation to ensnare the Israelites. They will be "barbs in your eyes and thorns in your sides" (v. 55).

In contrast with the Deuteronomic tradition, Israel in Numbers 33 is instructed to drive out, not to destroy, the land's inhabitants, and is warned of the danger of the remaining inhabitants if left unconquered. The chapter is also different from Exodus 23, in which God, not Israel, will drive out the local inhabitations of Canaan. Exodus portrays God as sending hornets before the people of Israel (23:28), lest the Canaanites lead Israel to sin and become a snare unto Israel (23:33). The Canaanites will harass Israel and entice them to follow their gods and their religious practices (23:33; 34:12; cf. Deut. 7:16). It is clear in Psalm 106, an exilic production reflecting God's anger and the resultant dispersion of Israel among the nations (vv. 41-42), that Israel did not carry out the command to eliminate the peoples of the land. They coexisted with the Canaanites, learned their customs, and "served their idols, which became a snare to them" (v. 36).

What, then, is the provenance of Num. 33:50-56, and when was it composed? Philip Budd (1984: 358) notices the presence of Priestly elements in Num. 33:50-51, 54, which is mixed with material foreign to P (vv. 52-53, 55-56). The latter has affinities with the Holiness Code in Lev. 26:1, 30. Some scholars prefer to ascribe the whole passage (vv. 50-56, except v. 55) to deuteronomic tradition, especially the command to destroy Canaanite objects of worship (e.g., Exod. 23:24, 31-33; 34:11-16; Deut. 7:1-6; 12:2-3) and dispossession of inhabitants (Budd 1984: 359). Martin Noth too sees strong deuteronomistic form and context in the whole section of Num. 33:50—34:29, which indicates a late editorial process at the stage when the pentateuchal narrative was brought together with the deuteronomistic historical work (Noth 1968: 248). Budd (1984: 360–61) concludes that "the message and imagery are essentially deuteronomistic, with embellishments from Lev 26:1, 30, and the priestly author wishes to enforce this passage in his own way."

Baruch Levine is of the opinion that Num. 33:50-56, exhibiting "a strong statement," resonates with deuteronomic and deuteronomistic themes on the conquest and settlement of Canaan.[15] "Figurative objects" and "molten images," together with cultic "high places" (1 Kgs. 22:44; 2 Kgs. 2:4; 14:4; 15:4, 35), are to be destroyed. Levine (2000: 524) points out that the formula "grant/to take possession" is used in the manner found in Deuteronomy (3:18; 5:28; 9:6; 12:1; 15:4; 25:19; 19:2, 4, 21). We have, however, noted that in contrast to the commandment to utterly exterminate the former inhabitants, to be found in the deuteronomistic work, here in Numbers 33 the emphasis is on "driving out" and "dispossessing" (v. 50) the former occupants of the land in order to have Israel take possession of and settle in it (v. 53; cf. Deut. 1:8, 22; 2:21, 24; 5:23).[16]

In discussing the conquest of the land and the total destruction of the Canaanites in the land, Moshe Weinfeld's understanding is worthy of consideration: "The implementation of the *ḥerem* of the Canaanites in the deuteronomistic sources (Josh 10:28-43; 11:11-23) is wishful thinking, an attempt to adjust reality to the ideal world, which was never implemented (cf. Judg 1:21-34; I Kgs 9:20-21)" (Weinfeld 1991: 365).

The *ḥerem* command intends to totally exterminate the Canaanites so that Israel will be left to worship God alone without temptation and threat from her neighbors. The term *ḥerem* has the basic meaning of "consecration" (Lev. 27:28) and subsequently (v. 29) exhibits the connotation of "annihilation" (Antonelli 1997: 393). This latter meaning is present in the case of the total destruction of Canaanite kings and their cities (Num. 21:21-35; Deut. 2:34; 3:3, 6).[17]

It is surprising to note that very few contemporary commentaries are critical of this horrifying *ḥerem* command and of the expulsion of the natives from the perspective of the Canaanite inhabitants. The command to drive out the inhabitants of Canaan is justified by the threat they would bring to Israel's religious life. Riggans (1983: 235) asserts, based on the Ten Commandments (Exod. 20:3-6), that this "comes from the very heart of a God who is holy and jealous for his people's love and loyalty"; and this very God cannot tolerate "perversion of his faith nor desertion to other gods and cults." To prevent Israel from sinning against God, the command to expel the Canaanites from the land is repeatedly stated in the Bible. The religious practices and ritual objects of the existing inhabitants are to be utterly destroyed and the land made vacant is to be allotted to Israel as their possession. Riggans endorses the text with the theological concept that "the land belonged to the Lord and it was his sovereign right to use it as he willed" (p. 236). He also refers to the "dangers of assimilation" and the belief that we are made in God's image as the basis for extermination of the Canaanites and devastating all their false images and idols.

Patrick Miller simply ignores the impending destruction brought about to the non-Israelites and concerns himself with "the possibility of all sorts of chauvinistic and arrogant misunderstandings," but he goes on to clarify the meaning of Israel's election and her special place in God's sight (Miller 1990: 111). Gerhard von Rad (1964: 68) only mentions the obvious misunderstanding: "This choice was not made because Yahweh might have allowed himself to be impressed by Israel in any respect, but simply from an impulse of love."

Terence Fretheim notes that in Num. 33:50-56 Israel is to drive out all the present inhabitants of Canaan. She has to destroy all images, idols, and high places before the land is apportioned by lots according the size of the tribes and clans. The threat of not driving out the inhabitants is the danger of the latter becoming "barbs in your eyes and thorns in your sides" (v. 55). Fretheim is of the opinion that not only this threat (cf. Judg. 2:11—3:6) but also the warning of Israel's destruction (v. 56) would come true, as fulfilled by the expulsion and exile (Fretheim 2001: 133). A. D. H. Mayes (1979: 183) tries to redeem the text by underlining the command as simply representing an idea and that "all forms of intermingling with non-Israelites are rejected."

Christoph Bultmann also holds the same view, but goes further to account for the functions of the passage: "It serves as a basis for explaining the defeat of Jerusalem in 587 BCE in terms of Israel's apostasy which is seen to have been induced by her assimilation to the nations of the land in defiance of a Mosaic Command (cf. 20:18; 29:25-8 [M.T 24.7]; Josh 23:1 to Judg 3:6) and it serves as a warning against assimilation for the community of those who are faithful to the law, probably at some time in the Second Temple period" (Bultmann 2001: 143).

In the Hebrew Bible, there are in general two different traditions of the conception of idolatry. The first has to do with the prohibition of worship of gods other than Yahweh, an indication of exclusive loyalty to Yahweh. The second involves the prohibition of any image representing Yahweh, the core of aniconism in the biblical worship of Yahweh (Chung 2010: 207). Recent studies tend to attribute the formulation of the prohibition on images of Yahweh to the monotheistic affirmation of the aniconic God, with the motivation to avoid any possible idea of equating Israel's ruin and material destruction in the exile with Yahweh's defeat by other gods.[18] Nathaniel Levtow's research in his book *Images of Others* (2008) is a good example for understanding the dynamics of Israel's iconic politics among the empires and their gods in the exile.

The exhortation serves to underline the warning about the danger of religious practices attributed to the local inhabitants, and affirms the identity of Israel in her commitment to the monotheistic God. The locals have led the first generation of Israelite settlers and subsequent generations away from Yahweh, resulting in the exile. These past generations of Israelite forefathers and foremothers were blamed for not driving out the local inhabitants and for not destroying their divine images and cultic practices. Now, to ensure that this present new generation survives and to avoid repetition of the same fate as that of the older generations, a radical break from foreign cults must be introduced. The command to drive out the "Canaanites" is for self-preservation. It is not, therefore, a challenge for the strong and powerful to conquer other people's religion and destroy their cultural practices, as the missionary movement during the colonialist expansion—mistakenly—attempted to accomplish.

CONCLUSION

Scholars have mostly admitted that Israel did not carry out the command of Yahweh (e.g., Psalm 106). They mingled with the inhabitants and followed their religious customs and cultic practices. The prohibition against idolatry in Num. 33:50-56 is commonly acknowledged by scholars as being a late editorial addition to the book, with the exile as its background. It represents the major concern of Israel in the exilic community, in the quest for religious and political identity vis-à-vis the foreigners and the other. The myth of an empty land is seen as at best an ideal, but, most important, as a constant reality encountered by the people of Israel. The central issue at stake is, how to relate to other people and their gods.

From the Chinese pluralistic religious context, we try to understand the historical circumstances that gave rise to the formation of the biblical iconoclastic stipulations in Numbers 33. The people of Israel were in the desperate situation of exile and loss, anticipating comfort and encouragement in redefining their identity vis-à-vis the oppressive and imperialist religions and cultures of the empire.

Christendom has an ideology contrary to the biblical circumstances. In fact, the expansionist and colonialist zeal of the missionary movement was armed with military power and filled with triumphalist spirit, crashing down the native culture and its religious practices. In a postcolonial perspective of seeing plurality as a God-designed reality in this world of diversity in culture and religion, any iconoclastic act against other people's religion should be condemned. It is ironic that words that were meant to encourage and comfort the weak have become swords to further empower the powerful.

Notes

1. The research for this paper was made possible with the support from the General Research Funds (GRF) of the Hong Kong Research Grants Council for the project on the Bible in China, 2009–2012.

2. Translations from the Hebrew in this essay are from NRSV unless otherwise stated.

3. This is a modified translation of that of Spence (1966: 69), based on the Chinese original.

4. Michael 1971: 2:150. Taiping documents quoted in this essay are based on the English translation of Franz Michael, with modifications by the present author.

5. See Spence's chapter "Judgments," 1966: 96–109.

6. On the controversy about the Chinese term for the biblical God, see Lee 2006: 1–17.

7. For a list of Taiping terms used see Boardman 1952: 81. See also Xia Chun-tao 2006: 26–27.

8. Boardman lists about sixteen of these terms that have sources in early Chinese Bible versions (83).

9. In *The Book of Heavenly Commandments*," Michael 1971: 2:120.

10. The phrase is used in the title of Spence's book (1966).

11. "Proclamation by Imperial Sanction," Michael 1971: 2:151.

12. For more on the Ba'al Peor incident and on Phinehas's role see essays by Dor, Gafney, Rees, and Vaka'uta in this volume.

13. Cf. also Amadi Ahiamadu's essay in this volume.

14. Graham Davis (1979: 94n2) understands the itinerary forms as the basis from which other itinerary segments of the journey in Exodus and Numbers are derived (Exod. 12:37a; 13:20; 14:2; 15:22-23a, 27; 16:1; 17:1; 19:1-2; Num. 10:12, 33a; 11:35; 12:16; 20:1, 22; 21:4a, 10-11; 22:1; 25:1).

15. Levine 2000: 522. See also Levine's comment on Numbers 33 and Deuteronomy 12 in his introduction, 57.

16. Moshe Weinfeld has a clear discussion on the differences between "expulsion" and "extermination." See his commentary on Deuteronomy 1–11 (1991: 382–84).

17. Antonelli sees the *ḥerem* of women captives in war as being "dedicated" or "consecrated" to God: "Killing the women rather than capturing them required a certain level of self-restraint and denial of gratification on men's part" (1997: 395); see also and otherwise Jacobs 2012: 237–57.

18. See Chung's conclusion, 2010: 204–8. Since all gods in West Asia were represented by symbols or images, there is practically no distinction between the prohibition of other gods and the ban on their images. Chung proves, based on the exhortation to Israel in the exile in Deut. 4:1-40, among others, "that there was no law designed to prohibit images of YHWH prior to the Exile" and that the crystallization of the prohibition of YHWH's image in the exile has the motive to underline the declaration of the uniqueness of the monotheistic YHWH (Deut. 4:35, 39). Chung also discusses the scholarly views on the origin of monotheistic faith (pp. 191–99).

Bibliography

Abramsky, Shmuel. 1975. "On the Kenite-Midianite Background of Moses' Leadership." In *EI* 12:35–39 (Heb.).

———. 1984. "The Ishmaelites and the Midianites."In *EI* 17:128–34 (Heb.).

Abravanel, Isaac. 1955. *Commentary on the Former Prophets*. Jerusalem: Torah vda'ath (Heb.).

———. 1964. *Commentary on the Torah*. 3 vols. Benei Arbal (Heb.).

———. 1979. *Commentary on Later Prophets*. Jerusalem: Benei Arbal [Heb.].

Abusch, Tzvi. 2002. "Sacrifice in Mesopotamia." In *Sacrifice in Religious Experience*, ed. A. I. Baumgarten, 39–48. Boston: Brill.

Aharoni, Yohanan. 1974. "Amalek." In *Encyclopaedia Biblica*, ed. E. L. Sukenik and U. M. D. Cassuto, 6:289–92. Jerusalem: Bialic Institute (Heb.).

Alberts, Rainer. 1992. *A History of Israelite Religion in the Old Testament Period*. Vol. 1, *From the Beginnings to the End of Monarchy*. Trans. John Bowden. Louisville: John Knox.

Allen, Diane. 2005. "Greek Tragedy and Law." In *The Cambridge Companion to Ancient Greek Law*, ed. Michael Gagarin and David Cohen, 374–93. New York: Cambridge University Press.

Allen, Leslie C. 1990. *Ezekiel 20–48*. WBC 29. Dallas: Word.

———. 2002. *Psalms 101–150*. WBC 21. Waco: Word.

Alster, Bendt. 1983. "The Mythology of Mourning." *Acta Sumerologica* 5: 1–16.

Alston, Philip. 2009. United Nations Document Reference A/HRC/11/2. "Promotion and Protection of All Human Rights, Civil, Political, Economic, Social and Cultural Rights, Including the Right to Development." *Report of the Special Rapporteur on Extrajudicial or Arbitrary Executions*. May 27. 11th Session of the UN HCR. http://www2 .ohchr.org/english/bodies/hrcouncil/docs/11session/A.HRC. 11.2.pdf.

Alter, Robert. 1981. *The Art of Biblical Narrative*. New York: Basic.

Amadi, E. 1982. *Ethics in Nigerian Culture*. London: Heinemans.

Amit, Yairah. 2003. "A Prophet Tested: Elisha, the Great Woman of Shunem, and the Story's Double Message." *BibInt* 11: 279–94.

Amnesty International. 11 February 2009. "Increasing Sorcery-Related Killings in Papua New Guinea." A/HRC/11/2 http://www.amnesty.org/en/ news-

and-updates/news/increasing-sorcery-related-killings-papua-new-guinea-20090211.

Anderson, Gary A. 1991. *A Time to Mourn, A Time to Dance: The Expression of Grief and Joy in Israelite Religion*. University Park: Pennsylvania State University Press.

Antonelli, Judith S. 1997. *In the Image of God: A Feminist Commentary on the Torah*. London: Jason Aronson.

Ashley, T. R. 1993. *The Book of Numbers*. NICOT. Grand Rapids: Eerdmans.

Austin, Alvyn. 2007. *China's Millions: The China Inland Mission and Late Qing Society, 1832–1905*. Grand Rapids: Eerdmans.

Avalos, Hector. 2007. *The End of Biblical Studies*. Amherst, NY: Prometheus.

Avalos, Hector, Sarah J. Melcher, and Jeremy Schipper, eds. 2007. *This Abled Body: Rethinking Disabilities in Biblical Studies*. SemeiaSt 55. Atlanta: Society of Biblical Literature.

Avioz, Michael. 2008. "'He Went into the House of the Lord and Prostrated Himself': Where Did David Go?" *Shnaton: An Annual for Biblical and Ancient Near Eastern Studies* 18: 3–11 (Heb.).

Ayandele, E. A. 1966. *The Missionary Impact in Modern Nigeria 1842–1914: A Political and Social Analysis*. London: Longmans.

Bach, Alice, ed. 1999. *Women in the Hebrew Bible: A Reader*. New York: Routledge.

Bahrani, Zainab. 2008. *Rituals of War: The Body and Violence in Mesopotamia*. New York: Zone.

Bal, Mieke, ed. 1989. *Anti-Covenant: Counter-Reading Women's Lives in the Hebrew Bible*. Sheffield: Almond.

———. 1993. "Myth à la Lettre: Freud, Mann, Genesis and Rembrandt, and the Story of the Son." In *A Feminist Companion to Genesis*, ed. A. Brenner, 343–78. Sheffield: Sheffield Academic. (Originally published in *Discourse in Psychoanalysis and Literature*, ed. S. Rimon-Kenan, 57–89. London: Methen, 1987).

Bar-Efrat, Shimon. 2009. *Das Zweite Buch Samuel, aus dem Neuhebräischen übersetzt von Johannes Klein*. Stuttgart: W. Kohlhammer.

Barr, J. 1999. *The Concept of Biblical Theology: An Old Testament Perspective*. Minneapolis: Fortress Press.

Batson, C. Daniel, Randy B. Floyd, Julie M. Meyer, and Alana L. Winner. 1999. "'And Who Is My Neighbor?': Intrinsic Religion as a Source of Universal Compassion." *JSSR* 38/4: 445–57.

Bell, Catherine. 1989. "Religion and Chinese Culture: Toward an Assessment of 'Popular Religion.'" *HR* 29: 35–57.

Ben David, Haim. 2008. "Sites of 'Medina' on the Springs of the Arnon—Midian Next to Moab?" In *In the Hill-Country, in the Plain and in the Arabah (Josh 12: 8): Studies and Researches Presented to Adam Zertal on the Thirtieth Anniversary of the Manasseh Hill-Country Survey*, ed. Shai Bar, 78–88. Jerusalem: Ariel (Heb.).

Bendann, E. 1930 (repr. 1969). *Death Customs: An Analytical Study of Burial Rites.* London: Dawsons of Pall Mall.

Berman, J. 2007. "Ancient Hermeneutics and the Legal Structure of the Book of Ruth." *ZAW* 119: 22–38.

Berman, Saul. 1992. "Jewish Environmental Values: The Dynamic Tension Between Nature and Human Needs." In *Human Values and the Environment: Conference Proceedings*, Madison, Wis.: Wisconsin Academy of Sciences, Arts and Letters, 8–11.

Bird, P. A. 1992. "Women in the OT." In *ABD* 6:951–57.

Blauner, Robert. 1966. "Death and the Social Structure." *Psychiatry* 29: 378–94.

Blenkinsopp, Joseph. 2008. "The Midianite-Kenite Hypothesis Revisited and the Origins of Judah." *JSOT* 33/2: 131–53.

Block, Daniel I. 1997. *The Book of Ezekiel: Chapters 1–24.* NICOT. Grand Rapids: Eerdmans.

Boardman, Eugene P. 1952. *Christian Influence upon the Ideology of the Taiping Rebellion, 1851–1864.* Madison: University of Wisconsin Press.

Boecker, H. J. 1976. *Law and Administration of Justice in the Old Testament and Ancient Near East.* London: SPCK.

Boniface-Malle, Anastasia. 2008. "From Violence and War to *Shalom* in the Hebrew Bible." In *Validating Violence—Violating Faith? Religion, Scripture and Violence*, ed. William W. Emilsen and John T. Squires, 77–94. Adelaide: ATF Press.

Bosco, Joseph, and Puay-peng Ho. 1999. *Temples of the Empress of Heaven, Images of Asia.* New York: Oxford University Press.

Bosman, H. L. 2002. "Appropriating the Decalogue According to African Proverbs." *Scriptura* 81: 354–61.

Boyarin, Daniel. 2012. *The Jewish Gospels: The Story of the Jewish Christ.* New York: New Press.

Branch, R. G. 2003. "Zelophehad, Daughters of." In *Dictionary of the Old Testament: Pentateuch*, ed. T. D. Alexander and D. W. Baker, 912–14. Downers Grove, IL: InterVarsity.

Brenner, Athalya. 1997. "Deviation from Socio-Sexual Boundaries I." In *The Intercourse of Knowledge: On Gendering Desire and Sexuality in the Hebrew Bible*, 90–130. Biblical Interpretation 26. Leiden: E. J. Brill.

———. 2003. "'On the Rivers of Babylon' (Psalm 137), or Between Victim and Perpetrator." In *Sanctified Aggression: Legacies of Biblical and Post-Biblical Vocabularies of Violence*, ed. Yvonne Sherwood and Jonneke Bekkenkamp, 76–91. JSOTSup 400. London: T&T Clark.

Brett, Mark G. 2009. *Decolonizing God: The Bible in the Tides of Empire*. Bible in the Modern World. Sheffield: Sheffield Phoenix.

Bridge, Edward J. 2012. "Female Slave vs Female Slave: אמה and שפחה in the Hebrew Bible." *Journal of Hebrew Scriptures* 12/2: 1–21.

Bromiley, G. W. 1999. *The Encyclopaedia of Christianity*. Grand Rapids: Eerdmans.

Brownlie, Ian, ed. 2010. *Basic Documents on Human Rights*. Oxford: Oxford University Press.

Brueggemann, Walter. 2002. *The Land: Place as Gift, Promise, and Challenge in Biblical Faith*. 2nd ed. Minneapolis: Fortress Press.

Buber, Martin. 1997. *On Zion: The History of an Idea*. Syracuse: Syracuse University Press.

Budd, Philip J. 1984. *Numbers*. WBC 5. Waco: Word.

Bultmann, Christoph. 2001. "Deuteronomy." In *The Oxford Bible Commentary*, ed. John Barton and John Muddiman, 135–58. Oxford: Oxford University Press.

Burney, Charles Fox.1970. *The Book of Judges: With Introduction and Notes*. Library of Biblical Studies. 3rd ed. New York: Ktav.

Burns, K., and L. Novick. 2011. *Prohibition*. DVD. Culver City, CA: PBS Home Video.

Bury, R. G., ed. and trans. 1926. *Plato: Laws, Books 7–12*. LCL 192. London: Heinemann.

Butler, Trent C. 1983. *Joshua*. WBC, 7. Waco, Nashville: Thomas Nelson.

Callicott, J. Baird. 1989. *In Defense of the Land Ethic: Essays in Environmental Philosophy*. Albany: State University of New York Press.

———. 1999. *Beyond the Land Ethic: More Essays in Environmental Philosophy*. Albany: State University of New York Press.

Carmichael, Calum M. 1985. *Law and Narrative in the Bible: The Evidence of Deuteronomic Laws and the Decalogue*. Ithaca, NY: Cornell University Press.

———. 1992. *The Origins of Biblical Law: The Decalogues and the Book of the Covenant*. Ithaca, NY: Cornell University Press.

———. 1996. *The Spirit of Biblical Law*. Athens: University of Georgia Press.

———. 1997. *Law, Legend, and Incest in the Bible. Leviticus 18–20*. Ithaca, NY: Cornell University Press.

———. 2010. *Sex and Religion in the Bible*. New Haven: Yale University Press.

Carroll, Robert P. 1986. *Jeremiah*. OTL 11. Philadelphia: Westminster Press.

Carter, Sarah. 2008. *The Importance of Being Monogamous: Marriage and Nation Building in Western Canada to 1915*. Edmonton: University of Alberta Press.

Cazelles, Henri. 1974. "'*Ashrê*." In *TDOT*, ed. G. Johannes Botterweck, Helmer Ringgren, and Heinz-Josef Fabry, 445–48. Grand Rapids: Eerdmans.

Chapman, Cynthia R. 2004. *The Gendered Language of Warfare in the Israelite-Assyrian Encounter*. HSM 62; Winona Lake, IN: Eisenbrauns.

Charles, R. H., ed. 1913. *The Apocrypha and Pseudepigrapha of the Old Testament in English*. 2 vols. Oxford: Clarendon.

Chung , Youn Ho. 2010. *The Sin of the Calf: The Rise of the Bible's Negative Attitude toward the Golden Calf*. London: T&T Clark.

Cohen, Menachem, ed. 1993. *Mikra'ot Gedolot "Haketer"—Samuel I & II*. Ramat-Gan: Bar-Ilan University Press (Heb.).

———. 2000. *Mikra'ot Gedolot "Haketer"—Ezekiel*. Ramat-Gan: Bar-Ilan University Press (Heb.).

Cohen, Paul A. 1978. "Christian Missions and Their Impact to 1900." In *The Cambridge History of China, Late Ch'ing 1800–1911*, ed. John K. Fairbank, 10:543–90. Cambridge: Cambridge University Press.

Collins, John J. 2003. "The Zeal of Phinehas: The Bible and the Legitimation of Violence." *JBL* 122/1: 3–21.

Confucius. 1967. *Li Chi: Book of Rites*. 2 vols. New Hyde Park, NY: University Books.

Cooke, G. A. 1936 (repr., 1967). *A Critical and Exegetical Commentary on the Book of Ezekiel*. ICC 17. Edinburgh: T&T Clark.

Cooper, Jerrold S. 2006. "Genre, Gender, and the Sumerian Lamentation." *JCS* 58: 39–47.

Countryman, L. William. 2008. *Dirt, Greed, and Sex: Sexual Ethics in the New Testament and Their Implications for Today*. Minneapolis: Fortress Press.

Craigie, Peter C. 1976. *Deuteronomy*. NICOT. Grand Rapids: Eerdmans.

Cross, Frank Moore. 1976. *Canaanite Myth and Hebrew Epic: Essays in the History of the Religion of Israel*. Cambridge, MA: Harvard University Press.

Curtis, A. H. W. 1994. *Joshua*. Sheffield: Sheffield Academic.

Dahood, Mitchell. 1960. "Textual Problems in Isaia." *CBQ* 22: 400–409.

Danby, Herbert (trans.). 1933. *The Mishnah*. Oxford: Oxford University Press.

Darwin, Charles R. 1874. *The Descent of Man, and Selection in Relation to Sex*. 2nd ed. London: John Murray, Ablemarle Street.

Davis, Ellen F. 2009. *Scripture, Culture and Agriculture: An Agrarian Reading of the Bible*. New York: Cambridge University Press.

Davis, Graham. 1979. *The Way of the Wilderness: A Geographical Study of the Wilderness Itineraries in the Old Testament*. Cambridge: Cambridge University Press.

Deist, F. 1990. *A Concise Dictionary of Theological and Related Terms*. Pretoria: van Schaik.

Dijk-Hemmes, Fokkelien van. 1994. "The Great Woman of Shunem and the Man of God: A Dual Interpretation of 2 Kings 4.8-37." In *A Feminist Companion to Samuel and Kings*, ed. Athalya Brenner, 218–30. Sheffield: Sheffield Academic.

Dobbs-Allsopp, F. W. 1993. *Weep, O Daughter of Zion: A Study of the City-Lament Genre in the Hebrew Bible*. Rome: Pontificio Istituto Biblico.

Dor, Yonina. 2006. *Were the "Foreign Women" Really Expelled? Separation and Exclusion in the Restoration Period*. Jerusalem: Magnes (Heb.).

———. 2011. "The Rite of Separation of the Foreign Wives in Ezra-Nehemiah." In *The Judeans in the Achaemenid Age: Negotiating Identity in an International Context*, ed. G. N. Knoppers, O. Lipschits, and M. Oeming, 173–88. Winona Lake, IN: Eisenbrauns.

Dorff, Elliot N. 1996. *Human Cloning: A Jewish Perspective*. Chicago: Park Ridge Center for Health, Faith, and Ethics.

———. 1996. *The Jewish Tradition: Religious Beliefs and Healthcare Decisions*. Chicago: Park Ridge Center for Health, Faith, and Ethics.

Douglas, Mary. 1999. *Leviticus as Literature*. New York: Oxford University Press.

———. 2002 (1966). *Purity and Danger: An Analysis of Concepts of Pollution and Taboo*. London: Routledge.

———. 2002. "Responding to Ezra: The Priests and the Foreign Wives." *BibInt* 10/1: 1–23.

Drew, S., ed. 1833. *The Imperial Magazine; and Monthly Record of Religious, Philosophical, History, Biographical, Topological, and General Knowledge; Embracing Literature, Science, and Art* 3. London: Caxton.

Duncan, P. 1994. "Shame." In *The Encyclopaedia of Aboriginal Australia*, ed. D. Horton. Canberra, 978–80. The Australian Institute of Aboriginal and Torres Islander Studies.

Durkheim, Émile. 1965 (1915). *The Elementary Forms of the Religious Life*. Trans. Joseph Ward Swain. New York: Free Press.

Dybdahl, J. L. 1981. "Israelite Village Land Tenure: Settlement to Exile." Ph.D. diss., Fuller Theological Seminary.

Elder, Bruce. 1988. *Blood on the Wattle: Massacres and Maltreatments of Australian Aborigines since 1788*. Frenchs Forest, N.S.W: Child & Associates.

Eliade, Mircea. 1963. *The Sacred and the Profane: The Nature of Religion*. Trans. Willard R. Trask. New York: Harcourt Brace Jovanovich.

Eusebius of Caesarea. 2003. *The Onomasticon*. Trans. G. Freeman-Grenville S.P., ed. Joan E. Taylor. In *Palestine in the Fourth Century A.D.* Jerusalem: Carta.

Evans, M. J. 2003. "Women." In *Dictionary of the Old Testament: Pentateuch*, ed. T. D. Alexander and D. W. Baker, 978–93. Downers Grove, IL: InterVarsity.

Falk, Ze'ev W. 1964. *Hebrew Law in Biblical Times: An Introduction*. Jerusalem: Wahrman.

Feld, Steven, and Aaron A. Fox. 1994. "Music and Language." *Annual Review of Anthropology* 23: 25–53.

Feldman, Emanuel. 1977. *Biblical and Post-Biblical Defilement and Mourning: Law as Theology*. New York: Yeshiva University Press.

Feuchtwang, Stephan. 2001. *Popular Religion in China: The Imperial Metaphor*. Richmond, Surrey: Curzon.

Fewell, Danna Nolan. 1987. "Feminist Reading of the Hebrew Bible: Affirmation, Resistance and Transformation." *JSOT* 39: 77–87.

Finkelstein, Israel. 2007. "When and How Did the Israelites Emerge?" In *The Quest for the Historical Israel: Debating Archaeology and the History of Early Israel*, ed. Israel Finkelstein, Amihai Mazar, and Brian B Schmidt, 73–84. Archaeology and Biblical Studies. Atlanta: Society of Biblical Literature.

Fischer, Stefan. 2012. Review of *Sex and Religion in the Bible*, by Calum Carmichael. *Review of Biblical Literature* (http://www.bookreviews.org/pdf/7431_8104.pdf).

Fishbane, Michael. 1999. "Accusations of Adultery: A Study of Law and Scribal Practice in Num. 5:11-31." In *Women in the Hebrew Bible: A Reader*, ed. Alice Bach, 487–502. New York: Routledge.

Foer, Jonathan Safran. 2009. *Eating Animals*. New York: Little, Brown.

Fokkelman, J. P. 1981. *Narrative Art and Poetry in the Books of Samuel, Vol. I—King David*. Assen: Van Gorcum.

Fonrobert, Charlotte E. 2007. "Regulating the Human Body: Rabbinic Legal Discourse and the Making of Jewish Gender." In *The Cambridge Companion* to the Talmud and Rabbinic Literature, ed. Charlotte Elisheva Fonrobert and Martin S. Jaffee. 270–94. Cambridge: Cambridge University Press.

Fontaine, Carole. 2008. *With Eyes of Flesh: The Bible, Gender, and Human Rights.* Sheffield: Sheffield Phoenix.

Foster, Douglas, and Anthony Dunnavant. 2004. "Slogans." In *The Encyclopedia of the Stone-Campbell Movement*, ed. Douglas A. Foster, Paul M. Blowers, Anthony L. Dunnavant, and D. Newell Williams. Grand Rapids: Eerdmans.

Fowler, Jeaneane D., and Merv Fowler. 2008. *Chinese Religions: Beliefs and Practices.* Brighton; Portland: Sussex Academic.

Fox, Everett. 1995. *The Five Books of Moses: Genesis, Exodus, Leviticus, Numbers, Deuteronomy; A New Translation with Introductions, Commentary, and Notes.* The Schocken Bible 1. New York: Schocken.

Fretheim, Terence E. 2001. "Numbers." In *The Oxford Bible Commentary*, ed. John Barton and John Muddiman. 110–34. Oxford: Oxford University Press.

———. 2005. *God and World in the Old Testament: A Relational Theology of Creation.* Nashville: Abingdon.

Frevel, Christian, ed. 2011. *Mixed Marriages: Intermarriage and Group Identity in the Second Temple Period.* New York: Continuum.

Friebel, Kalvin G. 1999. *Jeremiah's and Ezekiel's Sign-Acts.* JSOTSup 283. Sheffield: Sheffield Academic.

Frisch, Amos. 1999. "Midrashic Derivations of Solomon's Name in the Book of Kings." *Beit Mikra* 45: 84–96 (Heb.).

Frymer-Kensky, Tikva. 1999. "The Strange Case of the Suspected Sotah." In *Women in the Hebrew Bible: A Reader*, ed. Alice Bach, 463–74. New York: Routledge.

Frymer-Kensky, Tikva. 2002. *Reading the Women of the Bible.* New York: Schocken.

Gammie, John G. 1989. *Holiness in Israel.* Minneapolis: Fortress Press.

Gane, Roy. 2005. *Cult and Character: Purification Offerings, Day of Atonement, and Theodicy.* Winona Lake, IN: Eisenbrauns.

Ganuz, Itzchak. 1989. "The Personal Belongings of Tsaddikim as Treasures of Virtues." *Proceedings of the Tenth World Congress of Jewish Studies, Division D* 2: 29–31 (Hebrew section).

García Martínez, F. and Tigchelaar, E. J. C. 1997–1998. *The Dead Sea Scrolls Study Edition.* Vols. 1 and 2. Leiden: Brill.

Garsiel, Moshe. 1991. *Biblical Names: A Literary Study of Midrashic Derivations and Puns.* Trans. Phyllis Hackett, Ramat Gan: Bar-Ilan University.

Gaster, Theodor H. 1969. *Myth, Legend and Custom in the Old Testament*. New York: Harper & Row.

Gauguin, Paul. 1978. *Writings of a Savage*. New York: Viking.

———. 2009. *Noa Noa: The Tahitian Journal*. New York: Classic Books.

———. 2011. *Gauguin Tahiti*, ed. George Shackelford et al. Boston: MFA Publications.

Gerhards, Meik. 2005. "Über die Herkunft der Frau des Mose." *VT* 55/2: 162–75.

Ginat, Joseph. 1987. *Blood Disputes among Bedouin and Rural Arabs in Israel: Revenge, Mediation, Outcasting and Family Honor*. Pittsburgh: University of Pittsburgh Press; Jerusalem Institute for Israel Studies.

Goldingay, John. 2008. *Psalms*. Vol. 3, *Psalms 90–150*. Baker Commentary on the Old Testament Wisdom and Psalms. Grand Rapids: Baker Academic.

Goossaert, Vincent. 2005. "Chinese Religion: Popular Religion." In *Encyclopedia of Religion*, ed. L. Jones, 1613–21. Detroit: Macmillan Reference USA.

Gray, George B. 1956. *A Critical and Exegetical Commentary on Numbers*. ICC 4. 2nd. ed. Edinburgh: T&T Clark.

Greenberg, Moshe. 1997. *Ezekiel 21–37*. AB 22A. New York: Doubleday.

Greenstein, Edward L. 1982. "An Equivocal Reading of the Sale of Joseph." In *Literary Interpretations of Biblical Narratives*, ed. K. R. R. Gros Louis, 2:114–25. Nashville: Abingdon.

Grossman, Jonathan. 2007. "Divine Command and Human Initiative: A Literary View on Numbers 25–31." *BibInt* 15: 54–79.

Gruber, Mayer I., 1980. *Aspects of Nonverbal Communication in the Ancient Near East*. 2 vols. Rome: Biblical Institute Press.

Gutzwiller, Kathryn. 1996. "Comments on Rolf Rendtorff." In *Reading Leviticus: A Conversation with Mary Douglas*, ed. John F. A. Sawyer, 36–39. Sheffield: Sheffield Academic.

Hackett, Rosalind I. J. 2005. "Rethinking the Role of Religion in the Public Sphere: Local and Global Perspectives." In *Comparative Perspectives on Shari`ah in Nigeria*, ed. Philip Ostien, Jamila M. Nasir, and Franz Kogelmann, 74–100. Ibadan: Spectrum.

Hacohen, David Ben-Gad. 2006. "Eretz Hashasu Yehu." *Nile, Euphfrates and Tigris* 2: 1-22 (Heb.).

Halpern-Amaru, B. 1999. "Bilhah and Naphtali in Jubilees: A Note on 4QTNaphtali." *DSD* 6/1: 1–10.

Harrell, C. Stevan. 1974. "When a Ghost Becomes a God." In *Religion and Ritual in Chinese Society*, ed. A. P. Wolf, 193–206. Stanford: Stanford University Press.

Harrington, Hannah K. 1996. "Interpreting Leviticus in the Second Temple Period: Struggling with Ambiguity." In *Reading Leviticus: A Conversation with Mary Douglas*, ed. John F.A. Sawyer, 230–37. Sheffield: Sheffield Academic.

Harris, R. 1992. "Women in (Mesopotamia)." In *ABD* 6:947–57.

Harrison, David. 2008. "Nigeria's 'Child Witches' Seek Refuge." *The Telegraph.* http://www.telegraph.co.uk/news/worldnews/africaandindianocean/nigeria/3407882/Child-witches-of-Nigeria-seek-refuge.html (accessed April 30, 2012).

Hartley, John E. 1992. *Leviticus.* WBC 4. Dallas: Word.

Havea, Jione. 2004. "Numbers." In *The Global Bible Commentary*, ed. Daniel Patte et al., 43–51. Nashville: Abingdon.

Hays, J. Daniel, and Donald A. Carson. 2003. *From Every People and Nation: A Biblical Theology of Race.* New Studies in Biblical Theology. Downers Grove: InterVarsity.

Hawk, D. L. 1991. *Every Promise Fulfilled: Contesting Plots in Joshua.* Louisville: Westminster John Knox.

Hoffner, Harry A., Jr. 1997. "Hittite Laws." In *Writings from the Ancient World: Law Collections from Mesopotamia and Asia Minor*, ed. Martha T. Roth, 213–47. 2nd ed. Writings from the Ancient World Series. Atlanta: Scholars Press.

Horsley, Richard A. 2004. "The Origin of the Hebrew Scriptures in Imperial Relations." In *Orality, Literacy, and Colonialism in Antiquity*, ed. Jonathan A. Draper, 107–34. Atlanta: Society of Biblical Literature.

———. 2008. *Jesus in Context: Power, People, and Performance.* Minneapolis: Fortress Press.

Houston, Walter J. 1993. *Purity and Monotheism: Clean and Unclean Animals in Biblical Law.* JSOTSup 140. Sheffield: JSOT Press.

———. 2003. "Towards an Integrated Reading of the Dietary Laws of Leviticus." In *The Book of Leviticus: Composition and Reception*, ed. R. Rendtorff, R. A. Kugler, and S. S. Bartel, 142–61. Leiden: Brill.

———. 2008. *Contending for Justice: Ideologies and Theologies of Social Justice in the Old Testament.* Rev. ed.. London: T&T Clark.

Houtman, Cornelis. 1993. *Exodus.* Vol 1. Historical Commentary on the Old Testament. Trans. Rebel Johan and Sierd Woudstra. Kampen: Kok.

Howie-Willis, Ian. 1994a. "Family." In *The Encyclopaedia of Aboriginal Australia*, ed. D. Horton, 356. Canberra: The Australian Institute of Aboriginal and Torres Strait Islander Studies.

———. 1994b. "Marriage." In *The Encyclopaedia of Aboriginal Australia*, ed. D. Horton, 664. Canberra: The Australian Institute of Aboriginal and Torres Strait Islander Studies.

Huntington, Richard, and Peter Metcalf. 1979. *Celebrations of Death*. Cambridge: Cambridge University Press.

Hurowitz, Victor. 1992. *I have Built You an Exalted House: Temple Building in the Bible in the Light of Mesopotamian and Northwest Semitic Writings*. JSOTSup 115; Sheffield, Sheffield Academic Press.

Imhoff, D., ed. 2010. *The CAFO Reader: The Tragedy of Industrial Animal Factories*. Contemporary Issues. Healdsburg, CA: Watershed Media.

Instone-Brewer, David. 2002. *Divorce and Remarriage in the Bible: The Social and Literary Context*. Grand Rapids: Eerdmans.

Jackson, Bernard. 2007. "Gender Critical Observations on Tripartite Breeding Relationships in the Hebrew Bible." In *Gender and Difference in the Hebrew Bible and Beyond*, ed. Deborah W. Rooke, 39–52. Sheffield: Phoenix.

Jacobs, Sandra. 2012. "Terms of Endearment? The Desirable Female Captive (אשת יפת תאר) and her Illicit Acquisition." In *Exodus and Deuteronomy: Texts@Contexts*, ed. A. Brenner and G. A. Yee, 237–57. Minneapolis: Fortress Press.

Japhet, Sara. 1977. *The Ideology of the Book of Chronicles and Its Place in Biblical Thought*. Jerusalem: Bialik Institute (Heb.).

Jastrow, Marcus. 1903. "מעא." In *A Dictionary of the Targumim, the Talmud Babli and Yerushalmi, and the Midrashic Literature*, 812. London: Luzac and Co.

Jochim, Christian. 2003. "Chinese Beliefs." In *Macmillan Encyclopedia of Death and Dying*, ed. R. Kastenbaum, 158–63. New York: Macmillan Reference USA.

Joosten, Jan. 1996. *People and Land in the Holiness Code: An Exegetical Study of the Ideational Framework of the Law in Leviticus 17–26*. Leiden: Brill.

Jung, C. G. 1912. *The Theory of Psychoanalysis*. Nervous and Mental Disease Monograph 19. New York: The Journal of Nervous and Mental Disease Publishing Company.

Kaminsky, Joel S. 1995. *Corporate Responsibility in the Hebrew Bible*. Sheffield: Sheffield Academic Press.

———. 2008. "Loving One's Israelite Neighbor: Election and Commandment in Leviticus 19." *Int* 62/2: 123–32.

Karff, Samuel E. 1995. "Leviticus 10:1-20: Silence and Weeping before the Song." In *Preaching Biblical Texts: Expositions by Jewish and Christian Scholars*, ed. Fredrick C. Holmgren and Herman E. Schaalman, 105–16. Grand Rapids: Eerdmans.

Kasher, Rimon. 2004. *Ezekiel*. Mikra LeYisra'el. 2 vols. Tel Aviv: Am Oved (Heb.).

Kaufmann, Yehezkel. 1960. *The Religion of Israel: From Its Beginnings to the Babylonian Exile*. Translated by Moshe Greenberg. Chicago: University of Chicago (originally in Hebrew, from 1937 onwards).

Keel, Othmar. 1978. *The Symbolism of the Biblical World*. New York: Seabury.

Kimbrell, A., ed. 2002. *The Fatal Harvest Reader: The Tragedy of Industrial Agriculture*. Washington, DC: Island.

Kirk-Duggan, Cheryl. 2003. Introduction to *Pregnant Passion: Gender, Sex and Violence in the Bible*, ed. C. Kirk-Duggan, 1–10. Atlanta: Society of Biblical Literature.

Kirschner, Robert. 1983. "The Rabbinic and Philonic Exegeses of the Nadab and Abihu Incident (Lev. 10:1–6)." *JQR* 73: 375–93.

M. Kister, ed. 1997. Avot de-Rabbi Nathan Solomon Schechter Edition. New York: Schocken/JTS (also as e-book).

Klingbeil, Gerald A. 2007. "Not so Happily ever after . . . : Cross-Cultural Marriages in the Time of Ezra-Nehemiah." *Maarav* 14/1: 39–75.

Knohl, Israel. 2008. *The Bible's Genetic Code*. Or Yehuda, Israel: Kinneret & Zmora-Bitan & Dvir (Heb.).

Knoppers, Gary N. 2001. "Intermarriage, Social Complexity, and Ethnic Diversity in the Genealogy of Judah." *JBL* 120/1: 15–30.

Kovacs, David, trans. 1995. *Euripides: Children of Heracles. Hippolytus. Andromache. Hecuba*. LCL 484. Cambridge, MA: Harvard University Press.

———. 1998. *Euripides III. Suppliant Women. Electra. Heracles*. LCL 9. Cambridge, MA: Harvard University Press.

Kramer, Samuel Noah. 1982. "BM 98396: A Sumerian Prototype of the Mater-Dolorosa." *EI* 16:141*–46* (non-Heb. section).

———. 1983. "The Weeping Goddess: Sumerian Prototypes of the Mater Dolorosa." *BA* 46: 69–80.

Kruger, Paul. 2005. "The Inverse World of Mourning in the Hebrew Bible." *BN* 124: 41–9.

Kugel, James L. 1987. "On Hidden Hatred and Open Reproach: Early Exegesis of Leviticus 19." *Harvard Theological Review* 80/1: 43–61.

———. 1997. *The Bible as It Was*. Cambridge, MA: Belknap Press of Harvard University Press.

———. 2006. *The Ladder of Jacob: Ancient Interpretations of the Biblical Story of Jacob and His Children*. Princeton: Princeton University Press.

Lai, Chi-tim. 2003. "Hong Kong Daoism: A Study of Daoist Altars and Lü Dongbin Cults." *Social Compass* 50: 459–70.

———. 2005. "Cong Dajai Yishi Kan Daojiao Dui Siwang de Chuli" (Understanding the Daoist treatment on death from the purification rites). In *Ningshi Siwang: Siyu Renjian de Duoyuan Shengsi*, ed. M. Liang and C. Zhang, 55–78. Xianggang: Zhong Wen Da Xue Chu Ban She.

Lappé, A. 2010. *Diet for a Hot Planet: The Climate Crisis at the End of Your Fork and What You Can Do about It*. New York: Bloomsbury.

Lapsley, Jacqueline E. 2007. "A Feeling for God: Emotions and Moral Formation in Ezekiel 24:15-27." In *Character Ethics and the Old Testament: Moral Dimensions of Scripture*, ed. Daniel R. M. Carroll and Jacqueline E. Lapsley, 93–102. Louisville: Westminster John Knox.

Lasor, William S., ed. 1996. *Old Testament Survey*. Grand Rapids: Eerdmans.

Lawrence, Jonathan David. 2007. *Washing in Water: Trajectories of Ritual Bathing in the Hebrew Bible and Second Temple Literature*. Academia Biblica 23; Leiden: E. J. Brill.

Lee, Archie C. C. 1999. "Returning to China: Biblical Interpretation in Postcolonial Hong Kong." *BibInt* 7/2: 156–73.

———. 1999a. "Identity, Reading Strategy and Doing Theology," *BibInt* 7/2: 197–201.

———. 2000a. "Cross-Textual Hermeneutics." In *Dictionary of Third World Theologies*, ed. V. Fabella and R. S. Sugirtharajah, 60–62. Maryknoll, NY: Orbis.

———. 2000b. "Weaving of a Humanistic Vision: Reading the Hebrew Bible in Asian Religio-Cultural Context." In *Sacred Text, Secular Times: The Hebrew Bible in the Modern World*, ed. L. J. G. Greenspoon and B. F. Le Beau, 282–95. Omaha: Creighton University Press.

———. 2002. "Cross-Textual Interpretation and Its Implications for Biblical Studies." In *Teaching in Bible: Discourses and Politics of Biblical Pedagogy*, ed. F. F. Segovia and M. A. Tolbert, 247–54. Maryknoll, NY: Orbis.

———. 2006. "The Names of God and Bible Translation: Engaging the Chinese Term Question in the Context of Scriptural Interpretation." *Journal of Theologies and Cultures in Asia* 5: 1–17.

———. 2008. "Cross-Textual Hermeneutics and Identity in Multi-Textual Asia." In *Christian Theology in Asia: Emerging Forms and Themes*, ed. S. C. H. Kim, 179–204. Cambridge: Cambridge University Press.

———. 2010. "Presidential Address: Ecology, Economy, and Con/textual Asian Biblical Interpretation." In *Society of Asian Biblical Studies Conference Handbook*, 23–30. Hong Kong.

Leopold, Aldo, 1989. *A Sand County Almanac, and Sketches Here and There*. New York: Oxford University Press.

Levinas, Emmanuel. 2004. *Nine Talmudic Readings*. Bloomington: Indiana University Press.

Levine, Amy-Jill. 2006. *The Misunderstood Jew: The Church and the Scandal of the Jewish Jesus*. San Francisco: HarperSanFrancisco.

Levine, Baruch A. 1989. *Leviticus*. JPS Torah Commentary. New York: Jewish Publication Society.

———. 1993a. *Numbers 1–20*.AB. New York: Doubleday.

———. 1993b. "Silence, Sound, and Phenomenology of Mourning in Biblical Israel." *JANES* 22: 89–106.

———. 2000. *Numbers 21–36*. AB. New York: Doubleday.

Levine, Samuel J. 1998. "Unenumerated Constitutional Rights and Unenumerated Biblical Obligations: A Preliminary Study in Comparative Hermeneutics." *Constitutional Commentary* 15: 511–27.

Levinson, Bernard M. 1997. *Deuteronomy and the Hermeneutics of Legal Innovation*. New York: Oxford University Press.

Levtow, Nathaniel B. 2008. *Images of Others: Iconic Politics in Ancient Israel*. Winona Lake, IN: Eisenbrauns.

Licht, Jacob. 1995. *A Commentary on the book of Numbers (XXII–XXXVI)*. Jerusalem: Magnes; Hebrew University Press (Heb.)

Lipton, Diana. 2006. "Early Mourning? Petitionary Versus Posthumous Ritual in Ezekiel XXIV." *VT* 56: 185–202.

———. 2007a. "God's Influence on Influencing God." In *The God of Israel*, ed. Robert P. Gordon, 73–93. University of Cambridge Oriental Publications 64; Cambridge: Cambridge University Press.

———. 2007b. "*Ki Tetze*." In *The Torah: A Women's Commentary*, ed. Tamara Cohn Eskenazi and Andrea Weiss, 1185. New York: Union of Reform Judaism Press.

———. 2008. *Longing for Egypt and Other Unexpected Biblical Tales*. Sheffield: Sheffield Phoenix.

———. 2009. "Feeding the Green-Eyed Monster: Bitter Waters, Flood Waters, and the Theology of Exile." In *Embroidered Garments: Priests and Gender in Biblical Israel*, ed. Deborah W. Rooke, 102–18. Hebrew Bible Monographs 25. Sheffield: Sheffield Phoenix.

Liu, Tik-sang. 2003. "A Nameless but Active Religion: An Anthropologist's View of Local Religion in Hong Kong and Macau." In *Religion in China Today*, ed. D. L. Overmyer, 67–88. Cambridge: Cambridge University Press.

Liver, Jacob. 1974. "Midian." In *Encyclopaedia Biblica*, ed. E. L. Sukenik and U. M. D. Cassuto, 4:686–91. Jerusalem: Bialik Institute (Heb.).

London, Leslie. 2008. "What Is a Human-Rights Based Approach to Health and Does It Matter?" *Health and Human Rights* 10/1: 65–80.

Lopez, Davina C. 2011. "Pedagogy with the Repressed: Critical Reflections from a Post-9/11 Biblical Studies Classroom." In *Faith, Feminism, and Scholarship: The Next Generation*, ed. Melanie L. Harris, 163–80. New York: Palgrave Macmillan.

Ludemann, Gerd. 1997. *The Unholy in Holy Scripture: The Dark Side of the Bible*. Louisville: Westminster John Knox.

Lutzky, Harriet C. 1997. "The Name 'Cozbi' (Numbers XXV 15, 18)." *VT* 47/4: 546–49.

MacDonald, N. 2008a. *Not Bread Alone: The Uses of Food in the Old Testament*. Oxford: Oxford University Press.

———. 2008b. *What Did the Ancient Israelites Eat? Diet in Biblical Times*. Grand Rapids: Eerdmans.

Malul, Meir. 1988. "Foundlings and Adoptions in the Bible and in Mesopotamian Documents: Scrutiny of Some Legal Metaphors in Ezekiel 16:1-7." *Tarbitz* 57: 461–82.

Marshall, Mandy, and Nigel Taylor. 2006. "Tackling HIV and AIDS with Faith-Based Communities: Learning from Attitudes on Gender Relations and Sexual Rights within Local Evangelical Churches in Burkina Faso, Zimbabwe, and South Africa." *Gender & Development*, 14/3: 363–74.

Martens, E. A. 1997. "Numbers, Theology of." in *Dictionary of Old Testament Theology and Exegesis*, ed. W. A. Van Gemeren, 4:985–99. Grand Rapids: Zondervan.

Matthews, V. H. 1988. *Manners and Customs in the Bible*. Peabody: Hendrickson.

———. 2003. "Family Relationships." In *Dictionary of the Old Testament: Pentateuch*, ed. T. D. Alexander and D. W. Baker, 293–99. Downers Grove, IL: InterVarsity.

Mayer, Ann Elizabeth. 2007. *Islam and Human Rights: Tradition and Politics*. 4th ed. Boulder, Colo.: Westview.

Mayes, A. D. H. 1979. *Deuteronomy*. NCB. Grand Rapids: Eerdmans; London: Marshall, Morgan and Scott.

———. 1994. "Deuteronomy 14 and the Deuteronomic World View." In *Studies in Deuteronomy: In Honour of C. J. Labuschagne on the Occasion of His 65th Birthday*, ed. F. G. Martínez, A. Hilhorst, J. T. A. G. M. van Ruiten, and A. S. van der Woude, 165–81. Supplements to Vetus Testamentum 53. Leiden: Brill.

McClintock, Anne. 1995. *Imperial Leather: Race, Gender and Sexuality in the Colonial Contest*. London: Routledge.

McConville, J. G. 2002. *Deuteronomy*. Apollos Old Testament Commentary. Downers Grove, IL: InterVarsity.

McKim, Donald K. 1996. *Westminster Dictionary of Theological Terms*. Louisville: Westminster John Knox.

McNeill, John. 2010. "Homophobic Abuse and Distortion of Scripture." *Queering the Church* blog entry. March 7. http://queeringthechurch.com/2010/03/07/john-mcneill-homophobic-abuse-and-distortion-of-scripture/ (accessed April 30, 2012).

McNeur, George Hunter. 1934. *China's First Preacher, Leung A-fa (1789–1855)*. Shanghai: Kwang Hsueh Publishing House and Oxford University Press.

McNutt, Paula M. 1994. "The Kenites, the Midianites, and the Rechabites as Marginal Mediators in Ancient Israelite Tradition." *Semeia* 67: 109–32

Mead, Margaret. 1928 (repr., 1973). *Coming of Age in Samoa*. New York: American Museum of Natural History.

Meek, C. K. 1957. *Land Tenure and Administration in Nigeria and the Cameroons*. London: Her Majesty Press.

Meek, Theophile J. 1992. "Documents from the Practice of Law: Mesopotamian Legal Documents (Nuzi Akkadian)." In *The Ancient Near East*. Vol. 1, *An Anthology of Texts and Pictures*, ed. James B. Prichard, 167–70. Princeton: Princeton University Press.

Melamed, Abraham. 2002. *The Image of the Black in Jewish Culture: A History of the Other*. Haifa: Haifa University & Zmora-Bitan (Heb.).

Meyer, Birgit. 2004. "Christianity in Africa: From African Independent to Pentecostal-Charismatic Churches." *Annual Review of Anthropology* 33: 447–74.

Meyers, Carol. 1988. *Discovering Eve: Ancient Israelite Women in Context*. London: Oxford.

Michael, Franz, in collaboration with Chung-il Chang. 1966–1971. *The Taiping Rebellion: History and Documents*. Seattle: University of Washington Press.

Milgrom, Jacob. 1976. *Cult and Conscience: The Asham and the Priestly Doctrine of Repentance.* Leiden: Brill.

———. 1990. *Numbers.* JPS Torah Commentary. Philadelphia: Jewish Publication Society.

———. 1991. *Leviticus 1–16.* AB. New York: Doubleday.

———. 1999. "The Case of the Suspected Adulteress, Numbers 5:11-31: Redaction and Meaning." In *Women in the Hebrew Bible: A Reader*, ed. Alice Bach, 475–82. New York: Routledge.

———. 2000. *Leviticus 17–22.* AB. New York: Doubleday.

———. 2001. *Leviticus 23–27.*AB. New York: Doubleday.

———. 2004. *Leviticus: A Book of Ritual and Ethics.* Minneapolis: Fortress Press.

———. 2007. "Kipper." In *Encyclopaedia Judaica*, ed. M. Berenbaum and F. Skolnik, 180–83. Detroit: Macmillan Reference USA.

Miller, Patrick D. 1990. *Deuteronomy.* IBC. Louisville: John Knox.

Moberly, R. W. L. 2009. *The Theology of the Book of Genesis.* Old Testament Theology. Cambridge: Cambridge University Press.

Moiseraele, Prince Dibeela. 2001. "A Seswana perspective on Genesis 1–10." In *Bible in Africa: Transactions, Trends and Trajectories*, ed. G. West and M. W. Dube, 384–92. Leiden: Brill.

Moor, George F. 1949. *A Critical and Exegetical Commentary on Judges.* ICC 7. 2nd ed. Edinburgh: T&T Clark.

Na'aman, Nadav. 1999. "No Anthropomorphic Graven Image." *UF* 31: 391–415.

———. 2005. *Canaan in the Second Millennium B.C.E.* Winona Lake, IN: Eisenbrauns.

Nelson, R.D. 1997. *Joshua: A Commentary.* Louisville: Westminster John Knox.

Newsom, Carol A., and Sharon H. Ringe, eds. 1992, 1998. *The Women's Bible Commentary.* Louisville: Westminster John Knox. (2012: an updated and expanded 3rd ed., with Jacqueline E. Lapsley as third editor)

Nicholson, Ernest Wilson. 1986. *God and His People: Covenant and Theology in the Old Testament.* Oxford: Oxford University Press.

Niditch, Susan. 1993. *War in the Hebrew Bible.* New York: Oxford University Press.

Nihan, C. 2007. *From Priestly Torah to Pentateuch: A Study in the Composition of the Book of Leviticus.* FAT 2. Reihe 25. Tübingen: Mohr Siebeck.

Noth, Martin. 1968. *Numbers: A Commentary*. Trans. James D. Martin. OTL. London: SCM.

———. 1977. *Leviticus*. Trans. J. E. Anderson. OTL. Philadelphia: Westminster.

Nussbaum, Martha C. 1997. "Capabilities and Human Rights." *Fordham Law Review* 273. http://ir.lawnet.fordham.edu/flr/vol66/iss2/2 (accessed April 30, 2012).

———. 2000. *Women and Human Development: The Capabilities Approach.* Cambridge: Cambridge University Press.

Nwabueze, B. O. 1972. *Nigeria Land Law*. Enugu: Nwamife.

Nwaoru, E. O. 2002. "The Case of the Daughters of Zelophehad (Num 27:1-11) and African Inheritance Rights." *Voices from the Third World* 24/2: 63–78.

Nyitray, Vivian-Lee. 2000. "Becoming the Empress of Heaven: The Life and Bureaucratic Career of Mazu." In *Goddesses Who Rule*, ed. E. Benard and B. Moon, 165–80. New York: Oxford University Press.

Objects and Memory. 2008. Documentary, 62:04. Produced by Brian Danitz and Jonathan Fein. Broadcast September 8. http://www.pbs.org/programs/objects-and-memory/.

Odell, Margaret S. 2000. "Genre and Persona in Ezekiel 24:15–24." In *The Book of Ezekiel: Theological and Anthropological Perspectives*, ed. Margaret S. Odell and John T. Strong, 195–219. Atlanta: Society of Biblical Literature.

Okeke, Uju Peace. 2010. "A Case for the Enforcement of Women's Rights as Human Rights in Nigeria." Women's UN Report Network. http://www.wunrn.com/news/2010/04_10/04_05_10/040510_nigeria.htm (accessed April 30, 2012).

Olson, Dennis T. 1985. *The Death of the Old and the Birth of the New: The Framework of the Book of Numbers and the Pentateuch*. Chico, CA: Scholars.

———. 1996. *Numbers*.IBC. Louisville: Westminster John Knox.

———. 1997. "Negotiating Boundaries: The Old and New Generations and the Theology of Numbers." *Int* 51/3: 229–40.

Olyan, Saul M. 2004. *Biblical Mourning: Ritual and Social Dimensions*. Oxford: Oxford University Press.

Organ, Barbara E. 2001. "Pursuing Phinehas: A Synchronic Reading." *CBQ* 63/2: 203–19.

Ostwald, Martin. 2009. *Language and History in Ancient Greek Culture*. Philadelphia: University of Pennsylvania Press.

Otto, Rudolf. 1928. *The Idea of the Holy*. London: Oxford University Press.

Overmyer, Daniel L. 1986. *Religions of China: The World as a Living System, Religious Traditions of the World.* San Francisco: Harper & Row.

Paper, Jordan D. 1995. *The Spirits Are Drunk: Comparative Approaches to Chinese Religion.* SUNY series in Chinese Philosophy and Culture. Albany: State University of New York Press.

Pardes, Ilana. 1995. "Zipporah and the Bridegroom of Blood: Women Giving Birth to a People in the Book of Exodus." *Theory and Criticism: An Israeli Forum* 7: 93–94 (Heb.).

Patrich, Joseph. 1990. *The Formation of Nabatean Art: Prohibition of a Graven Image among the Nabateans.* Jerusalem: Magnes.

Patte, Daniel, et al., eds. 2004. *The Global Bible Commentary.* Nashville: Abingdon.

Payne, Elizabeth J. 1983. "The Midianite Arc in Joshua and Judges." In *Midian, Moab and Edom: The History and Archaeology of Late Bronze and Iron Age, Jordan and North-West Arabia,* ed. John F. A. Sawyer and David J. A. Clines, 163–72. JSOTSup 24. Sheffield: JSOT Press.

Pearce, R. G. 1995. "To Save a Life: Why a Rabbi and a Jewish Lawyer Must Disclose a Client Confidence." *Loyola Los Angeles Law Review* 29: 1771.

Penner, Todd, and Caroline Vander Stichele, eds. 2005. *Her Master's Tools? Feminist and Postcolonial Engagements of Historical-Critical Discourse.* Global Perspectives on Biblical Scholarship. Atlanta: SBL

Perdue, Leo G., Joseph Blenkinsopp, John J. Collins, and Carol Meyers. 1997. *Families in Ancient Israel.* Louisville: Westminster John Knox.

Pham, Xuan Huong Thi. 1999. *Mourning in the Ancient Near East and the Hebrew Bible.* JSOTSup 302. Sheffield: Sheffield Academic.

Phillips, Anthony. 2002. "Uncovering the Father's Skirt." In *Essays on Biblical Law,* 245–50. JSOTSup Series 344. Sheffield: Sheffield Academic.

Pollan, Michael. 2006. *The Omnivore's Dilemma: A Natural History of Four Meals.* New York: Penguin.

———. 2008. *In Defense of Food: An Eater's Manifesto.* New York: Penguin.

Powell, James N. 2009. "Tahitian Tantra." *Lunacies* blog entry. December 8. http://slowloveblog.blogspot.co.nz/2009/12/tahitian-tantra.html.

Pritchard, James B., ed. 1969. *Ancient Near Eastern Texts Relating to the Old Testament with Supplement.* 3rd ed. Princeton: Princeton University Press.

———. 1992. *The Ancient Near East. Volumes I and II: An Anthology of Texts and Pictures.* Princeton: Princeton University.

Quesada, Jan Jaynes. 2002. "Body Piercing: The Issue of Priestly Control Over the Acceptable Family Structure in the Book of Numbers." *BibInt* 10/1: 24–35.

Rad, Gerhard von. 1964. *Deuteronomy*.OTL. London: SCM.

———. 1966. *The Problem of the Hexateuch: And Other Essays*. Trans. E. W. Trueman Dicken. London: Oliver and Boyd.

———. 2001 (1962). *Old Testament Theology*. Vol. 1. Louisville: Westminster John Knox Press.

Rajavi, Maryam. 2012. "International Solidarity with Women in Iran, and the 1000 Vanguard Women in Ashraf, Iraq." Paper delivered at Les femmes, force du changement Conference, Auvers-sur-Oise, France.

Ratzel, Friedrich. 1896. *The History of Mankind*. London. http://inquirewithin.biz/history/american_pacific/oceania/courtship-weddings.htm

Redford, Donald B. 1992. *Egypt, Canaan and Israel in Ancient Times*. Princeton: Princeton University Press.

Reif, Stefan C. 1971. "What Enraged Phinehas: A Study of Numbers 25:8." *JBL* 9/2: 200–206.

Reilly, Thomas. 2004. *The Taiping Heavenly Kingdom: Rebellion and Blasphemy of Empire*. Seattle: University of Washington Press.

Rendtorff, Rolf. 1996. "Is It Possible to Read Leviticus as a Separate Book?" In *Reading Leviticus: A Conversation with Mary Douglas*, ed. John F.A. Sawyer, 22-35.JSOTSup 227. Sheffield: Sheffield Academic.

Riggans, Walter. 1983. *Numbers*. Daily Study Bible. Philadelphia: Westminster Press.

Rhoads, David, et al.,eds. 2005. *From Every People and Nation: The Book of Revelation in Intercultural Perspective*. Minneapolis: Fortress Press.

Roberts, J. P. 1981. *Massacres to Mining: The Colonisation of Aboriginal Australia*. Updated ed. Melbourne: Dove Communications.

Rodale, M. 2010. *Organic Manifesto: How Organic Food Can Heal Our Planet, Feed the World, and Keep Us Safe*. New York: Rodale.

Rogerson, J. W. 2010. *A Theology of the Old Testament: Cultural Memory, Communication, and Being Human*. Minneapolis: Fortress Press.

Rooke, Deborah W., ed. 2009. *Embroidered Garments: Priests and Gender in Biblical Israel*. Sheffield: Sheffield Phoenix.

Rosenblatt, Paul C. R., Patricia Walsh, and Douglas A. Jackson. 1976. *Grief and Mourning in Cross-Cultural Perspective*. New Haven: HRAF.

Roth, Martha T. 1997. *Writings from the Ancient World: Law Collections from Mesopotamia and Asia Minor.* 2nd ed. Writings from the Ancient World. Atlanta: Scholars.

Roux, Georges. 1992. *Ancient Iraq.* London: Penguin.

Said, Edward W. 1994. *Culture and Imperialism.* London: Vintage.

Sangren, Paul Steven. 1987. *History and Magical Power in a Chinese Community.* Stanford: Stanford University Press.

———. 2000. *Chinese Sociologics: An Anthropological Account of the Role of Alienation in Social Reproduction.* New Brunswick, NJ: The Athlone.

Sarna, Nahum M. 1991. *Exodus.* JPS Torah Commentary. Philadelphia: Jewish Publication Society.

Sasson, Jack. 1999. "Numbers 5 and the Waters of Judgment." In *Women in the Hebrew Bible: A Reader,* ed. Alice Bach, 483–86. New York: Routledge.

Sawyer, John F. A., ed. 1996. *Reading Leviticus: A Conversation with Mary Douglas.* JSOTSup 227. Sheffield: Sheffield Academic.

Schenker, Adrian. 2003. "What Connects the Incest Prohibitions with the Other Prohibitions Listed in Leviticus 18 and 20?" In *The Book of Leviticus: Composition and Reception,* ed. Rolf Rendtorff and Robert A. Kugler with Sarah Smith Bartel, 162–88. Leiden: Brill (also SBL, 2006, 2011).

Scholz, Susanne. 2004. "Gender, Class, and Androcentric Compliance in the Rapes of Enslaved Women in the Hebrew Bible." *Lectio Difficilior* 1: 312–24. http://www.lectio.unibe.ch/04_1/Scholz.Enslaved.htm.

Scott, Janet Lee. 2007. *For Gods, Ghosts and Ancestors: The Chinese Tradition of Paper Offerings.* Seattle: University of Washington Press.

Seri, Andrea. 2011. "Domestic Female Slaves During the Old Babylonian Period." In *Slaves and Households in the Near East,* ed. Laura Culbertson, 49–67. Oriental Institute Seminars 7. Chicago: Oriental Institute of the University of Chicago.

Sharon, Diane M. 1999. "When Fathers Refuse to Eat: The Trope of Rejecting Food and Drink in Biblical Narrative." *Semeia* 86: 135–48.

Segovia, Fernando F., ed. 1995. *Reading from This Place.* Vol. 1, *Social Location and Biblical Interpretation in the United States.* Minneapolis: Fortress Press.

Segovia, Fernando F., and Mary Ann Tolbert, eds. 2000. *Reading from This Place.* Vol. 2, *Social Location and Biblical Interpretation in Global Perspective.* Minneapolis: Fortress Press. (Orig. pub. 1995.)

———, eds. 2004. *Teaching the Bible: The Discourses and Politics of Biblical Pedagogy.* Repr. Eugene, OR: Wipf & Stock. (Orig. pub. 1997.)

Shemesh, Yael. 1999. "Measure for Measure in Biblical Narrative." *Beit Mikra* 44: 261–77 (Heb.)

———. 2008. "The Elisha Stories as Saints' Legends." *JHS* 8:1–41. http://www.arts.ualberta.ca/JHS/Articles/article_82.pdf.

———. 2011. "Achsah, from Object to Subject: A Story about a Wise Woman, a Field, and Water (Judges 1:10–15)." *Studies in Bible and Exegesis* 10: 23–48 (Heb.).

Shields, Mary E. 1993. "Subverting a Man of God, Elevating a Woman: Role and Power Reversals in 2 Kings 4." *JSOT* 58: 59–69.

Shih, Vincent Y. C. 1967. *The Taiping Ideology: Its Sources, Interpretation, and Influences*. Seattle: University of Washington Press.

Shinan, Avigdor. 1978–79, "The Sins of Nadab and Abihu in Rabbinic Literature." *Tarbiz* 48: 201–14 (Heb.).

Sivan, Helena Zlotnick. 2001. "The Rape of Cozbi (Numbers XXV)." *VT* 51/1: 69–80.

Skinner, John. 1910. *A Critical and Exegetical Commentary on Genesis*. ICC. Edinburgh: T&T Clark.

Sklar, Jay. 2005. *Sin, Impurity, Sacrifice, and Atonement: The Priestly Conceptions*. Ed. D. J. A. Clines, J. C. Exum, and K. W. Whitelam. Hebrew Bible Monographs. Sheffield: Sheffield Phoenix.

Smith-Christopher, Daniel L. 2008. "Abolitionist Exegesis: A Quaker Proposal for White Liberals." In *Still at the Margins*, ed. R. S. Sugirtharajah, 128–38. London: T&T Clark.

Smith, Christian. 2011. *The Bible Made Impossible: Why Biblicism Is Not a Truly Evangelical Reading of Scripture*. Grand Rapids: Brazos.

Smith, J. M. 2003. *Seeds of Deception: Exposing Industry and Government Lies about the Safety of the Genetically Engineered Foods You're Eating*. Fairfield, IA: Yes Books.

Smith, Roger W. 1994. "Women and Genocide: Notes on an Unwritten History." *Holocaust and Genocide Studies* 8/3: 315–34.

Snaith, Norman H. 1967. *Leviticus and Numbers*. NCB. Greenwood, SC: The Attic.

Soggin, J. Alberto. 1987. *Judges: A Commentary*. OTL. Trans. John Bowden. 2nd. ed. London: SCM.

Sommer, B. D. 2009. "Dialogical Biblical Theology: A Jewish Approach to Reading Scripture Theologically." In *Biblical Theology: Introducing the Conversation*, 1-53. Library of Biblical Theology. Nashville: Abingdon.

Spence, Jonathan. 1966. *God's Chinese Son: The Taiping Heavenly Kingdom of Hong Xiuquan*. London: HarperCollins.

Stager, Laurence E. 1998. "Midianites, Moses, and Monotheism." In *The Oxford History of the Biblical World*, ed. Michael D. Coogan, 142–48. New York: Oxford University Press.

Stein, David E., ed. 2006. *The Contemporary Torah: A Gender-Sensitive Adaptation of the JPS Translation*. Philadelphia: Jewish Publication Society.

Steinberg, A. 1991. "Jewish Medical Ethics." In *Bioethics Yearbook*, Vol. 1, *Theological Developments in Bioethics*, ed. B. A. Brody et al., 179–99. Alphen aan den Rijn: Kluwer Academic.

Stewart, Pamela J., and Andrew Strathern. 2007. *Asian Ritual Systems: Syncretisms and Ruptures*. Carolina Academic Press Ritual Studies Monographs. Durham, NC: Carolina Academic.

Stone, M. E. 1996. "215. 4QTestament of Naphtali." In *Qumran Cave 4: XVII, Parabiblical Texts, Part 3*, 73–82. pl. V. DJD 22. Oxford: Clarendon.

Storr, F., trans. 1932 (1912). *Sophocles I: Oedipus the King; Oedipus at Colonus; Antigone*. LCL 20. London: Heinemann.

———. 1967. *Sophocles II: Ajax; Electra; Trachiniae, Philoctetes*. LCL 21. London: Heinemann.

Stroete, G. A. te. 1977. "Ezekiel 24: 15–27: The Meaning of a Symbolic Act." *Bijdragen* 38: 163–75.

Sturdy, John. 1976. *Numbers*. CBC. Cambridge: Cambridge University Press.

Sugirtharajah, R. S. 2012. *Exploring Postcolonial Biblical Criticism*. Oxford: Wiley-Blackwell.

Sweeney, M. A. 2011. *Tanakh: A Theological and Critical Introduction to the Jewish Bible*. Minneapolis: Fortress Press.

Szonyi, Michael. 2007. "The Virgin and the Chinese State: The Cult of Wang Yulan and the Politics of Local Identity on Jinmen (Quemoy)." In *Asian Ritual Systems: Syncretisms and Ruptures*, ed. P. J. Stewart and A. Strathern, 183–208. Durham, NC: Carolina Academic.

Tetlow, Elisabeth Meier. 2004. *Women, Crime and Punishment in Ancient Law and Society*.Vol. 1, *The Ancient Near East*. New York: Continuum.

Thompson, J. A. 1980. *The Book of Jeremiah*. NICOT. Grand Rapids: Eerdmans.

Tigay, Jeffrey H. 1996. *Deuteronomy*. JPS Torah Commentary. Philadelphia: Jewish Publication Society.

Tong, Chee-Kiong. 2004. *Chinese Death Rituals in Singapore*. Anthropology of Asia. New York: RoutledgeCurzon.

Tosato, A. 1984. "The Law of Leviticus 18:18: A Reexamination." *CBQ* 46: 199–214.

Uchem, R. N. 2001. "Overcoming Women's Subordination in Igbo African Culture and in the Catholic Church: Envisioning an Inclusive Theology with Reference to Women."Ph.D. diss., Mishawaka, IN, Graduate Theological Foundation.

Ukpong, J. S. 2001. "Developments in Biblical Interpretation in Africa: Historical and Hermeneutical Directions." In *The Bible in Africa*, ed.G. O. West and M. Dube, 11–28. Leiden: Brill.

United Nations Document Reference A/CONF.177/20/Rev.1. 1996. *Report of the Fourth World Conference on Women, Beijing (4–15 September 1995)*. http://www.un.org/womenwatch/daw/beijing/pdf/ Beijing%20full%20report% 20E.pdf (accessed May 13, 2012).

University of Chicago Oriental Institute and Ignace Jay Gelb. 1956. *The Assyrian Dictionary of the Oriental Institute of the University of Chicago*. Chicago: J. J. Augustin; Oriental Institute.

Van Houten, Christiana. 1991. *The Alien in Israelite Law*. JSOTSup 107. Sheffield: JSOT Press.

Vaux, Roland de. 1961. *Ancient Israel: Its Life and Institutions*, trans. John McHugh. New York: McGraw-Hill.

Veenhof, Klass, R. 2005. *Letters in the Louvre*. AbB 14. Leiden: Brill, 2005.

Walker, Alice. 1983. *In Search of Our Mothers' Gardens: Womanist Prose*. San Diego: Harcourt Brace Jovanovich.

Ward, Eileen F. de. 1972. "Mourning Customs in 1, 2 Samuel." *JJS* 23: 1–27, 145–66.

Watson, Alan. 1996. "Leviticus in Mark: Jesus' Attitude to the Law." In *Reading Leviticus: A Conversation with Mary Douglas*, ed. John F.A. Sawyer, 263–71. JSOTSup 227. Sheffield: Sheffield Academic.

Watson, James L. 2004. "Standardizing the Gods: The Promotion of Tian Hou ('Empress of Heaven') along the South China Coast, 960–1960." In *Village Life in Hong Kong: Politics, Gender, and Ritual in the New Territories*, ed. J. L. Watson and R. S. Watson, 269–310. Hong Kong: Chinese University Press.

Weinfeld, Moshe. 1991. *Deuteronomy 1–11*. AB. New York: Doubleday.

Weldon, Terence. "Clobber Texts." *Queering the Church* blog entry. http://queeringthechurch.com/queer-faith/queer-scripture/clobber-texts/.

Weller, Robert P. 1987. *Unities and diversities in Chinese Religion*. Seattle: University of Washington Press.

Wellhausen, Julius. 1885. *Prolegomena to the History of Israel*. Trans. J. Sutherland Black and Allan Menzies. Edinburgh: Adam & Charles Black.

Wells, Bruce. 2006. "The Covenant Code and Near Eastern Legal Traditions: A Response to David P. Wright." *Maarav* 13: 85–118.

Westbrook, Raymond. 1988. *Old Babylonian Marriage Law*. AfOB 23. Horn: Berger & Söhne.

———. 1991. *Property and the Family in Biblical Law*. Sheffield: Sheffield Academic.

———. 1998. "The Female Slave." In *Gender and Law in the Hebrew Bible and the Ancient Near East*, ed. Victor Matthews, Bernard Levinson, and Tikva Frymer-Kensky. 177–93. Sheffield: Sheffield Academic.

Westenholz, Joan. 1989. "Tamar Qedesa, Qadistu, and Sacred Prostitution in Mesopotamia." *HTR* 83: 245–65.

Wolf, Arthur P. 1974. "Gods, Ghosts, and Ancestors." In *Religion and Ritual in Chinese Society*. ed. A. P. Wolf, 131–82. Stanford: Stanford University Press.

Wolkstein, Diane, and Samuel Noah Kramer. 1983. *Inanna, Queen of the Heaven and Earth: Her Stories and Hymns from Sumer*. New York: Harper & Row.

World Bank Poverty Reduction and Equity Group. 2011. *Food Price Watch* (August 2011). http://siteresources.worldbank.org/INTPOVERTY/ Resources/ 335642-1210859591030/FPW_August2011.pdf (accessed September 26, 2011).

Wright, Christopher. 1996. *Deuteronomy*. NIBCOT. Peabody: Hendrickson.

Wright, David P. 2003. "The Laws of Hammurabi as a Source for the Covenant Collection (Exodus 20:23–23:19)." *Maarav* 10 (2003): 11–87.

———. 2009. *Inventing God's Law: How the Covenant Code of the Bible Used and Revised the Laws of Hammurabi*. New York: Oxford University Press.

Xia, Chun-tao. 2006. *The Fall of the Heavenly Kingdom: Re-examination of the Religion of Taiping Kingdom*. Beijing: People's University Press (Chinese).

Yakubu, M. G. 1985. *Land Law in Nigeria*. London: Macmillan.

Zhang, Huaicheng. 1998. *Tian Ren Zhi Bian: Zhongguo Chuantong Lunli Daode de Jindai Zhuanxing* (The change from heaven to human being: modern transformation of traditional morality and ethics in China). Changsha Shi: Hunan Jiao Yu Chu Ban She.

Zimmerli, Walther. 1979. *Ezekiel*. Vol. 1. Trans. Ronald E. Clements. Philadelphia: Fortress Press.

Author Index

Scripture Index